# Industrial Management

**Series editor**
H. Biedermann, Leoben, Austria
C. Ramsauer, Graz, Austria
W. Sihn, Wien, Austria

Die Schriftenreihe behandelt Themen des gesamten Lebenszyklus von Produkten aus und in der produzierenden Industrie. Damit umfasst das Industrial Management die Produktinnovation, die Produktionsüberleitung, von der eigentlichen Produktion und Auslieferung der industriell produzierten Erzeugnisse bis hin zum Recycling. Die Beherrschung der neuen Themen wie Digitalisierung, Agilität, Interdisziplinarität, demographischer Wandel und Offenheit beeinflussen den Erfolg im Produktentstehungsprozess. In der Produktentwicklung stehen modernste technische Methoden zur Verfügung gepaart mit Rapid-Prototyping-Maschinen, um beispielsweise in FabLabs und anderen öffentlichen oder privaten Makerspaces Prototypen zu bauen. Das Anlaufmanagement beschäftigt sich damit, wie man rasch Produkte mit maximaler Kapazitätsauslastung produzieren kann. Die industrielle Produktion benötigt meist hochverfügbare Maschinen mit hohem Investitionsbedarf. Das strategisch-operative Asset Management spielt dabei eine entscheidende Rolle. Aus ökonomisch-ökologischer Sicht hat die Ressourceneffizienz (insbesondere Material und Energie) hohe Bedeutung. Die in der Industrie beschäftigten Mitarbeiter bedürfen wegen des hohen Innovationsgrades weiterer Befähigung und benötigen ergonomisch gestaltete Arbeitsplätze. Die Kostenposition wird nicht zuletzt von der Wahl des Industriestandorts und der richtigen Fabriksplanung beeinflusst. Die Digitalisierung betrifft die gesamte Wertschöpfungskette und ist die Voraussetzung für neue Geschäftsmodelle und ein agiles Unternehmen. Das Industrial Management entwickelt zu all diesen Themen Theorien, Konzepte, Modelle, Methoden und praxisrelevante Instrumente.



More information about this series at http://www.springer.com/series/16058

Markus Hammer

# Management Approach for Resource-Productive Operations

## Design of a Time-Based and Analytics-Supported Methodology Grounded in Six Sigma

With a foreword by
Univ.-Prof. Dipl.-Ing. Dr. techn. Christian Ramsauer
and Prof. Dipl.-Wirt.-Inf. Dr. Christian Terwiesch

Springer Gabler

Markus Hammer
Graz, Austria

Dissertation Graz University of Technology, Austria, 2017

ISSN 2523-3866 ISSN 2523-3874 (electronic)
Industrial Management
ISBN 978-3-658-22938-2 ISBN 978-3-658-22939-9 (eBook)
https://doi.org/10.1007/978-3-658-22939-9

Library of Congress Control Number: 2018949896

Springer Gabler


Printed on acid-free paper

This Springer Gabler imprint is published by the registered company Springer Fachmedien Wiesbaden GmbH part of Springer Nature
The registered company address is: Abraham-Lincoln-Str. 46, 65189 Wiesbaden, Germany

# Foreword

Academics often spend too much time developing complex mathematical models while failing to recognize that business leaders struggle with very different decisions. One of these under-researched decisions that we see many business leaders facing, relates to their search for management approaches that help them connect their operational decision making with their corporate financial performance.

The research work of Mr. Hammer presents a unique implementation methodology of a management approach that aims to optimize profits using a financial, time-based target operating parameter, e.g., profit per hour. By connecting the decision making with real time data, this work provides decision makers with a simple yard stick they can use to run their operations.

The research of Mr. Hammer is clearly conceptual and application focused and we view it as an important contribution on how to implement performance management systems. The work also touches on related topics that, in our view, have received insufficient attention from the performance management literature, including Big Data, Data Analytics, as well as Industry 4.0.

The abundance of data that modern plant managers in theory have access to is in sharp contrast to the sophistication of their current planning methodologies. This deficit is especially becoming a challenge in times of increasing volatility and complexity.

Throughout the document, Mr. Hammer uses relevant sources of literature and builds upon the current body of international publications in the field. Through his careful referencing and citations, Mr. Hammer demonstrates a high degree of academic integrity. He only claims credit for what he contributes himself, while being generous pointing to the contributions of those who went before him.

The work submitted by Mr. Hammer provides a significant contribution to the field of industrial operations management.

Univ.-Prof. Dipl.-Ing. Dr.techn. Christian Ramsauer
Institute of Innovation and Industrial Management

Prof. Dipl.-Wirt.-Inf. Dr. Christian Terwiesch
The Wharton School of the University of Pennsylvania

## Acknowledgements

I would like to thank my supervisor Prof. Dr. Christian Ramsauer for being a role model and for his support and trust. I thank Prof. Dr. Christian Terwiesch for being my second assessor and early thought partner on pursuing a PhD. Furthermore, I would like to acknowledge Prof. Dr. Stefan Vorbach, for his advice and for being the head of the examination board.

Being part of the team at the Institute for Innovation and Industrial Management has been a fantastic experience. Thank you Alex, Christian, Christoph, Daniela, Elma, Hans, Hugo, Jasmin, Kerstin, Mario, Martin, Matthias, Nils, Patrick, Philipp, Sascha, Silke, Stefan, Thomas, et al. I would also like to thank my work colleagues, in particular, Joris, Ken, Olivier, and Robert and the three industrial companies who agreed to contribute with the practical cases.

I owe deep gratitude to my family, my parents Roswitha and Helmut, my loving wife Raquel, and my two sons Lucas and David, to whom I dedicate this work.

Dipl.-Ing. Dr. techn. Markus Hammer

# Abstract

The objective of this doctoral thesis is to investigate a time-based and analytics-supported operations management approach and develop a structured implementation methodology.

In the context of digitization, the Industry 4.0 and the Industrial Internet of Things the amount of available technology and data is continuously rising. At the same time increasing volatility, uncertainty and complexity demand making operations decisions in ever shorter intervals trending towards real-time.

This research explores five perspectives, the needs of industry, in particular manufacturing in process industries; the impact of digitization, with focus on Big Data and analytics; the management of operations through time-based performance metrics; how operations improvement methods and advanced process control help achieve resource-productive operations; and learning from practice based on two empirical case studies.

Next an implementation methodology for a time-based and analytics-supported operations management approach is conceived, explained and tested. The methodology is structured around five phases known from Six Sigma: Define, Measure, Analyze, Improve, Control and contains 17 specific steps which are explained and subsequently validated in an industrial case study.

This thesis discusses the criteria when this approach is meaningful, for example, situations when trade-off decisions between conflicting targets are required, time is the constraint, close to real time decision making is required, cumulative profit maximization is the desired long term goal, and where invested capital and/or resource intensity is high.

Pre-conditions for implementations are stated, for example, infrastructure such as sensors, meters, or data storage; data to compute the metric; access to advanced algorithms required to solve for profit per hour as a target function; an implementation process; and the required skills.

It can be concluded that a time-based and analytics-supported operations management approach for maximizing profits is meaningful if the pre-conditions are met. The final case study proves that the developed implementation methodology works in practice.

# Contents

## List of Figures

# List of Tables

## List of Equations

# List of Abbreviations

| | |
|---|---|
| APC | Advanced Process Control. |
| APICS | American Production and Inventory Control Society. |
| APL | Action-Profit-Linkage. |
| BI | Business Intelligence. |
| BSC | Balanced ScoreCard. |
| CAGR | Compound Annual Growth Rate. |
| CM2025 | China Manufacturing 2025. |
| CoV | Coefficient of Variation. |
| CPPS | Cyber-Physical Production Systems. |
| CPS | Cyber-Physical Systems. |
| CRISP-DM | Cross Industry Standard Process for Data Mining. |
| CTQ | Critical-to-Quality. |
| DBR | Drum-Buffer-Rope. |
| DCS | Distributed Control System. |
| DELTTA | Data, Enterprise, Leadership, Targets, Technology, Analytics and data scientists. |
| DMAIC | Define, Measure, Analyze, Improve, Control. |
| DOE | Design of Experiments. |
| EBIT | Earnings before interest and taxes. |
| EFQM | European Foundation for Quality Management. |
| ERP | Enterprise Resource Planning. |
| EVO | Efficiency Valuation Organization. |
| FMEA | Failure Mode Effect Analysis. |
| GDP | Gross Domestic Product. |
| IIoT | Industrial Internet of Things. |
| IoT | Internet of Things. |
| IPMVP | International Performance Measurement and Verification Protocol. |
| ISA | International Society of Automation. |
| ISO | International Organization for Standardization. |
| IT | Information Technology. |
| ITU | International Telecommunication Union. |
| KDD | Knowledge Discovery in Databases. |
| KPI | Key Performance Indicator. |

| | |
|---|---|
| M2M | Machine-to-machine. |
| MES | Manufacturing Execution System. |
| MIS | Management Information System. |
| MIT | Massachusetts Institute of Technology. |
| MPC | Model Predictive Control. |
| MSR | Maximum Sustainable Rate. |
| OEE | Overall Equipment Effectiveness. |
| OEM | Original Equipment Manufacturer. |
| OLAP | Online Analytical Processing. |
| OM | Operations Management. |
| OPC | OLE (Object Linking and Embedding) for Process Control. |
| OT | Operational Technology. |
| PDCA | Plan, Do, Check, Act. |
| PDSA | Plan, Do, Study, Act. |
| PIMS | Process Information Management System. |
| PMA | Performance Management Analytics. |
| PMM | Performance measurement and management. |
| PPE | Property, Plant, and Equipment. |
| R&D | Research & Development. |
| ROA | Return on Assets. |
| ROE | Return on Equity. |
| ROIC | Return on Invested Capital. |
| RQ | Research Question. |
| RTO | Real-Time Optimization. |
| S&OP | Sales & Operations Planning. |
| SCVI | Supply Chain Volatility Index. |
| SEMMA | Sample, Explore, Modify, Model, Analyze. |
| SIGMA | Source of data, Innovation, Growth mindset, Market opportunities, Analytics. |
| SIPOC | Supplier, Input, Process, Output, Customer. |
| SIPOC | Supplier-Input-Process-Output-Customer. |
| SMART | Start with strategy, Measure metrics and data, Analyze your data, Report your results, Transform your business and decision making. |
| SPC | Statistical Process Control. |
| SQL | Structured Query Language. |
| TA | Throughput Accounting. |
| TEEP | Total Effective Equipment Performance. |
| TOC | Theory of Constraints. |
| TPS | Toyota Production System. |
| TQM | Total Quality Management. |

| | |
|---|---|
| USAF | United States Air Force. |
| VDMA | Verband Deutscher Maschinen- und Anlagenbau e.V. (German Mechanical Engineering Industry Association). |
| VPN | Virtual Private Network. |
| VUCA | Volatile, Uncertain, Complex, Ambiguous. |
| WAN | Wide Area Network. |
| WEF | World Economic Forum. |

# 1 Introduction

Chapter 1 provides an introduction to this thesis in four sections. Section 1.1 describes the initial situation and motivation for this research. Section 1.2 defines the objective of the research, section 1.3 articulates the research questions, and section 1.4 lays out the research design and structure of the thesis.

## 1.1 Initial Situation and Motivation

Industrial companies are currently facing challenging times due to globalization, rapid changes in both, supplier and customer markets, and innovation in technology (Westkämper, Zahn 2009, V). Key challenges like volatility and uncertainty are steadily increasing in today's business environment (Abele, Reinhart 2011, 5-32). As an example, the volatility of revenues and profitability in US firms doubled between 1960 and 2000 (Sull 2009, p. 9). The pressure on manufacturing industries has been intensifying due to their typically high capital employed and resulting costs (Friedli, Schuh 2012, p. 12). Industrial companies in high cost countries need to consider topics such as agility, automation and resource efficiency to remain competitive (Ramsauer 2013a, pp. 3–4). In this constant state of change, organizations which recognize and react quickly and intelligently to market swings increase their competitiveness (Davenport 2014b, p. 48). More effective and quicker decisions might be achieved through transformation of currently available data into information and knowledge (Vercellis 2009, XIV). The availability of data is driven by innovation in advanced manufacturing technologies. The integration of digital and intelligent technologies enables companies to raise the level of management with the objective of finding its best operating model (Zhou 2013, p. 6). Digitalization, and the creation of the Internet of Things in manufacturing leading to the fourth industrial revolution, is commonly discussed under the umbrella term "Industry 4.0" (Kagermann et al. 2013, p. 13). However, according to a recent study of more than 500 companies, only 13% of industrial companies have, for example, adopted Big Data initiatives as part of their business routines (Bange et al. 2015, p. 11). The goal of this research is to enable smart operational decision making to optimize operations for maximum profitability using a time-based and analytics-supported operations management approach.


M. Hammer, *Management Approach for Resource-Productive Operations*,
Industrial Management, https://doi.org/10.1007/978-3-658-22939-9_1

> "The search for the one objective is essentially a search for a magic formula that will make judgement unnecessary. But the attempt to replace judgement by formula is always irrational; all that can be done is to make judgement possible by narrowing its range and the available alternatives, giving it clear focus, sound foundation in facts and reliable measurements of the effects and validity of actions and decisions" (Drucker 1966, p. 59).

The rise of Industry 4.0 and in particular Big Data analytics of production parameters offers exciting new ways for optimization. Currently, the majority of factories, for example in process industries, aim either for output maximization, yield increase, or cost reduction. With the availability of real time data and opportunity to process it online with advanced algorithms a profit per hour management approach becomes possible. Profit per hour as a target control metric enables running factories at the optimal currently available operating point taking all revenue and cost drivers into account.

This thesis describes a methodology to implement profit per hour as target key performance indicator in production in process industries. The author explains how this management approach helps to make better operational decisions, trading off yield, energy, throughput among other factors, and the resulting cumulative benefits. He also lays out how Big Data and advanced algorithms are the key enablers to this new approach. With profit per hour an agile control approach is presented which aims to optimize the performance of industrial manufacturing systems in a world of ever increasing volatility.

## 1.2 Objective of the Research

The objective of this thesis is to derive a structured implementation methodology for an operational management approach leveraging advanced analytics and a time-based profit key performance indicator (KPI), Figure 1, in the context of Industry 4.0 and Big Data.

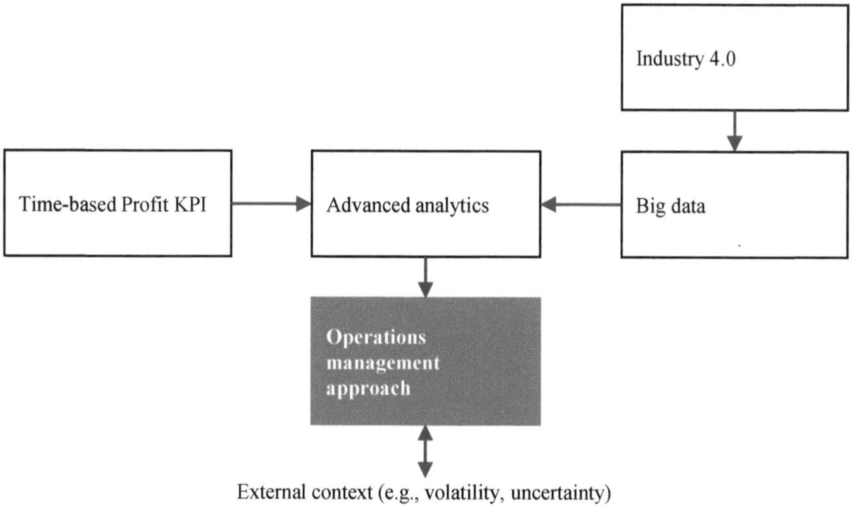


Figure 1: Framing the objective

"Developing a structured management process for using measures to support decision makers, set goals, allocate resources and inform management" has been stated as academic research priority (Busi, Bititci 2006, p. 20). For industrial companies this is equally a priority as they "struggle to incorporate data-driven insights into day-to-day business processes" (Henke et al. 2016a, vi). Diab et al emphasize that

> "Industrial analytics, especially at its early stage of development, requires a systematic and architectural approach that is flexible to meet the operational and business requirements and forward looking in accommodating usage changes and technological advances" (Diab et al. 2017, p. 15).

Horvath et al. see a need to integrate predictive analytics into performance management and to further develop value driver models considering interdependences between operative KPIs and profit (Horvath et al. 2015, p. 105). These research needs should be addressed as part of techno-economic research. According to Bauer, the term techno-economics results from the intersection between the scientific areas of technology and economics and are grounded in realism and experience. Fundamentally, there are 3 questions to be answered: (1) is the idea technically solvable, (2) is it economically feasible, and (3) does it serve people and society? (Bauer 2013, pp. 10–11).

For this research and the resulting methodology, four objectives can be defined:

Objective 1: Identification of criteria *(when meaningful?)*
Objective 2: Identification of pre-conditions *(what is needed?)*
Objective 3: Conception of a methodology *(how to implement?)*
Objective 4: Validation of the developed methodology *(does it work?)*

In line with the general operations management research process, the next step is to determine research questions and to choose a research approach (Karlsson 2016, pp. 16–17).

## 1.3 Research Questions

Research questions are the pre-cursor of research design and serve as guardrails for targeted research (Töpfer 2012, pp. 155–157). Research questions can be classified in four types (exploratory, descriptive, explanatory, prescriptive) and six forms (who, what, where, when, how, why) (Åhlström 2016, p. 66). Based on the objectives of the research from the previous section three research questions (RQ) have been formulated:

RQ1: Under what conditions does a profit per hour management approach help to take the best decisions? When does it fail?
RQ2: In practice, what keeps companies from implementing a profit per hour approach? What are the pre-conditions and why?
RQ3: How would companies implement a profit per hour operations management approach?

While the first two research questions are of exploratory and explanatory nature, the third question aims to be prescriptive.

## 1.4 Research Design and Structure

The techno-economic research efforts at TU-Austria-Universities is considered to be mainly application oriented. The aim is to apply economic theories to technical-natural scientific problems and to find answers to the question of practical implementability in industrial practice (Bauer 2013, pp. 18–19). As per Ulrich, the applied research process begins with the identification of relevant practical problems, which are subsequently investigated from a scientific perspective building on existing literature and relevant theories. The derived models are validated in the specific application context. The result of applied research is to provide guidance to practitioners based on the learning from the research (Ulrich 1981, p. 20). Academics in production research ask for applied research, that is "less armchair research and more empirical and experimental work out there in the field" (Akkermans, van Wassenhove 2013, p. 6754). This is the intention of this thesis: investigating a relevant practical problem based on real-life case studies, developing a suitable methodology grounded in theory to solve the problem, and to demonstrate the applicability in practice. According to Yin case study research is

> "an empirical inquiry that investigates a contemporary phenomenon within its real-life context [..., that] copes with [a] technical distinctive situation [...,] relies on multiple sources of evidence [...and that] benefits from the prior development of theoretical propositions" (Yin 2003, pp. 13–14).

This thesis includes three industrial case studies from manufacturers in process industries. Table 1, gives an overview of the cases studied as part of this research, their location, investigation time interval, subject, focus, and the role of the researcher. As part of this research, the author was consultant, observer and sounding board/partner as defined by Karlsson 2016, pp. 15–16.

| | **Cement** | **Ammonia** | **Pulp** |
|---|---|---|---|
| **Location** | Northern Europe | Western Europe | Western Europe |
| **Investigation duration**[1] | May – Aug 2016 | Sep. – Dec. 2016 | Apr – Jul. 2017 |
| **Investigation subject** | Proof-of-concept | Pilot implementation | Ongoing continuous process improvement |
| **Investigation focus** | Analytics based process control | Profit per hour modelling | Validation of methodology |
| **Role of researcher** | Consultant | Observer | Sounding board and partner |

Table 1: Overview of case studies

The cement and the ammonia cases are of explorative nature providing valuable empirical insights for defining requirements and identifying design elements of the developed methodology. The third case of pulp manufacturing serves to

1 Note that project periods extend beyond investigation duration

describe and validate the derived methodology in practice. Yin points out the advantage of multiple case studies (Yin 2003, p. 19). For the review of theory and related work a heuristic, conceptual framework is used, which is a defined step in the research process by Karlsson 2016, p. 17. Heuristics such as Figure 2 are helpful in research “enabling a person to discover or learn something for them”[2], “involving or serving as an aid to learning, discovery, or problem-solving”[3].

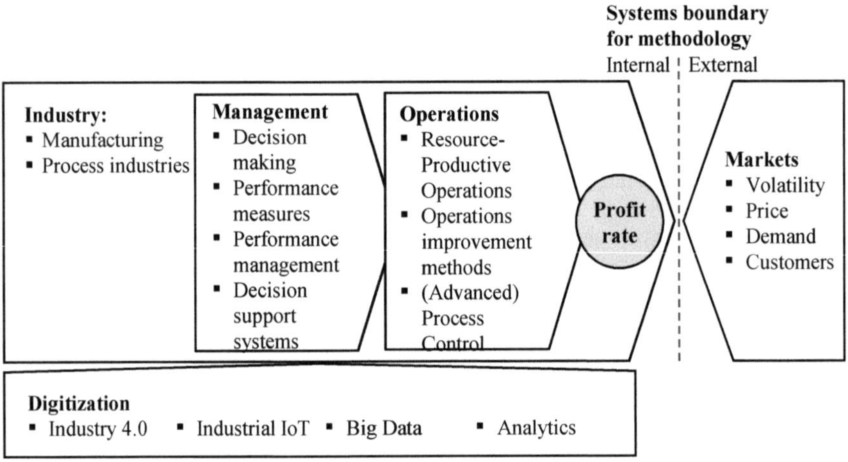


Figure 2: Conceptual framework (heuristic) of this research

The literature review for the terms and concepts related to industry, management, operations and digitization was conducted in the period of April 2015 and April 2017. Next to the library sources of Graz University of Technology[4], common scientific search engines such as Google Scholar[5], Science Direct[6] and Scopus[7], were used as they cover a wide range of relevant electronic and printed documents with free full-text access to the author.Figure 3, gives an overview of the overall timeline of the research.

---

2 https://en.oxforddictionaries.com/definition/heuristic, last accessed 16.08.2017
3 https://www.merriam-webster.com/dictionary/heuristic, last accessed 16.08.2017
4 http://ub.tugraz.at
5 http://scholar.google.com
6 http://www.sciencedirect.com
7 http://www.scopus.com

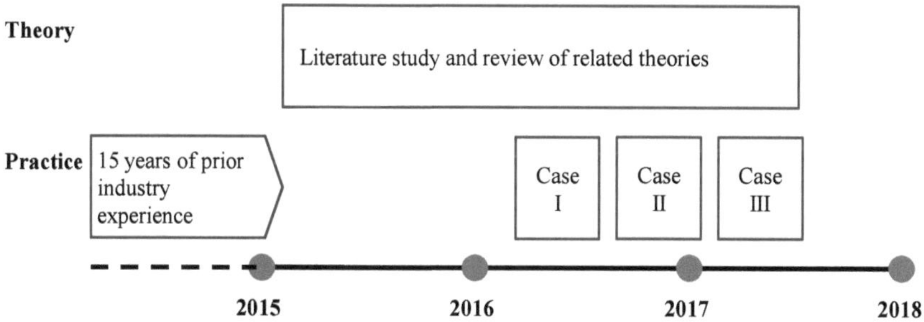


Figure 3: Research timeline

The design research methodology follows four phases: (1) research clarification defining goals, (2) descriptive study to gain deeper understanding, (3) prescriptive study resulting in a methodology, and (4) descriptive study for empirical evaluation (Blessing, Chakrabarti 2009, p. 15). Application-oriented research, according to Ulrich follows seven steps: (1) identification of relevant problems; (2) identification and interpretation of problem-relevant theories; (3) identification and specification of problem-relevant methodologies; (4) identification and investigation of application context; (5) derivation of evaluation criteria, design rules and models; (6) validation of rules and models in the application context; and (7) advice for practice. The research design for this thesis integrates the aspects of Ulrich, Blessing and Chakrabarti, and takes practical considerations such as access, skills and interest into account (Åhlström 2016, p. 72). Furthermore, it aims to address relevant criteria for exploratory and descriptive case study research: justification of the research approach, construct validity defining the unit of analysis and using multiple sources of evidence, external validity by using the theory to define domain for generalization and applicability, and reliability of the case study research by making the research process transparent (Yin 2003, p. 28, Voss et al. 2016, p. 192).

## 1.5 Thesis Outline

This thesis is structured in eleven chapters as indicated in Figure 4 on the next page. Chapter 1 serves as an introduction to the topic commencing with the initial situation, problems identified, research gap and motivation for this thesis stating its objectives, design, research questions and structure. Chapter 2 takes a look at current challenges from an industrial perspective. It starts with reviewing current megatrends and the impact of external factors such as increased volatility, uncertainty or complexity. Chapter 3 reviews the impact of digitization driven by Industry 4.0 and the Industrial Internet of Things leading to the rise of Big Data and advanced analytics. Chapter 4 provides a management view on the topic dealing with decision making based on performance measures, management systems and decision support systems. Chapter 5 deals with operations and how to make them resource-productive. It includes a coverage of relevant operational improvement methods, e.g., lean, Six Sigma and the Theory of Constraints and in addition, it looks at advanced process control systems. Chapter 6 adds practical insights drawing from two cases studies of manufacturing in process industries, cement and ammonia. Chapter 7 syntheses the theoretical concepts, literature and practical learning in order to define the scope of work, specific requirements and its delimitation. Chapter 8 conceives the methodology, looks at criteria when it is meaningful, and derives pre-conditions for implementation. Chapter 9 explains the implementation methodology and its underlying steps in detail. In chapter 10, the methodology is validated through an industrial case study from pulp manufacturing. Chapter 11 concludes this thesis with a summary, critically reviews answers to the research questions, and provides an outlook for further research.

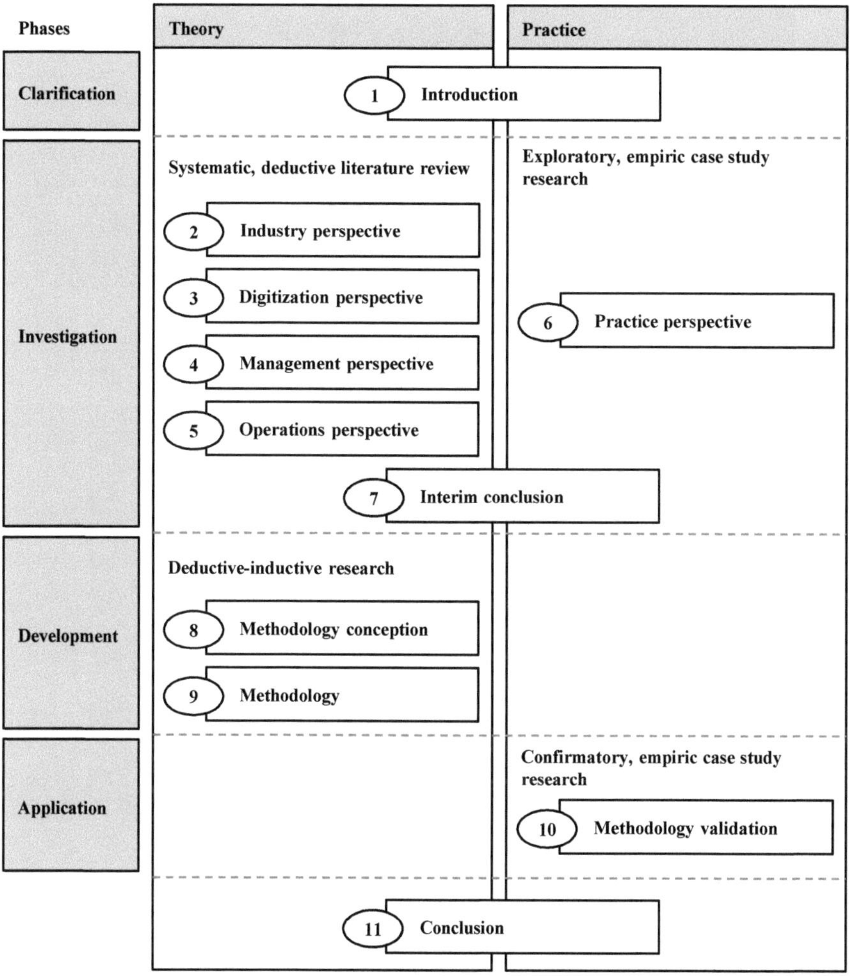


Figure 4: Research design and structure of this thesis

# 2 Industry Perspective: Challenges in Manufacturing in Process Industries

This chapter frames the setting for this thesis. Section 2.1 looks at mega trends such as the increasingly dynamic environment industrial companies are exposed to. Section 2.2 gives an overview of manufacturing industries. Section 2.3 focuses specifically on process industries. Section 2.4 provides a summary of the challenges faced by manufacturers in process industries.

## 2.1 Megatrends in Industry

The context in which companies operate, according to Adam et al., is getting more and more dynamic resulting in a need for quick reactions. However, they should not only be based on static analysis at a given point in time, but should rather be dynamic analyses reflecting meaningful future development paths of companies. The aim is to create potential in the future and leverage previously achieved benefits. Future success depends on decisions today (Adam et al. 1998, p. 6). But as Gordon points out: "Our decisions are only as good as the view of the future they rest on" (Gordon 2009, p. 6). The future is significantly impacted by technology as the main engine for development of the modern world economy. Especially, the rapid growth in information and communication technologies influences the standard of living, allocation of resources and internationalization (Dunning 2002, p. 61). Chapter 3 of this document focuses on technology, more specifically on digitization. Other megatrends affecting industrial production include ageing populations, environmental sustainability, and individualization and are listed in Table 2.


M. Hammer, *Management Approach for Resource-Productive Operations*,
Industrial Management, https://doi.org/10.1007/978-3-658-22939-9_2

| Global mega trends | Effect on production |
|---|---|
| **Ageing society** | • Future markets and products<br>• Workflow and management of production |
| **Individualization** | • Individual and customer specific products<br>• Complexity of products and production<br>• Synchronization of global production networks |
| **Knowledge** | • Knowledge based product development<br>• Knowledge based production systems |
| **Sustainability** | • Economic, ecological and social efficiency of production<br>• Changing availability and cost of raw materials and energy<br>• Global competition for resources |
| **Globalization** | • Products and production technologies for global markets<br>• Global process standards in OEMs<br>• Local circumstances and location factors in global competition |
| **Urbanization** | • Local infrastructure<br>• Emissions, mobility and traffic near to factories<br>• Production/work in mega-cities |
| **Finance** | • Highly dynamic economic cycles<br>• Financing of investments in R&D and PPE |
| **Public debt** | • More value-added – more employment<br>• Economic politics, public spending<br>• Competition between locations |

Table 2: Megatrends beyond technology with effects on industrial production (Westkämper 2013b, p. 8)

Next to the megatrends the operating conditions across industries are changing and can be described as VUCA volatile, uncertain, complex, and ambiguous). This expression was first used in the 1990s by the U.S. Army War College (Whiteman 1998, p. 15) and resulted in requirements for strategists "to exercise influence over the volatility, manage the uncertainty, simplify the complexity, and resolve the ambiguity" (Yarger 2006, p. 18). Bennett and Lemoine, summarized the main characteristics of VUCA, Figure 5, in the Harvard Business Review in 2014.

How well can you predict the results of your actions? (+ top, - bottom)

| | |
|---|---|
| **COMPLEXITY**<br><br>**Characteristics:** The situation has many interconnected parts and variables. Some information is available or can be predicted, but the volume or nature of it can be overwhelming to process.<br><br>**Example:** You are doing business in many countries, all with unique regulatory environments, tariffs, and cultural values.<br><br>**Approach:** Restructure, bring on or develop specialists, and build up resources adequate to address the complexity. | **VOLATILITY**<br><br>**Characteristics:** The challenge is unexpected or unstable and may be of unknown duration, but it's not necessarily hard to understand; knowledge about it is often available.<br><br>**Example:** Prices fluctuate after a natural disaster takes a supplier off-line.<br><br>**Approach:** Build in slack and devote resources to preparedness - for instance, stockpile inventory or overbuy talent. These steps are typically expensive; your investment should match the risk. |
| **AMBIGUITY**<br><br>**Characteristics:** Causal relationships are completely unclear. No precedents exist; you face "unknown unknowns."<br><br>**Example:** You decide to move into immature or emerging markets or to launch products outside your core competencies.<br><br>**Approach:** Experiment. Understanding cause and effect requires generating hypotheses and testing them. Design your experiments so that lessons learned can be broadly applied. | **UNCERTAINTY**<br><br>**Characteristics:** Despite a lack of other information, the event's basic cause and effect are known. Change is possible but not a given.<br><br>**Example:** A competitor's pending product launch muddies the future of the business and the market.<br><br>**Approach:** Invest in information – collect, interpret, and share it. This works best in conjunction with structural changes, such as adding information analysis networks, that can reduce ongoing uncertainty. |

\- **How much do you know about the situation?** +

Figure 5: What VUCA really means for you (Bennett, Lemoine 2014, p. 27)

## Volatility

In their book "No Ordinary Disruption" Dobbs et al state that: "The external environment is volatile, with capital markets increasingly characterized by more extreme events" (Dobbs et al. 2015, p. 88) and the World Economic Forum (WEF) sees increased volatility as the new normal for globalized and interconnected supply chains (World Economic Forum 2013, p. 9). In order to illustrate the degree of overall turbulence in the business environment Christopher and Holweg created the Supply Chain Volatility Index (SCVI) based on the coefficient of variation (CoV) as a normalized and scale-free measurement of volatility. In 2011 they observed unprecedented levels of volatility in several key business parameters simultaneously, and postulated an era of turbulence: "As of 2008, we have left an almost 30-year lasting period of stability behind and are now entering a period of turbulence that was last seen during the oil crisis of 1973" (Christopher, Holweg 2011, pp. 65–67). In fact, the worldwide real gross domestic product (GDP) saw its sharpest decline during the crisis years 2008-2009. While there seems to have been an initial return to more stability since then, the SCVI index as shown in Figure 6, paints a different picture. The rise of the index above the "crisis level" of 10 per cent as of 2016 suggests that the "era of turbulence" with high volatility is not over yet (Christopher, Holweg 2017, pp. 9–10).

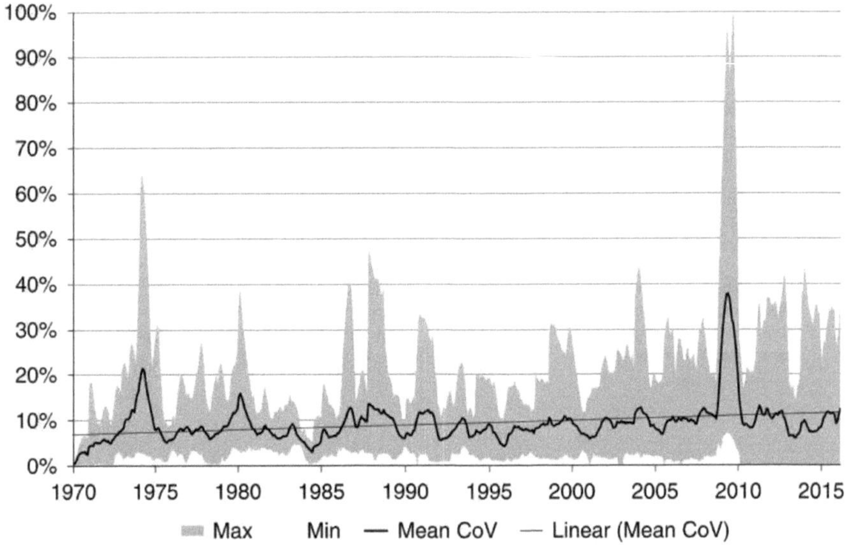


Figure 6: Supply Chain Volatility Index 1970-2015 (Christopher, Holweg 2017, p. 8)

Looking behind possible reasons for volatility, there is a wide range of external and internal change drivers, for example: shifts in customer demand with regard to product volumes, variants, mix, order entries, or delivery due dates; market pressure on prices and costs for oil, electricity, raw materials; political and regulatory factors, e.g., globalization or climate change; financial fluctuations in currency exchange rates and capital availability; pressure on short term positive financial results from capital markets; more frequent changes in ongoing production programs; or technological disruptions and innovations (Westkämper, Zahn 2009, p. 9; Christopher, Holweg 2011, p. 69). Volatility causes costs in supply chains either in the form of recovery costs, e.g., lost sales, idle capacity, overtime, or resilience costs, e.g., hedging/insurance cost, or access to extra capacity (Christopher, Holweg 2017, p. 14).

**Uncertainty**

Uncertainty is an important concern for managers and has significantly increased over recent years due to increased customer expectations demanding shorter product life-cycles and higher product variety; globalization resulting in more complex and longer supply chains; and non-conventional disruptions such as terror attacks (Sheffi, Rice Jr. 2005, p. 41). Uncertainty presents a risk and the WEF′s 2017 Global Risks Report calls for actions along five dimensions: (1) growing and reforming the economy, (2) rebuilding communities and society, (3) managing the technological disruption, (4) strengthening geopolitical cooperation, (5) accelerating environmental action (World Economic Forum 2017, p. 3). Overall the increasing feeling of uncertainty can be associated with: an unstable business environment; intransparent cause-effect interrelationships; and uncertain developments (Kremsmayr 2017, pp. 37–39). Dubeauclard et al. 2014, pp. 37–38, framed questions to help companies understand the effects of uncertainty on operations, for example:

- "How can operations preserve margin in down cycles while capturing disproportionate volume in up cycles?"
- "How can operations quickly react to minimize the impact on volume of an internal disruption to supply?", or
- "How can operations increase [their] ability to predict equipment and process failures?"

Figure 7 shows the effects of uncertainty on operations along six dimensions.

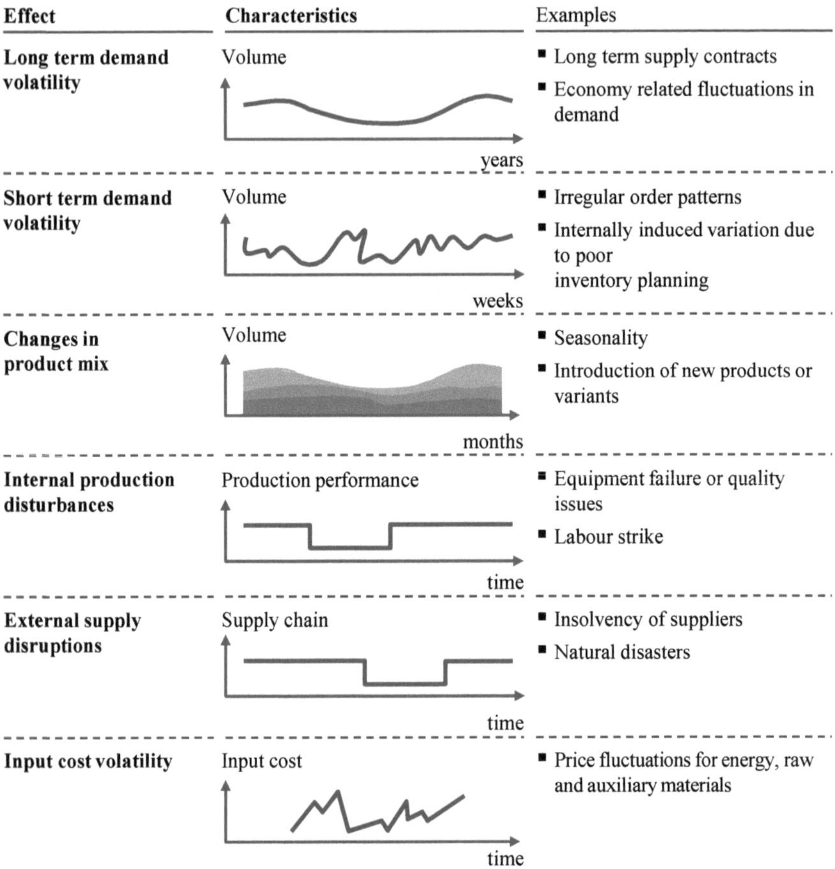


Figure 7: Effects of uncertainty on operations (Kremsmayr 2017, p. 59)

## Complexity

"Complexity arises when links between an intervention and an impact are difficult to identify and quantify", which is a common phenomenon in decision-making (Maier et al. 2016, p. 157). In organizations, complexity is concerned with "(1) interrelationships of the individuals, (2) their effect on the organization, and (3) the organization's interrelationships with its external environment"[8].

8 http://www.businessdictionary.com/definition/complexity.html, last accessed 10.05.2017

Understanding the 'who, what, where, how, and why', and the causes and effects of complexity is hard. However, major drivers such as mobility, technology (Codreanu 2016, p. 32) or globalization in general are known.

**Ambiguity**

Ambiguity, the lack of simple yes/no answers, is the result of volatility, uncertainty and complexity (Codreanu 2016, p. 32). For Ferrari et al., "causal relationships are not only unclear, but even the assumption that they exist in social systems cannot be verified" (Ferrari et al. 2015, p. 24). Ambiguity in general is defined as: "The quality of being open to more than one interpretation; inexactness"[9]. This thesis helps decision makers address ambiguity by solving trade-offs based on a profit per hour metric.

**Reframing VUCA as Opportunity**

After looking at the challenges of a VUCA world characterized by volatility, uncertainty, complexity, and ambiguity – it is important to also look at the opportunities. Johansen frames them as leadership opportunities using the very same VUCA acronym: vision, understanding, clarity, and agility (Johansen 2007, p. 45). The first three (i.e. vision, understanding, clarity) can be seen as necessary prerequisites while the last term (i.e. agility) can be viewed as the tangible result (Codreanu 2016, p. 33). Agility is a critical success factor for companies and their management in a context where volatility and uncertainty are the new "normal" (Ramsauer et al. 2017, p. 7). The increased volatility, uncertainty, complexity and ambiguity will present an ongoing challenge for industrial manufacturing companies. The opportunity lies in finding effective ways for coping with these circumstances, combining technologies, methods and capabilities to become more agile.

9 https://en.oxforddictionaries.com/definition/ambiguity, last accessed 28.04.2017

## 2.2 Manufacturing Industries

Manufacturing is a basic means of human existence and a major contributor to wealth creation (Hitomi 1996, p. 497). This is highlighted, for example in the Industrial Development Report 2016 (United Nations Industrial Development Organization 2015, p. 12):

- Global manufacturing value added (MVA) reached an all-time high of $9,228 billion in 2014. By 2014, the MVA of developing and emerging industrial economies (DEIEs) increased 2.4 times from 2000, while their GDP doubled.
- World export growth rates averaged 7.7 percent over 2005–2013, and in 2013 world trade reached a peak of more than $18 trillion, with 84.0 percent comprising manufacturing products.
- Manufacturing exports by industrialized countries expanded by an annual average of 4.3 percent over 2005–2013, reaching $11,998 billion in 2013. In the same period, DEIEs expanded their manufactured exports by an average 11.5 percent, to peak at $6,327 billion, 2.4 times more than in 2005.

**Definitions**

"Manufacturing can be defined as the application of mechanical, physical, and chemical processes to convert the geometry, properties, and/or appearance of a given starting material to make finished parts or products" (Rao 2011, p. 1). Hitomi specifies manufacturing as "the process of producing economic goods, including tangible goods and intangible services, from resources of production […] creating utility by increasing valued added" (Hitomi 1996, p. 8). The German Institute for Standardization classifies methodologies to manufacture goods in into six major groups: (1) primary shaping like casting or generative methodologies like 3D printing; (2) forming such as rolling, hammering or deep-drawing; (3) separating for example cutting, drilling or milling; (4) joining like welding or soldering; (5) coating such as galvanizing or powder coating; (6) changing material properties like tempering (DIN 8580:2003-09).

**Value Chain**

Manufacturing spans the entire value chain, Figure 8, and thus goes beyond the physical production of a product. Manufacturing is a "series of productive activities: planning, design, procurement, production, inventory, marketing, distribution, sales, management" (Hitomi 1996, p. 4).

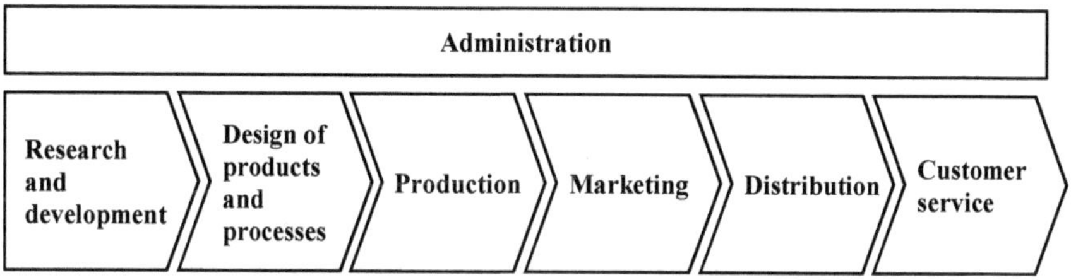


Figure 8: Different parts of the value chain (Horngren et al. 2015, p. 28)

Manufacturing is generally seen as a transformation process to create value (Westkämper 2013a, p. 15). It is an input-output system, as shown in Figure 9, "converting resources of production into economic goods [...] creating utilities" (Hitomi 1996, p. 7). The type of manufacturing varies by product and services provided. The success of a company depends on the efficiency of its operations (Rao 2011, p. 1) with its three distinct flows of materials, information, and cost (Hitomi 1996, p. 5).

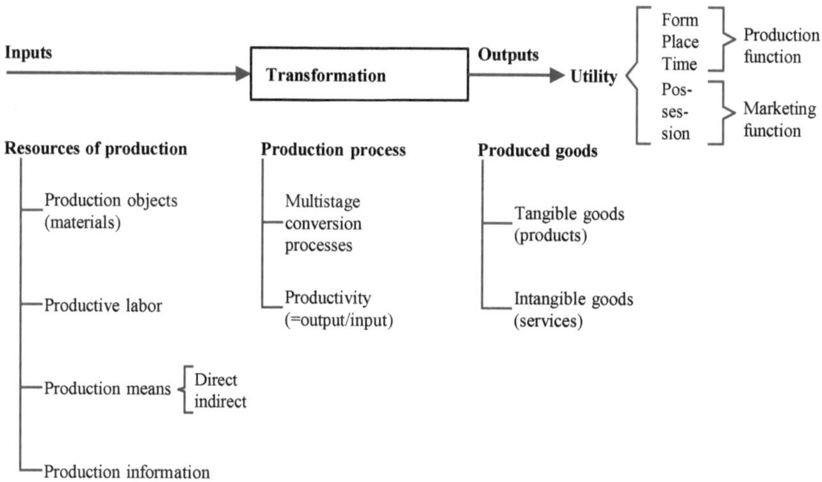


Figure 9: Definition/basic meaning of production (Hitomi 1996, p. 7)

**Objectives**

There are two categories of objectives of a company, which are: (1) a profit objective to be maximized by management, and (2) a social objective to be used to contribute to the welfare of society (Hitomi 1996, p. 13). Similarly, change in manufacturing is either profit driven based on market conditions or non-profit driven by regulations and policies (United Nations Industrial Development Organization 2015, p. 123). The profit objective has already been debated by Marx in his famous book "Capital" where he lays out the formula for capital circulation and creation of surplus (Marx 1990, p. 321), see Figure 10.

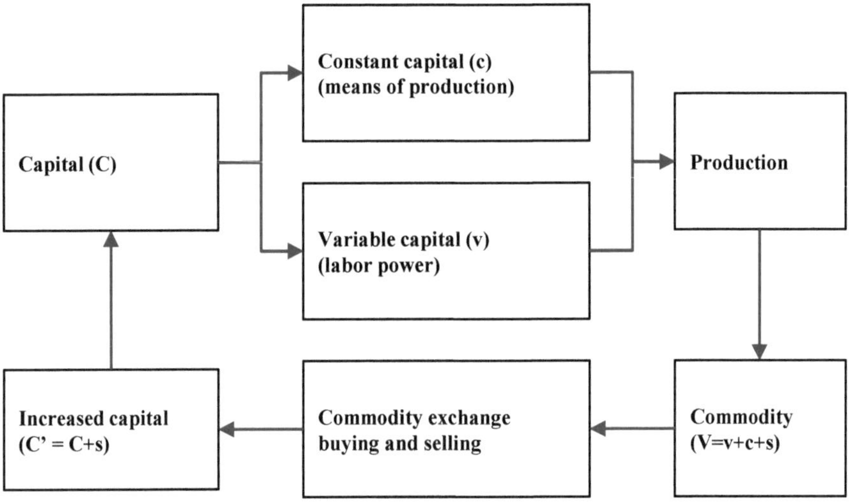


Figure 10: Capital circulation Karl Marx (Marx 1990, p. 321; Hitomi 1996, p. 10)

In the book "Capital in the 21st century" Piketty, argues that capitalism drives inequalities in situations when the rate of return on capital exceeds the rate of growth of output and income (Piketty, Goldhammer 2014, p. 1).

**Challenges and Opportunities in Manufacturing Industries**

The majority of root causes of manufacturing issues, for example, product availability, delivery performance, quality, efficiencies, etc. are related to transactional processes such as new product development, sales and operations planning, outsourcing, or other (Burton 2011, p. 359). Overarching challenges for the manufacturing sector are the maturity and saturation of industrial products; de-industrialization, unattractiveness of employment in manufacturing; and environmental impact (Hitomi 1996, pp. 497–498). A variety of factors hit production, e.g., cost pressure, new technologies with high complexity, time constraints for ramp-up/changeovers/delivery, quality standards, innovation, globalization, and organizational factors. Due to these factors further development of production concepts and systems is necessary (Wildemann 2010, p. 10). Wiendahl established several guidelines for future production, e.g., reacting fast to exceed the standard delivery performance of the market; being flexible to dominate volume and product mix changes; taking physical limits as point of orientation; designing products and processes to operate in a sustainable, energy and resource-efficient manner throughout the entire life cycle (Wiendahl et al. 2014, p. 74). In the "New Profit Imperative in Manufacturing", Wise and Baumgartner, argue that smart manufacturers have to go downstream, towards the customer, for the very simple reason: "that's where the money is". This results in exploiting valuable economic activity beyond manufacturing across the entire product life cycle (Wise, Baumgartner 1999, 133). Hitomi lays out 6 approaches to manufacturing excellence: (1) automated production/computer integrated manufacturing systems, (2) flexible/human-centered production, (3) high added-value production, (4) manufacturing for customer satisfaction, (5) green pro-duction, and (6) socially appropriate production (Hitomi 1996, pp. 500–501). According to Westkämper, the enablers of the production of the future are fundamentally driven by the innovations in information and communication technology leading to knowledge based technical and organizational processes; interconnected internal and external process chains; quick supply of information accessible from any location at any time; interactive ways of working with a high degree of visualization of complex processes; connection of real technical world with virtual display via sensor-linkage; and connection of suppliers and users during the life cycle of all technical products. As a consequence the boundaries of manufacturing extend to the entire life cycle and information technology supports the reduction in resource consumption (Westkämper 2013b, p. 9). But there is more than just technology. Skinner framed it as the productivity paradox, a "40 40 20" rule, stating that competitive advantage in manufacturing is driven 40% by structural factors such as manufacturing footprint, another 40% by process and equipment technology, and 20% by productivity improvement (Skinner 1986, 56). This document will focus the discussion on the 60% consisting of increasing productivity and technology and will not cover the area of manufacturing footprint. Driving productivity through operational measures has always been critical in manufacturing and resulted in the fact that a lot of performance management methods have been developed in this sector (Yadav, Sagar 2013, p. 956).

## 2.3 Process Industries

Process industries account for a significant portion of GDP in many countries and embrace a variety of businesses from small batch manufacturing in pharmaceuticals, to large batch manufacturing in steel production, up to continuous processing facilities in the petrochemical industry. However, "operations management (OM) research has traditionally paid very little attention to this large group of industries" (van Donk, Fransoo 2006, p. 211).

**Definitions**

Process industries are defined as "Manufacturers that produce products by mixing separating, forming, and/or performing chemical reactions" (Pittman, Atwater 2016, p. 141) and include large industrial scale processes in sectors such as: oil and gas production; mid-stream oil and gas processing; refining; petrochemicals; chemical and plastic production; food and drink processing; pharmaceuticals; water and waste water; paper production; nuclear power and other forms of power generation; and mining (Edmonds, Wilkinson 2016, pp. 13–14). "All process industries, whether batch or continuous, use nondiscrete materials", e.g., liquids, pulps, slurries, gases, and powders (Dennis, Meredith 2000a, p. 1086).

**Characteristics of Process vs. Discrete Industries**

Process industries are typically distinguished from discrete industries, which work with distinct solid materials that do not readily change and that maintain their shape and form without containerization. In contrast, process industries handle nondiscrete materials that expand, contract, settle out, absorb moisture, or dry out and cannot be held without containerization (Dennis, Meredith 2000a, p. 1086). Another common view is that process industries produce a variety of products from few raw materials whereas discrete industries assemble few product out of many input materials (Fransoo, Rutten 1994, p. 49). Changes to raw materials in process industries are transformational and frequently time dependent compared to reconfigurational and time independent changes in mechanical manufacturing, such as assembly industries (Floyd 2010, p. 16). Many companies in process industries "are actually hybrids due to the fact that their non-discrete units become discrete at some point during the manufacturing process" (Dennis, Meredith 2000b, p. 687). Table 3 summarizes further differences between the two industries (Ashayeri et al. 1996, p. 3312).

| | Process industries | Discrete industries |
|---|---|---|
| **Relationship with the market** | | |
| Product type | Commodity | Custom |
| Product assortment | Narrow | Broad |
| Demand per product | High | Low |
| Cost per product | Low | High |
| Order winners | Price | Speed of delivery |
| | Delivery guarantee | Product features |
| Transporting costs | High | Low |
| New products | Few | Many |
| **The production process** | | |
| Routings | Fixed | Variable |
| Lay-out | By product | By function |
| Flexibility | Low | High |
| Production equipment | Specialized | Universal |
| Labor intensity | Low | High |
| Capital intensity | High | Low |
| Changeover times | High | Low |
| Work in process | Low | High |
| Volumes | High | Low |
| **Quality** | | |
| Environmental demands | High | Low |
| Danger | Sometimes | Hardly |
| Quality measurement | Sometimes long | Short |
| **Planning & Control** | | |
| Production | To stock | To order |
| Long term planning | Capacity | Product design |
| Short term planning | Utilization capacity | Utilization personnel |
| Starting point planning | Availability capacity | Availability material |
| Material flow | Divergent + convergent | Convergent |
| Yield variability | Sometimes high | Mostly low |
| Explosion' via | Recipes | Bill of material |
| By and co-products | Sometimes | Not |
| Lot tracing | Mostly necessary | Mostly not necessary |

Table 3: Differences between process industries and discrete industries (Ashayeri et al. 1996, p. 3312)

**Batch vs. Continuous Processing**

Within process industries two modes of operations, batch and continuous processing, are distinguished. Fransoo and Rutten compare the key characteristic in Table 4.

| Process/flow businesses are characterized by | Batch/mix businesses are characterized by |
|---|---|
| • High production speed, short throughput time<br>• Clear determination of capacity, one routing for all products, no volume flexibility<br>• Low product complexity<br>• Low added value<br>• Strong impact of changeover times<br>• Small number of production steps<br>• Limited number of products | • Long lead time, much work in process<br>• Capacity is not well-defined (different configurations, complex routings)<br>• More complex products<br>• High added value<br>• Less impact of changeover times<br>• Large number of production/ process steps<br>• Large number of products |

Table 4: Characteristics continuous vs. batch (Fransoo, Rutten 1994, p. 53)

**The Element of Time**

Floyd points out three aspects of time in production that are relevant in process manufacturing such as in the chemical industry: (1) residence time, the time between initiation and completion of a chemical reaction; (2) persistence, time required to start or stop a reaction; and (3) continuity, i.e., continuous transformation of raw materials into products (Floyd 2010, p. 19,21). Also from a production and inventory management systems perspective, Dennis and Meredith concluded that a time-based system view might be most appropriate compared with a material-/capacity-dominated view (Dennis, Meredith 2000b, p. 697).

**Challenges and Opportunities in Process Industries**

One of the key challenges of process industries is their typically high capital intensity resulting in long amortization times of 10 to 15 or more years and high fixed costs putting pressure on companies to run their factories at the highest possible asset utilization (Friedli, Schuh 2012, p. 12). With capital and materials representing approximately 70% of the factory cost and labor the remaining 30% (Floyd 2010, p. 140), making resources more productive becomes paramount (Hammer, Somers 2015, p. 14). An essential requirement for operations in process industries is to remain within design and safety limits through tight process control of variables such as flow, temperature or pressure (Edmonds, Wilkinson 2016, p. 15). Improving safety, reducing variability, as well as documenting and sharing best-practices helps factories become more agile and more cost efficient (Ferdows, Thurnheer 2011, p. 922). Although the strategic value of agility varies between industries (Luczak 2017, p. 19), Floyd affirms that, given the large cost base and high capital intensity in process industries, the application of operations improvement principles "will yield higher benefits compared to discrete manufacturing" (Floyd 2010, pp. xv–xvi). However, Dennis and Meredith found that process industries face difficulties in realizing these benefits (Dennis, Meredith 2000b, p. 683). A positive example illustrating the opportunities that can be achieved, is a case study of a long term operations improvement effort for factory fitness at Hydro Aluminum Extrusion Group worldwide. Between 1986 and 2001, the factories did not only significantly improve safety, but also achieved a doubling of labor productivity (4.6 percent per year) and an output increase of 70 percent (4 percent per year) (Ferdows, Thurnheer 2011, p. 923).

## 2.4 Summary: Manufacturing in Process Industries

Manufacturing is an economically highly relevant sector. Private companies follow the profit maximization objective. A series of mega trends including globalization, environmental sustainability and digitalization have profound effects on manufacturing. Process industries embrace a wide range of sectors, such as the chemicals, metals, mining and pharmaceuticals industries, thus they represent a large and significant industrial sector. Due to the nature of the industry and continuous operations, time is an important factor in optimization as it is the ultimate constraint. In general, the sector already captures a lot of process data which can be used for analysis and are part of Big Data. There is further opportunity to apply lean, Six Sigma and agile principles, which will be covered under operations optimization in chapter 5.

| **Learning** | **Delimitations** | **Requirements** |
|---|---|---|
| • Megatrends affect industry, e.g., digitization<br>• Increased volatility, uncertainty, complexity and ambiguity (VUCA)<br>• Manufacturers have a social and/ or profit objective<br>• Process industries include a wide range or sectors and differ significantly from discrete industries<br>• Process industries are capital and asset intense<br>• Time is a critical constraint<br>• There is a need to make resources more productive<br>• Process industries generate a lot of data | INCLUDES<br>• Manufacturing at a process industry plant, regardless of geography and sector<br><br>EXCLUDES<br>• Discrete manufacturing, the larger supply chain, and service industries | • Leverage digital technologies<br>• Help manufacturers cope with VUCA context<br>• Maximize profits<br>• Focus on time utilization<br>• Develop a generic improvement approach for process industries, independent from sector, location or plant size |

Table 5: Summary of conclusions from industry perspective

# 3 Digitization Perspective: Impact of Digital Technologies in Manufacturing

This chapter provides a perspective on digitization and the impact on manufacturing. Section 3.1 introduces digitization and the subsequent chapters cover Industry 4.0 (section 3.2), Industrial Internet of Things (section 3.3), Big Data (section 3.4), advanced analytics (section 3.5) and a summary (section 3.6).

## 3.1 Digitization

Digitization presents an enormous financial opportunity. The World Economic Forum estimated the potential benefits, Figure 11, for industry and society as high as $100 trillion in the period to 2025 (World Economic Forum 2016, p. 2). Digitization also presents an attractive opportunity from a regional point of view. The 2016 study "Digital Europe – Pushing the frontier, capturing the benefits" found that Europe operates at only 12 percent (Bughin et al. 2016, p. 7) and the US economy at 18 percent of the potential shown by the digital frontier (Bughin et al. 2016, p. 12). Improvement opportunities can be grouped by categories, Table 6, including improved asset efficiency, resource management, better operations and supply-chain optimization (Bughin et al. 2016, p. 33).

This profit per hour research addresses a number of categories mentioned in Table 6, for instance, improved asset efficiency, resource management and operations optimization through real-time monitoring and control of production.


M. Hammer, *Management Approach for Resource-Productive Operations*, Industrial Management, https://doi.org/10.1007/978-3-658-22939-9_3

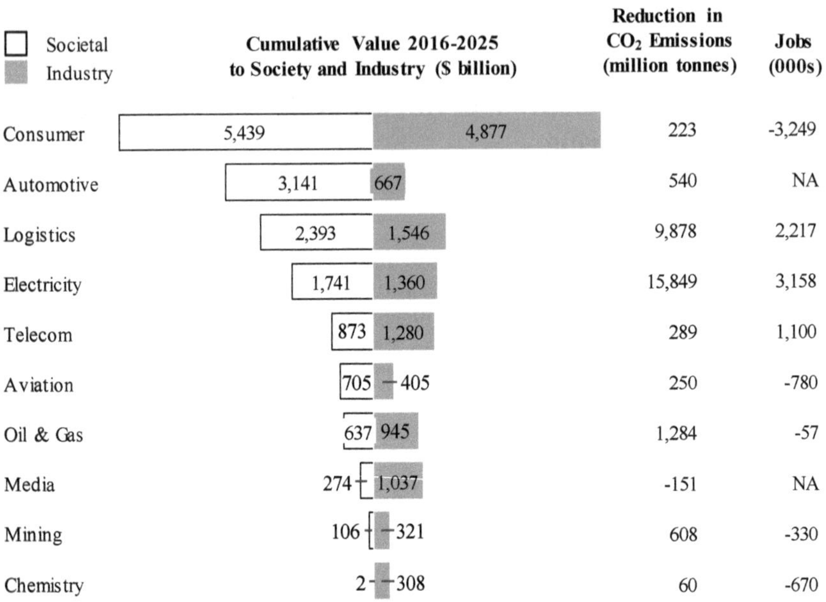


Figure 11: Value opportunity of digital transformation to 2025 (World Economic Forum 2016, p. 61)

| **Labor** | **Multifactor productivity** |
|---|---|
| Increased supply and productivity<br>• Increased labor-force participation<br>• Better and faster matching of workers with employers<br>• Increased productivity of workers in the labor force | R&D and product development<br>• Better use of data leads to new inventions<br>• Faster product development cycles enabled by better testing and quality control<br>Operations and supply-chain optimization<br>• Real-time monitoring and control of production lines<br>• Better logistics routing through path optimization and prioritization<br>Resource management<br>• Improved energy efficiency through intelligent building systems<br>• Increased fuel efficiency<br>• Decreased waste of raw materials |
| **Capital** | |
| Improved asset efficiency<br>• Preventive maintenance decreases downtime and reduces expenditure on maintenance<br>• Increased use of assets | |

Table 6: Improvement opportunities by categories (Bughin et al. 2016, p. 33)

**Technologies**

Slack defines disruptive technologies as "technologies which in the short term cannot match the performance required by customers but may improve faster than existing technology to make that existing technology redundant" (Slack et al. 2010, p. 660). New technologies are also being adopted at ever higher speed. While it took 38 years for the radio to reach fifty million users, it was only 13 years for television, 3 years for the internet and 1 year for Facebook (Dobbs et al. 2015, p. 43). The World Economic Forum studied "Technology Tipping Points and Societal Impact" and identified six megatrends: (1) people and the internet; (2) computing, communications and storage everywhere; (3) the Internet of Things; (4) artificial intelligence and Big Data; (5) the sharing economy and distributed trust, and (6) the digitization of matter (World Economic Forum 2015, p. 5).

**From Digitization to Digital Transformation**

Digitization goes back to the binary numerical system developed by Leibniz (Khan 2016, pp. 3–4). Through the conversion of information into 1s and 0s, digitization results in the creation of Big Data and close to zero cost information processing capability (Dobbs et al. 2015, p. 39). The book "Digital Economy" (Tapscott 2014, pp. 78–80) lays out twelve themes explained in Table 7. On top of digitization there is digital transformation, which is "the use of technology to radically improve performance or reach of enterprises" (MIT Center for Digital Business and Capgemini Consulting 2011, p. 5). Burton points out that "technology is most successful when it is integrated with process improvement and enables a fact-based solution to a business problem or challenge" (Burton 2011, p. 378). This requires organizational change, leadership, a compelling vision, and a process helping with the "how" rather than "the what" (MIT Center for Digital Business and Capgemini Consulting 2011, p. 5). The building blocks of a digital transformation are shown in Figure 12.

| | |
|---|---|
| **1. Knowledge** | There is a shift from brawn to brain. Knowledge becomes an important element of products. The gap between consumers and producers blurs. |
| **2. Digitization** | Human communication, delivery of government programs, execution of health care, business transactions, exchange of funds, etc., become based on ones and zeros. |
| **3. Virtualization** | Physical things can become virtual—changing the metabolism of the economy, the types of institutions and relationships possible, and the nature of economic activity itself. |
| **4. Molecularization** | Replacement of the mass media, mass production, monolithic governments, by molecular media, production, governance, etc. |
| **5. Integration/ Inter-networking** | The new economy is a networked economy with deep, rich interconnections within and between organizations and institutions. Wealth creation, commerce, and social existence are based on a ubiquitous public infrastructure. |
| **6. Disinter-mediation** | Elimination of intermediaries in economic activity including agents, brokers, wholesalers, some retailers, broadcasters, record companies, and anything that stands between producers and consumers. |
| **7. Convergence** | Convergence of key economic sectors—computing, communications, and content. |
| **8. Innovation** | Innovation is the key driver of economic activity and business success. Rather than traditional drivers of success such as access to raw materials, productivity, scale, and the cost of labor, human imagination becomes the main source of value. |
| **9. Prosumption** | The gap between consumers and producers blurs in a number of ways. For example, consumers become involved in the actual production process as their knowledge, information, and ideas become part of the product specification process. Human collaboration on the Net becomes a part of the international repository of knowledge. |
| **10. Immediacy** | The new economy is a real-time economy. Commerce becomes electronic as business transactions and communications occur at the speed of light rather than of the post office. |
| **11. Globalization** | Knowledge knows no boundaries. As knowledge becomes the key resource, there is only a world economy, even though the individual organization operates in a national, regional, or local setting. New economic and political regions and structures (such as the European Union) are leading to a decline in the importance of the nation-state and increasing the interdependencies among countries. |
| **12. Discordance** | Massive social contradictions are arising. New, highly paid employment versus the inappropriate skills of laid-off workers. Gulfs are growing between haves and have-nots, knowers and know-nots, those with access to the internet and those without it. |

Table 7: Themes of the Digital Economy (Tapscott 2014, pp. 78–80)

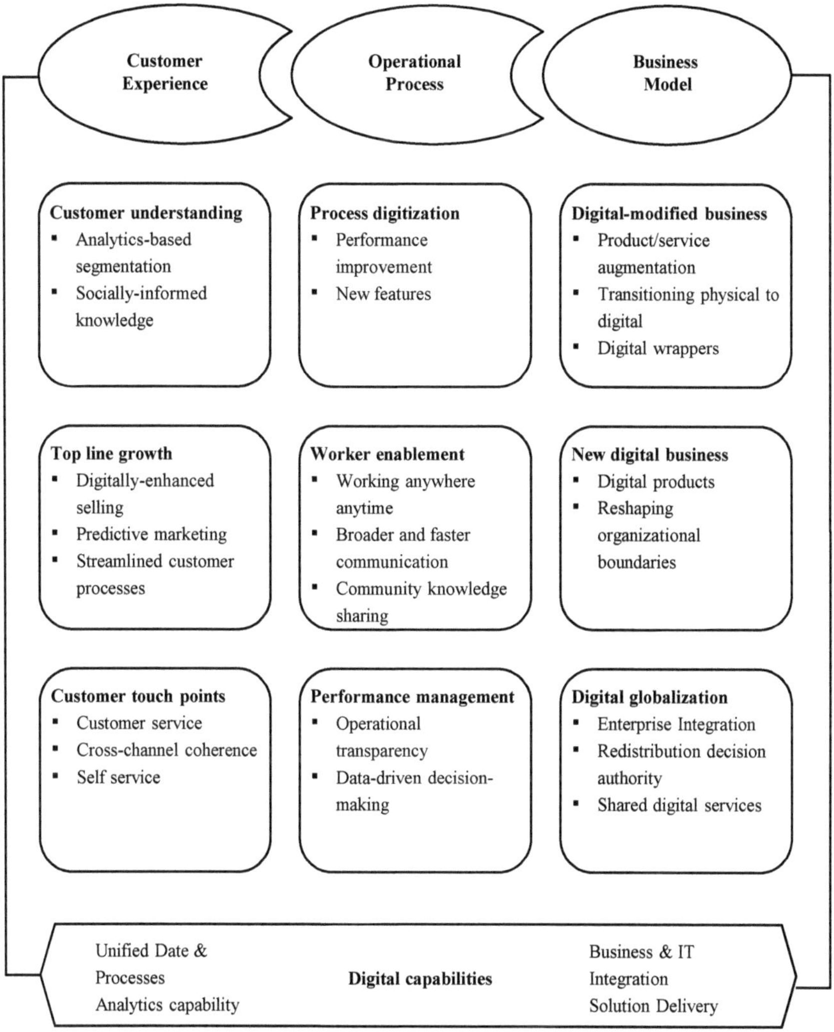


Figure 12: Building blocks of digital transformation
(MIT Center for Digital Business and Capgemini Consulting 2011, p. 17)

**Current State, Challenges and Opportunities**

For Porter and Heppelmann, digitization will lead to a new era of lean production systems, enabled by smart, connected products. By providing data on their activities, location, or maintenance needs, these products will reduce waste and lead to productivity increases in the area of materials, energy, labor, and assets (Porter, Heppelmann 2015). For asset-heavy industries and public sector-like businesses, digitization is of particular relevance, as they are considered as digital laggards (Bughin et al. 2016, p. 10). The digital economy also requires people to change. According to Tapscott, yesterday's managers need to become tomorrow's leaders, who carefully balance business objectives with needs of employees, customers and society in the face of the digital disruption (Tapscott 2014, xv).

## 3.2 Industry 4.0

The first three industrial revolutions are associated with mechanization, electrification and the rise of information technology, Table 8. The fourth industrial revolution is driven by the introduction of the Internet of Things and Services in the manufacturing environment (Kagermann et al. 2013, p. 5). Industry 4.0 is made possible by advancements in hardware and software technologies, such as miniaturization, sensors, storage capacities and computing power, that are now cheap enough for deployment at scale in production (Neugebauer et al. 2016, p. 4).

| **1. Industrial revolution**<br><br>follows introduction of water- and steam-powered mechanical manufacturing facilities | **2. Industrial revolution**<br><br>follows introduction of electrically-powered mass production based on the division of labor | **3. Industrial revolution**<br><br>uses electronics and IT to achieve further automation of manufacturing | **4. Industrial revolution**<br><br>based on Cyber-Physical Systems |
|---|---|---|---|
| End of 18th century | Start of 20th century | Start of 1970s | Today |

Table 8: The four stages of the industrial revolution (Kagermann et al. 2013, p. 13)

Industry 4.0, according to Kagermann et al., promises huge potential through new business models and increases in resource productivity and cross-value chain efficiencies. Smart factories will be capable of profitably producing custom specific items in an agile way, and smart assistance systems will help workers to focus on really value-added activities instead of routine tasks (Kagermann et al. 2013, p. 5). Table 9 gives an overview of the estimated cost optimization potential through Industry 4.0.

| Cost type | Effects | Potentials |
|---|---|---|
| Inventory | • Reduction of safety stocks<br>• Avoidance of Bullwhip and Burbridge effects | -30 to -40% |
| Production | • Increase in Overall Equipment Effectiveness (OEE)<br>• Process control loops<br>• Improvement in vertical and horizontal labor flexibility | -10 to -20% |
| Logistics | • Higher degree of automation (milk run, picking, …) | -10 to -20% |
| Complexity | • Enhanced span of control<br>• Reduced trouble shooting | -60 to -70% |
| Quality | • Real-time quality control loops | -10 to -20% |
| Maintenance | • Optimization of spare part inventories<br>• Condition-based maintenance (process data, measurement data)<br>• Dynamic prioritization | -20 to -30% |

Table 9: Estimated benefits of Industry 4.0 (Bauernhansl 2014, p. 31)

## Regional Perspectives Related to Industry 4.0

Industry 4.0 originated as a “strategic initiative” of the German government, part of the High-Tech Strategy 2020 Action Plan, which was approved in November 2011 (Kagermann et al. 2013, p. 77). Ernst Burgbacher, at the time Parliamentary State Secretary in the Federal Ministry of Economics and Technology declared that

> “Germany’s economy is characterized by its strong industrial base, particularly its machinery and plant manufacturing, automotive and energy industries. Implementation of Industry 4.0 will be absolutely key to its future development – we cannot allow industry to come to a standstill” (Kagermann et al. 2013, p. 30).

Other regions are pursuing similar initiatives, Table 10.

| USA | Europe, specifically Germany | China | Japan and South Korea |
|---|---|---|---|
| "Radical Innovation" | "Engineering Excellence" | "Speed" | "Ability to Scale" |
| **Bringing digital innovation into the physical world**<br>Start-ups for the Internet of Things and manufacturing Renaissance | **Bringing engineering excellence into the digital world**<br>Visionary concepts integrating technology, society and economy | **Pragmatic application of quick-wins and long-term strategy**<br>Application of mature technologies. strategic development of key technologies | **Innovation by application**<br>Massive construction of smart factories and very large manufacturers, strengthening products through domestic demand |

Table 10: Current focuses of selected countries and regions in the context of Industry 4.0 (Gausemeier, Klocke 2016, p. 33)

The Chinese government established a program called China Manufacturing 2025 (CM2025), which Chu, considers as "China's answer to Germany's Industry 4.0" (Chu 2016, p. 7). But CM2025 goes beyond the technological aspects of Industry 4.0 in that it includes the restructuring of manufacturing industry to make it more competitive (European Union Chamber of Commerce in China 2017, p. 7). CM2025 priority areas include: improving manufacturing innovation; integrating IT and industry; strengthening the industrial base; fostering Chinese brands; enforcing green manufacturing; promoting breakthroughs in 10 key sectors; advancing restructuring of the manufacturing sector; promoting service-orientated manufacturing and manufacturing-related service industries; and internationalizing manufacturing (European Union Chamber of Commerce in China 2017, p. 9).

In the United States, the President's Council of Advisors on Science and Technology promoted the term "advanced manufacturing" in a report in 2011:

> "We believe that advanced manufacturing provides the path forward to revitalizing U.S. leadership in manufacturing, and will best support economic productivity and ongoing knowledge production and innovation in the Nation" (Executive Office of the President: President's Council of Advisors on Science and Technology 2011, ii).

The recommendations of the Advanced Manufacturing Partnership across communities, academia, businesses, and government follow three pillars: (1) enabling innovation, (2) securing the talent pipeline, and (3) improving the business climate (Executive Office of the President: President's Council of Advisors on Science and Technology 2014, pp. 17–19). Advanced manufacturing covers both new production technologies and new products and is broadly defined as "a family of activities that (a) depend on the use and coordination of information, automation, computation, software, sensing, and networking, and/or (b) make use of cutting edge materials and emerging capabilities enabled by the physical and biological sciences, for example nanotechnology, chemistry, and biology" (Executive Office of the President: President's Council of Advisors on Science and Technology 2011, ii).

**Definition**

According to agiplan, Industry 4.0 is a meta term, referring to the advancement of production and value creation systems through combining physical and digital worlds (agiplan et al. 2015, p. 12). The integration of cyber-physical systems into manufacturing, as part of Industry 4.0, effects business models and value creation in both production and services (Kagermann et al. 2013, p. 14). Industry 4.0 covers multiple dimensions: technology, e.g., highly interconnected systems from sensors/actuators to machines/equipment and users; organization, e.g., self-controlled, autonomous systems; humans, e.g., their qualification; business models such as individualized production (agiplan et al. 2015, p. 1). Baur and Wee consider Industry 4.0 "as the next phase in the digitization of the manufacturing sector" based on four trends: (1) the rise in data volumes, computational power, and connectivity, (2) the emergence of analytics and business-intelligence capabilities; (3) new forms of human-machine interaction such as augmented-reality systems; and (4) improvements in transferring digital instructions to the physical world, such as advanced robotics and 3-D printing (Baur, Wee 2015, p. 1). Research into academic publications resulted in the following terms that define what Industry 4.0 means: real-time data, Big Data, machine-to-machine, the Internet of Things, cyber physical systems, cloud computing, and smart grid (Tschöpe et al. 2015, p. 148). Bauernhansl points out that it is not the digitalization that is revolutionary, but the possibilities offered by interconnected technical systems, communication, services, and humans as part of Industry 4.0 (Bauernhansl 2016, p. 454). The journey towards Industry 4.0, turning traditional factories into smart factories, is expected to be gradual and evolutionary (Lee et al. 2015b, p. 8). A study commissioned by the IMPULS foundation of the German Mechanical Engineering Industry Association VDMA framed the following dimensions of Industry 4.0: smart factory, smart products, smart operations, data-driven services, strategy and organization, and employees (Lichtblau et al. 2015, p. 21). The study conducted by IW Consult (a subsidiary of the Cologne Institute for Economic Research) and the Institute for Industrial Management (FIR) at RWTH Aachen University developed a readiness model based upon these six dimensions, Figure 13.

Figure 13: Dimensions and associated fields of Industry 4.0 (Lichtblau et al. 2015, p. 22)

**Smart Factories**

Smart factories offer significant potential ranging from individualized production in dynamic business environments to continuous improvement through optimal decision making (Monostori et al. 2016, p. 625). Kagermann et al highlighted smart factories as a key feature of Industry 4.0 (Kagermann et al. 2013, p. 19). However, the idea of „Smart Factories" existed even prior to Industry 4.0. In 2009 Westkämper and Zahn saw it as a new generation of knowledge-based factories based on information available anytime, anywhere through ubiquitous computing (Westkämper, Zahn 2009, p. 12). A smart factory is a cyber-physical manufacturing system enabling agile production through the integration of equipment, machines, products with information systems such as MES and ERP (Wang et al. 2016, p. 159). A smart factory is defined as a "factory whose degree of integration has reached a level which makes self-organizing functions possible in production and in all business processes relating to production" (VDI/VDE-Gesellschaft Mess- und Automatisierungstechnik 2016a, p. 20). Self-x properties can include adaptation, organization, optimization, configuration, protection, healing, discovery, description (Friess 2013, p. 63). Table 11offers a comparison between a typical factory and a smart factory.

| | | **Today´s factory** | | **Industry 4.0** | |
|---|---|---|---|---|---|
| | **Data source** | **Attributes** | **Technologies** | **Attributes** | **Technologies** |
| **Component** | Sensor | Precision | Smart sensors and fault detection | Self-aware<br>Self-predict | Degradation monitoring & remaining useful life prediction |
| **Machine** | Controller | Producibility & performance | Condition-based monitoring & diagnostics | Self-aware<br>Self-predict<br>Self-compare | Up time predictive health monitoring |
| **Production system** | Networked system | Productivity & OEE | Lean operations: work and waste reduction | Self-configure<br>Self-maintain<br>Self-organize | Worry-free productivity |

Table 11: Comparison of today´s with an Industry 4.0 factory (Lee et al. 2015a, p. 19)

For Gilchrist, the smart factory of the future unlike any traditional factories has already arrived (Gilchrist 2016, p. 194).

**Smart Products**

Smart products are another element of Industry 4.0. For Kagermann et al., products are smart if they "know the details of how they were manufactured and how they are intended to be used" (Kagermann et al. 2013, p. 19). A smart product is characterized as a "produced or manufactured (intermediate) product which in a smart factory delivers the (outward) communication capability to network and to interact intelligently with other production participants" (VDI/VDE-Gesellschaft Mess- und Automatisierungstechnik 2016a, p. 21). According to Porter and Heppelman, smart, connected products have 4 capabilities as shown in Table 12.

| **1. Monitoring** | **2. Control** | **3. Optimization** | **4. Autonomy** |
|---|---|---|---|
| Sensors and external data sources enable the comprehensive monitoring of:<br>• The product's condition<br>• The external environment<br>• The product's operation and usage<br>Monitoring also enables alerts and notifications of changes | Software embedded in the product or in the product cloud enables:<br>• Control of product functions<br>• Personalization of the user experience | Monitoring and control capabilities enable algorithms that optimize product operation and use in order to:<br>• Enhance product performance<br>• Allow predictive diagnostics, service, and repair | Combining monitoring, control, and optimization allows:<br>• Autonomous product operation<br>• Self-coordination of operation with other products and systems<br>• Autonomous product enhancement and personalization<br>• Self-diagnosis and service |

Table 12: Four capabilities of smart, connected products (Porter, Heppelmann 2014)

**Smart Operations**

Smart operations in production are achieved through a continuous exchange of information, "a dialogue between smart factory and smart product" (VDI/VDE-Gesellschaft Mess- und Automatisierungstechnik 2016a, p. 21). This is achieved through a "systems of systems", i.e. the integration of devices, sensors and software, providing real-time visibility of equipment condition, operating parameters, factory or product status (Biron, Follett 2016, p. 13). As of 2015 only 0.9% of companies had reached the highest maturity level for smart operations, that is characterized by complete system-integrated information sharing; autonomous control and self-reacting processes; and comprehensive IT security and cloud solutions (Lichtblau et al. 2015, p. 40). Autonomous control maximizing profit per hour is the envisioned end-state of the approach derived in this thesis.

**Data-Driven Services**

The goal of data-driven services, as per Lichtblau et al., is to provide additional value to customers through after-sales and services. This is made possible by the analysis of data collected from the usage phase of products (Lichtblau et al. 2015, p. 13). Data-driven services comprise the aspects of tele-maintenance; reduced resource consumption; and availability, performance, and quality enhancements through optimized parameter settings (Lichtblau et al. 2015, p. 66). The last aspect will be directly related to the goal of profit per hour maximization as part of this work.

**Employees**

The working environment and required employee skills and qualifications will be significantly impacted through Industry 4.0 (Lichtblau et al. 2015, p. 52). According to Gorecky et al., employees will have to take on a higher degree of responsibility as their role changes to determine the overarching production strategy, supervise the strategy implementation and status of the cyber-physical system, and intervene if needed. Companies will need to help their employees in this transition through interdisciplinary training and qualification, and provision of appropriate supporting human-technology solutions (Gorecky et al. 2014, p. 527). One of the aims of this work is to support employee decision making through the profit per hour approach.

**Strategy and Organization**

Industry 4.0 is a strategic topic, especially when it comes to identifying new business models based on innovation and use of new technologies (Lichtblau et al. 2015, p. 29). Baur and Wee recognize eight value areas for Industry 4.0: (1) resource/process efficiency, e.g., smart energy consumption or real-time yield optimization; (2) asset utilization, e.g., predictive maintenance, augmented reality for the maintenance and repair organization; (3) labor, e.g., human-robot collaboration and digital performance management; (4) inventories, e.g., real-time supply chain optimization and in situ 3-D printing; (5) quality, e.g., statistical process control (SPC) and advanced process control (APC); (6) supply/demand match, e.g., data-driven demand prediction and data-driven design to value; (7) time to market, e.g., rapid experimentation and simulation; and (8) service/aftersales, e.g., predictive maintenance, remote maintenance and virtually guided self-service (Baur, Wee 2015, p. 3).

**Current State, Challenges and Opportunities**

Industry 4.0 is a major opportunity to increase profitability in manufacturing. It goes far beyond the adoption of particular technologies as it encompasses disruptive business models and significantly affects humans and society at large. The chances are manifold, so are the risks. Challenges includes data protection, cyber-security, system reliability (agiplan et al. 2015, p. 79), and additional technological or organizational barriers in the supply chain (Kersten et al. 2014, p. 114). The key to increased performance in Industry 4.0 is the optimal collaboration between humans and cyber-physical systems. The vision of a self-controlling production plant with humans and technical components working synergistically together in a socio- technical unit, delivering creative value-added by working seamlessly together, is compelling (Eßer 2015, p. 3). R&D challenges consist of the handling of time, computational dynamical systems theory, standardization, and security issues (Monostori et al. 2016, p. 637). The biggest potential benefit of digitalization in the context of Industry 4.0 is to become more agile, thus reacting faster to external dynamics through analytics-based decision-making and increased efficiency (Schuh et al. 2017, p. 10). Turning factories into smart factories in Industry 4.0 is directly related to the Industrial Internet of Things (Wan et al. 2016, V).

## 3.3 Industrial Internet of Things

Intelligent systems connecting factories, machines, products and people with each other in real time, across all industries, is the vision of the Internet of Things (IoT) (Biron, Follett 2016, p. 1). According to the latest forecasts, "8.4 billion connected things will be in use worldwide in 2017, up 31 percent from 2016, and will reach 20.4 billion by 2020" (Gartner 2017). "Interest in IoT is higher than ever: 28% of businesses already have live projects, with a further 35% less than a year away from launch" according to the 4th edition of the Vodafone IoT Barometer in 2016. The survey concludes that IoT drives large-scale business transformation with measurable results, that it is a business topic and not a technology topic, and that one major focus is on Big Data and analytics to support decision making (Vodafone 2016, pp. 4–5). This is also reflected in a 22 percent compound annual growth rate (CAGR) for analytics and IoT from 2015 to 2020, a 2.7-fold growth (Cisco 2016). The estimated total potential economic impact is $3.9 trillion to $11.1 trillion per year in 2025 (Manyika et al. 2015, p. 2).

**Definitions**

According to Biron and Follett the term "Internet of Things" was developed by Kevin Ashton of the Massachusetts Institute of Technology (MIT) in 1999 (Biron, Follett 2016, p. 2). But similar concepts such as machine-to-machine (M2M) connectivity go back even further (Perry 2016, p. 1). Nowadays, the terms machine-to-machine communication and the Internet of Things are often used interchangeably (Höller et al. 2014, p. 10), although M2M only refers to communication between devices of the same type (Höller et al. 2014, p. 11). IoT, as per the International Telecommunication Union (ITU) is about communication between any type of thing (ITU-T 2012, p. 3), as shown in Figure 14.

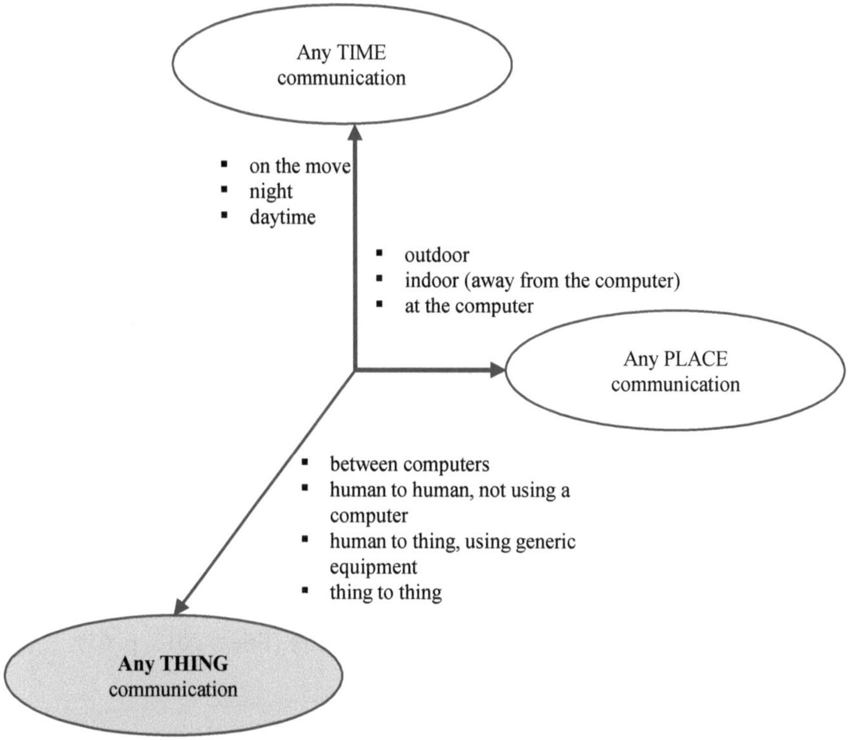


Figure 14: The new dimension introduced in the Internet of things (ITU-T 2012, p. 3)

A popular definition is for the Internet of Things is provided by Gartner: "The Internet of Things (IoT) is the network of physical objects that contain embedded technology to communicate and sense or interact with their internal states or the external environment[10]."

Formal definitions are provided by the standardization sector of the International Telecommunication Union (ITU-T 2012, p. 1):

> **Internet of Things (IoT)**: A global infrastructure for the information society, enabling advanced services by interconnecting (physical and virtual) things based on existing and evolving interoperable information and communication technologies.
> NOTE 1 – Through the exploitation of identification, data capture, processing and communication capabilities, the IoT makes full use of things to offer services to all kinds of applications, whilst ensuring that security and privacy requirements are fulfilled.
> NOTE 2 – From a broader perspective, the IoT can be perceived as a vision with technological and societal implications.
> **Thing**: With regard to the Internet of things, this is an object of the physical world (physical things) or the information world (virtual things), which is capable of being identified and integrated into communication networks.
> **Device**: With regard to the Internet of things, this is a piece of equipment with the mandatory capabilities of communication and the optional capabilities of sensing, actuation, data capture, data storage and data processing.

The Internet of Things brings together consumer, business and Industrial Internet (Friess 2013, pp. 8–9). The creation of the term Industrial Internet is attributed to General Electric (Gilchrist 2016, p. 1) and the application of IoT to the industrial area is now commonly known as the *Industrial Internet of Things,* or IIoT (Chu 2016, p. 11). The IIoT covers all sectors such as energy and utilities, manufacturing, agriculture, health care, retail and, transportation and logistics (Gilchrist 2016, p. 2). Usually retrofitting existing infrastructure with the sensors and communication modules is required to achieve smart, connected operations (Biron, Follett 2016, p. 12). Next to the self-x properties already mentioned, autonomy is a vital element of IoT systems in industry (Friess 2013, p. 63).

**Technology**

"One of the most significant advances in the development of computer science, information and communication technologies is represented by cyber-physical systems (CPS)" (Monostori et al. 2016, p. 621). A cyber-physical system is

10 http://www.gartner.com/it-glossary/internet-of-things, last accessed 10.03.2017

defined as a "system which links real (physical) objects and processes with information-processing (virtual) objects and processes via open, in some cases global, and constantly interconnected information networks" (VDI/VDE-Gesellschaft Mess- und Automatisierungstechnik 2016a, p. 18). The application of CPS in production results in cyber-physical production systems (CPPS), Figure 15, where employees interact with both physical and virtual system components (Thiede et al. 2016, p. 8).

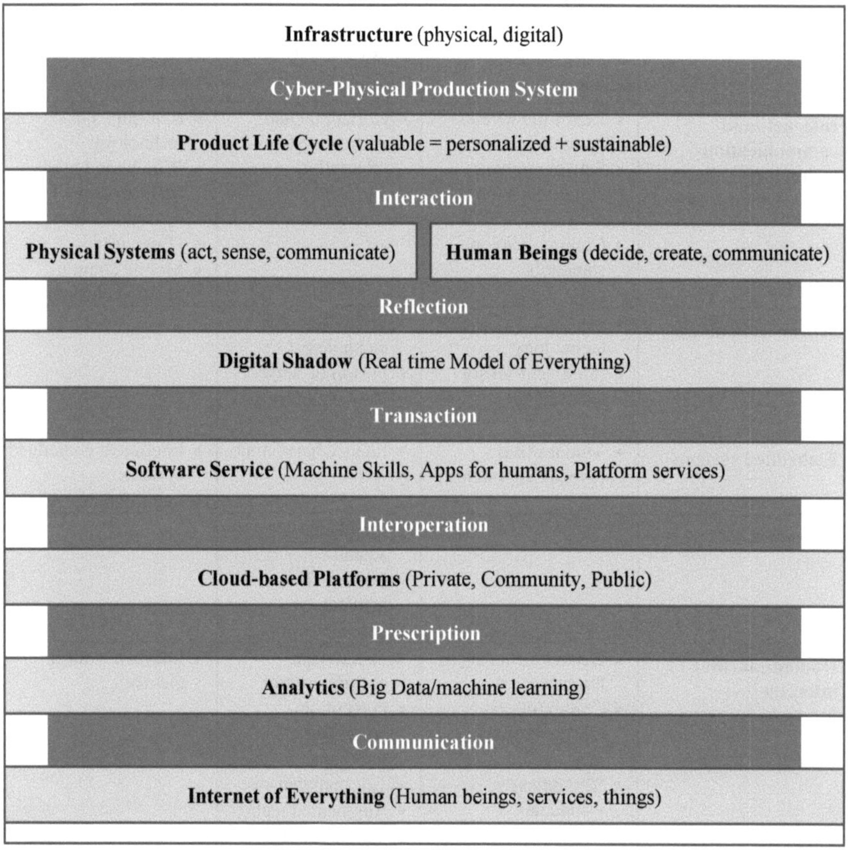


Figure 15: Functionalities of CPPS (Bauernhansl 2016, p. 454)

CPPS need to be smart, autonomous and able to collaborate with all users and elements of the system (Monostori et al. 2016, p. 624). In this context, the term digital twin or digital shadow is used for a "dynamic software model of a physical thing or system that relies on sensor data to understand the state of the thing or system, respond to changes, improve operations, and add value" (Gartner 2016). The capabilities of CPPS depend on the progress of the underlying technologies and their readiness level for application, Table 13.

| Technology-field | Technology-readiness level 1-3<br>(Basics) | Technology-readiness level 4-6<br>(Evaluation) | Technology-readiness level 7-9<br>(Implementation) |
|---|---|---|---|
| **Internet- and communication-technology** | • Real-time wireless communication<br>• Self-organizing communication-networks<br>• Communication standards | • Horizontal and vertical system-integration | • Real-time bus-technology<br>• Wire bound high-performance communication<br>• IT-security<br>• Mobile communication channels |
| **Sensor technology** | • Miniaturized sensor technology<br>• Intelligent sensor technology | • Linked-up sensor technology<br>• Fusion of sensors<br>• New security-sensors | |
| **Embedded systems** | • Miniaturized embedded systems | • Energy-harvesting | • Intelligent embedded systems<br>• Identification means |
| **Actuators** | | • Intelligent actuators<br>• Linked-up actuators<br>• Safe actuators | |
| **Human-machine interface** | • Behavior-models of humans<br>• Context-based representation of information<br>• Semantics-visualization | • Speech- and gesture-control<br>• Perception-controlled interfaces<br>• Tele-maintenance<br>• Augmented reality<br>• Virtual reality | • Intuitive control-elements |

| | | | |
|---|---|---|---|
| **Software/system-technology** | • Simulation-environment<br>• Multi-criteria evaluation of situations | • Multi-agent systems<br>• Machine-learning and pattern-recognition | • Big-Data storage- and analysis-methods<br>• Cloud-computing and -services<br>• Ontologies<br>• Mobile commun-ication-channels |
| **Automation, production technology and robotics** | • Autonomous robots<br>• Humanoid robots<br>• Cloud robotics<br>• Deep learning | • Additive manufacturing<br>• Sensitive robotics | • Multiple-axes robots |

Table 13: Maturity of technologies (agiplan et al. 2015, p. 24)

**Technology Convergence**

In the broad spectrum of technological developments in the IoT ranging from cloud computing to CPS, Friess identified a trend of convergence (Friess 2013, p. 17). This convergence will help with both horizontal integration end-to-end across the value chain and vertical integration of IT systems within a company. Kagermann et al., specify that horizontal integration of IT systems includes all stages of the business lifecycle within a company and their network, such as planning, inbound logistics, production, outbound logistics and marketing. On the other hand, vertical integration connects systems across hierarchical levels, e.g. the actuator and sensor, process control, production management, manufacturing execution and corporate planning levels (Kagermann et al. 2013, p. 20). This brings together, so called, Operational Technology (OT) with Information Technology (IT), shown in Figure 16, which will need to act as one (Gilchrist 2016, p. 192). Prior to the IIoT, there was limited learning and business insight due to separate processes, systems and organizations for OT and IT (IIC - Industrial Internet Consortium 2016, p. 17). The Gartner IT glossary defines IT and OT in the following ways:

> **IT** (information technology) "is the common term for the entire spectrum of technologies for information processing, including software, hardware, communications technologies and related services."[11]
> **OT** (operational technology) "is hardware and software that detects or causes a change through the direct monitoring and/or control of physical devices, processes and events in the enterprise."[12]

11 http://www.gartner.com/it-glossary/it-information-technology/, last accessed 16.08.2017
12 http://www.gartner.com/it-glossary/operational-technology-ot/, last accessed 16.08.2017

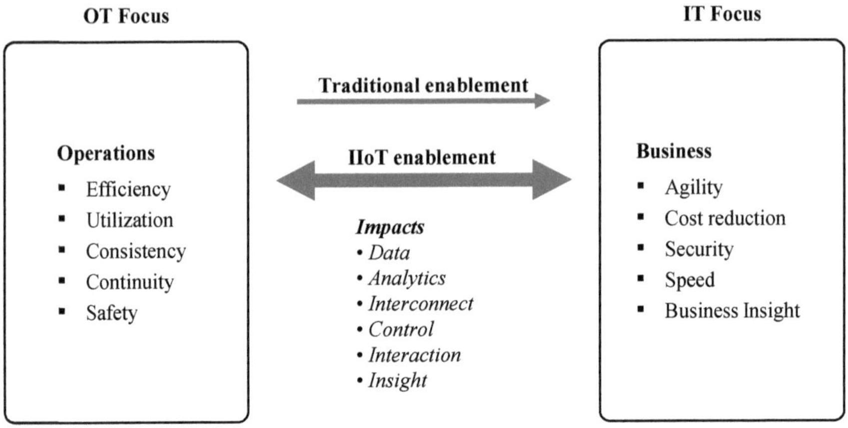


Figure 16: Current IT/OT state and transformation potential (IIC - Industrial Internet Consortium 2016, p. 18)

**Current State, Challenges and Opportunities**

"The potential benefits of IoT are almost limitless" according to Vermesan and Friess. The successful adoption of the IoT in their opinion, will be enabled by regulation that helps to build trust, privacy, security and interoperability within a broader ecosystem (Vermesan, Friess 2014, xiii). Furthermore, as per Manyika et al., the upgradability of existing equipment will affect the IoT adoption rate, as factories are in general capital-intensive with low rates of equipment replacement. They estimate an adoption rate of 65 to 90 percent in advanced economies and 50 to 70 percent in developing economies by 2025 (Manyika et al. 2015, p. 72). Table 14 provides an overview of 5 types of enablers.

| | |
|---|---|
| **Software and hardware technology** | • Low-power, inexpensive sensors and computers<br>• Ubiquitous connectivity/low-cost mesh connectivity<br>• Additional capacity and bandwidth in the cloud<br>• Confidence in security across entire IoT ecosystem |
| **Interoperability** | • Standardization in the technology stack and ability to integrate across technology vendors<br>• Standard protocols for sharing between IoT systems<br>• Standard access to external data sources |
| **Intellectual property, security, privacy, and confidentiality** | • Establishing trust with consumers for sharing data<br>• Collaboration across companies and industry verticals<br>• Horizontal data aggregators<br>• Data commerce platforms |
| **Business organization and culture** | • Industry structure, e.g., organized labor cooperation, third-party servicing<br>• Hardware-focused companies developing core competency in software<br>• Companies committing to up-front investment based on clear business cases |
| **Public policy** | • Regulation for autonomous control of vehicles and other machinery<br>• Government and payer subsidy of health-care IoT<br>• Agreements on fair practices for data sharing and use |

Table 14: Five types of enablers are needed for maximum IoT impact (Manyika et al. 2015, p. 101)

Companies are currently already shifting from "if" to "how" to best use IoT technology; from "technology" to "business outcome" focused approaches; from "caution" to "action" on cybersecurity as part of an overall IT security strategy; and from "optimizing" to "engaging" employees and customers in process improvements (Vodafone 2016, p. 33). IoT technologies will play a fundamental role in business improvement, next generation performance measurement systems (Dweekat, Park 2016, p. 1). Decision-making systems will increasingly leverage self-learning, cognitive capabilities to deal with real-time data and complex interactions (Höller et al. 2014, p. 26). The convergence of OT and IT will bring together advanced process control systems (APC) with advanced analytics.

## 3.4 Big Data

In the context of Industry 4.0 companies show great interest in the topic of Big Data (Jäger et al. 2016, p. 119). Mayer-Schönberger sees Big Data as game changer: “Big Data is poised to reshape the way we live, work, and think. [...] The possession of knowledge, which once meant an understanding of the past, is coming to mean an ability to predict the future” (Mayer-Schönberger, Cukier 2013, p. 190). The underlying drivers of Big Data go back to an observation of Gordon E. Moore about doubling the power and memory of computer semiconductors every 18 months, since then called Moore´s law (Schaller 1997, p. 57) that led to a sharp decline in the price of memory[13]. In 2005 Walter coins the effort of “cramming of as many bits as possible onto shrinking magnetic hard drives” as Kryders´ law: “Since the introduction of the disk drive in 1956, the density of information it can record has swelled from a paltry 2,000 bits to 100 billion bits (gigabits), all crowded in the small space of a square inch. That represents a 50-million-fold increase” (Walter 2005, p. 32). The global storage capacity for data increased 18-fold and the global computing power by a factor of 1600 in the time period from 1993 to 2007 (Hilbert, Lopez 2011). While this is impressive, Gandomi and Haider rightly point out that “Big Data are worthless in a vacuum. Its potential value is unlocked only when leveraged to drive decision making” (Gandomi, Haider 2015, p. 140). However, a recent study from an oil rig with approx. 30,000 sensors found that <1 % of data is actually used for decision making. That means 99% of data remains unused because it is not stored, streamed, made accessible and analyzed (Manyika et al. 2015, p. 25). Next to capturing more data, Franks underlines that “New Information Is What Makes Big Data So Powerful”, i.e. information that was not available before or information with a higher level of detail (Franks 2014, p. 41). Smart factories will become one of the major producers of real-time data by 2020 (BDVA Big Data Value Association 2016, p. 38).

**Definitions**

There are many different definitions for Big Data, focusing on different aspects, such as

(a) data: “Big Data refers to datasets whose size is beyond the ability of typical database software tools to capture, store, manage, and analyze” (Manyika et al., p. 1).

(b) process: “Collecting, storing and processing massive amounts of data for the purpose of converting it into useful information” (Pittman, Atwater 2016, p. 16).

---

13 http://www.aei-ideas.org/2013/04/chart-of-the-day-the-falling-price-of-memory/, last accessed 16.08.2017

(c) technology: "Big Data technologies as a new generation of technologies and architectures, designed to economically extract value from very large volumes of a wide variety of data by enabling high-velocity capture, discovery, and/or analysis" (Gantz, Reinsel 2012, p. 9).

**Characteristics**

Common attributes of Big Data are phrased as Vs and summarized in Figure 17.

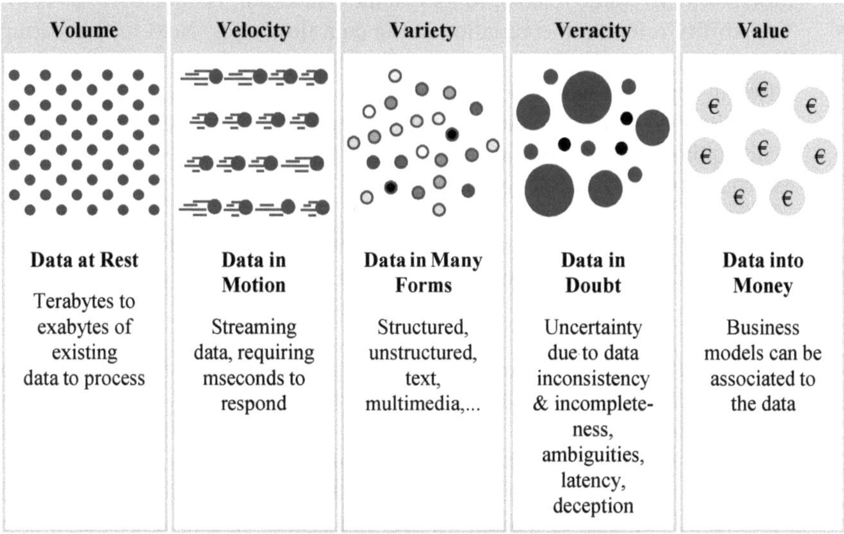


Figure 17: 5 Vs of Big Data (BDV PPP & BDVA 2016, p. 19)

One of the first authors to discuss data volume, velocity and variety was Laney in 2001 (Laney 2001, p. 1). Since then, several additional properties of Big Data have been mentioned and expressed as Vs.

- **Volume** refers to the magnitude of data. There is no specific threshold for Big Data, as the data volumes are relative and dependent on time, type and industry (Gandomi, Haider 2015, p. 138).
- **Velocity** refers to the rate at which data are generated [,...] analyzed and acted upon. Big Data technologies are able to process high volumes of real-time, 'perishable' data feeds instantaneously (Gandomi, Haider 2015, p. 138).

- **Variety** refers to the structural heterogeneity in a dataset. Data can be structured, semi-structured, or unstructured data (Gandomi, Haider 2015, p. 138).
- **Veracity** [...] represents the unreliability inherent in some sources of data. E.g., social media data can be imprecise, judgement based and uncertain (Gandomi, Haider 2015, p. 139).
- **Value**. High value is derived by analyzing Big Data, which in its original form has a low value relative to its volume (Gandomi, Haider 2015, p. 139).
- **Variability** refers to the variation in the data flow rates. Next to fluctuating data velocity, there is the complexity of connecting and processing data from different sources (Gandomi, Haider 2015, p. 139).
- **Visibility**. By visualizing data in an easily readable format people understand trends quicker, gain better insights and can share information internally and externally (Gilchrist 2016, pp. 52–54).

"Regardless of the number of Vs in Big Data, the essential point here is that Big Data can be expected to vary considerably" (Guzzo 2016, p. 347).

**Types of Data**

- **Structured and unstructured data:** "Structured data is information that exists in fixed fields of a computer record, file or database. Structured data also includes data that can be easily looked up, processed, analyzed and reported with little uncertainty. Examples of structured data include records of product prices, customer names and postal codes. Unstructured data are data that do not exist in fixed fields within a record or file, or are difficult to label. Examples of unstructured data include audio and video files, photographs and text-based data (documents, journals, emails and reports)" (APICS Suppy Chain Council 2015, p. 57).
- **Internal and external data**. With Big Data "internal data can be profitably supplemented with external data" (Davenport 2014a, p. 21). Marr establishes a logical sequences for analysis: (1) internal structured data, (2) internal semi-structured, (3) internal unstructured, (4) External structured, (5) External unstructured (Marr 2015, p. 84).

Within value chains data relates, for example, to customers, products, production, inventory, usage, quality, environment, knowledge, logistics (agiplan et al. 2015, p. 75).

**Value of Data**

"There are three classes of value: cost reductions, decision improvements, and improvements in products and services" (Davenport 2014a, p. 22), which are all relevant to this research. Further aspects of value include, for example, the availability, access and processing of data; legal aspects such as data ownership or intellectual property rights; technical features such as interoperability of data sets and solutions; private and public ecosystems; and societal impact by helping to solve challenges such as climate change or public sector efficiencies (BDVA Big Data Value Association 2016, pp. 5–6).

Data value is a matter of timing: "In most cases data has a life span" to be useful (Marr 2015, p. 28). Walker frames a window of opportunity, Figure 18, before the value of high velocity data decays to the residual value of historic data (Walker 2015, p. 42).

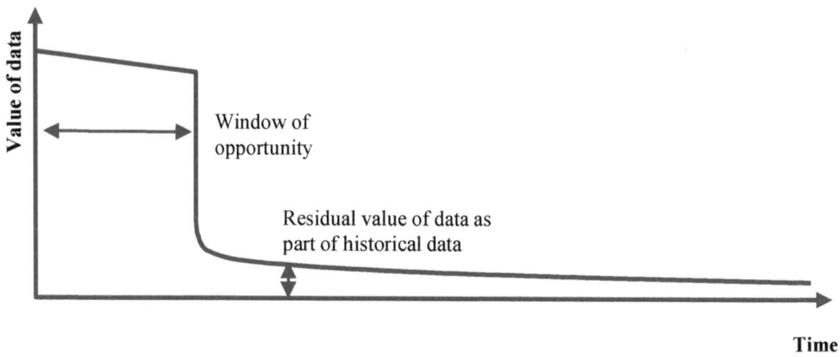


Figure 18: Value of data over time (Walker 2015, p. 42)

As data value declines over time it is important to actively reduce the latencies related to data, analytics, decisions, and actions when events occur (Iafrate 2014, p. 32), see also Figure 37 in chapter 4.4 (Decision support systems). Changes in decision-making culture together with Big Data analytics can significantly enhance corporate performance (McAfee, Brynjolfsson 2010, p. 61). Recent research confirmed that investments in Big Data and analytics lead to a 6% higher profitability (Bughin 2016, p. 3). As illustrated in Figure 19, highest returns can be achieved through optimal decisions supported by increases in both data velocity and data precision (Walker 2015, p. 52).

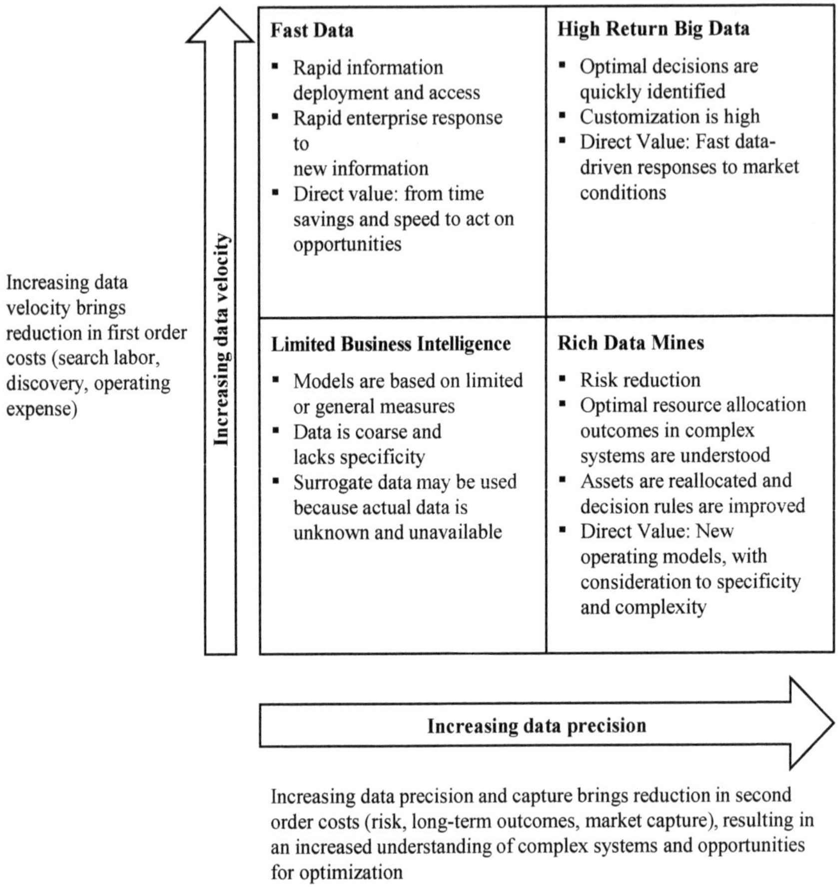


Figure 19: Achieving high return on Big Data by leveraging high velocity and high precision in Big Data (Walker 2015, p. 52)

## Smart Data

"We don´t need Big Data - we need SMART Data!" (Marr 2015, p. 79). Smart data is created through the application of analytical skills and tools and enables business intelligence and real-time process interventions (Iafrate 2014, p. 26). Smart data is essentially about the transformation of data into information and knowledge. Davenport, Prusak 2000, offer the following definitions:

- **Data** is “a set of discrete, objective facts about events”. It can be considered as raw material for information as it does not yet include judgement, interpretation or actionable recommendations.
- **Information** is data with meaning. Information is data that is contextualized with a clear purpose; categorized in defined components; calculated through analyses; corrected by removing errors; or condensed to conclusions.
- **Knowledge** comes from human experience, values, and information that is compared to the past or benchmarks; has consequences for actions; has connections to other related topics; and adds to conversations among people.

Additionally, Big Data becomes smart data through the automation of real-time, forward looking data analyses as basis for operational decision-making (Iafrate 2014, pp. 32–33).

**Small Data**

"Small is beautiful in a Big Data world" (Marr 2015, p. 27). This can refer to several aspects of the V-characteristics, e.g., less variety, the focus on only a few key parameters. Alternatively it can also refer to smaller volume, as per Biron and Follett in the case of construction equipment leases, daily location information can be sufficient (Biron, Follett 2016, p. 47).

**Data Quality**

“'Dirty Data' is a Business Problem, Not an IT Problem”, according to Gartner. Data quality is about

> “existence (whether the organization has the data), validity (whether the data values fall within an acceptable range or domain), consistency (for example, whether the same piece of data stored in multiple locations contains the same values), integrity (the completeness of relationships between data elements and across data sets), accuracy (whether the data describes the properties of the object it is meant to model), and relevance (whether the data is the appropriate data to support the business objectives)” (Gartner 2007).

**Use Case Selection**

"Don´t start with data [...] Start with strategy” (Marr 2015, p. 229). Managers need to demonstrate value and then operationalize (Loshin 2013, p. 19). Sources of value, Figure 20, can be found from both strategic and operational perspectives (Omri 2015, p. 104).

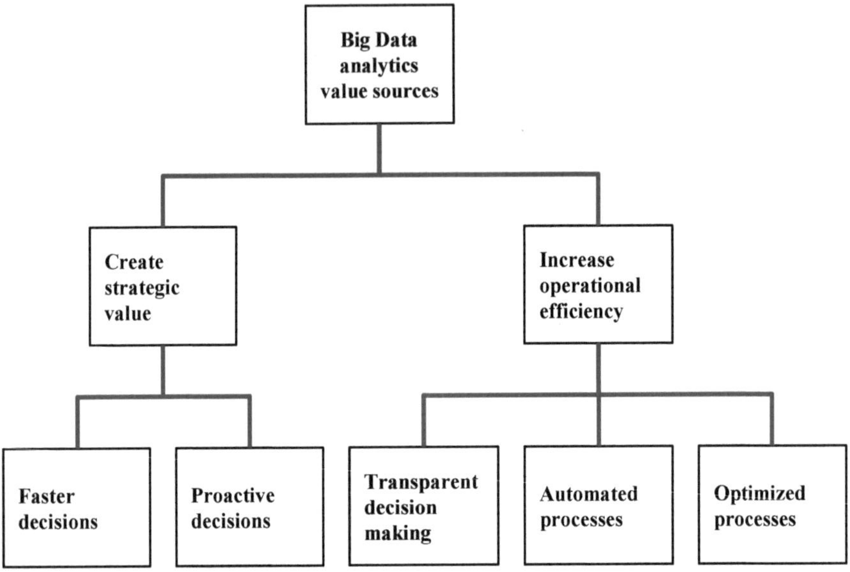


Figure 20: Sources of value of Big Data analytics for companies (Omri 2015, p. 104)

Most companies justify Big Data solutions through business cases built upon the following three arguments: (1) more intelligent and better quality decisions through the use of new data sources; (2) faster decisions through the capture and analysis of real-time data to support decisions; and (3) focus on fundamental decisions that allow real differentiation (IBM Institute for Business Value 2012, p. 17). According to Davenport, many organizations are still in the proof-of-concept stage of Big Data projects and often they are not identified using a structured approach nor take strategy into account (Davenport 2014a, p. 144). Marr offers the SMART model as potential solution: (S) Start with strategy, (M) Measure metrics and data, (A) Analyze your data, (R) Report your results, and (T) Transform your business and decision making (Marr 2015, p. 21). "The genuinely SMART business will therefore apply the data to their existing strategy and improve performance AND integrate those insights to improve day-to-day operational efficiency" (Marr 2015, p. 219). Agile companies monitor Big Data from the external environment and also use Big Data from their internal operations for optimization (Heldmann et al. 2017, p. 80). Approaches for identifying Big Data use cases are explained by Heldmann et al. 2017, pp. 81–82, and are based on a strategic and an operational perspective. As part of the Sales & Operations Planning process, insights can be gained from both perspectives, e.g. external demand predictions provide the boundaries of optimization in production, or sensitivities of internal parameters in a ROIC-tree trigger additional observations of external resource prices (Heldmann et al. 2017, p. 84).

### Current State, Challenges and Opportunities

"The proliferation of data in every corner of every sector represents both an opportunity and a problem" (Stanton 2016, pp. 160–161). Table 15 gives an overview of applications along the value chain.

| Value creation step | Application of Big Data analytics |
|---|---|
| **Research** | Generating new product ideas with trend- and market-analysis (e.g. patent-analysis); analysis of product data to improve future products; risk minimization of research activities. |
| **Sales / Marketing** | Identification of customers that might leave; identification of patterns in customer-requests; increasing efficiency of service-activities - automatic answering of requests; personalization of sales/marketing activities. |
| **Design** | Improved design by understanding of how users interact with the product; |
| **Development** | Potential-analysis for pricing and product development; optimization of development costs. |
| **Construction** | Using project data on future work – eliminating rework; enhancing iterative design by capturing and analyzing key building performance metrics, such as energy use intensity. |
| **Manufacturing** | Predictive maintenance by analyzing machine-data; reporting and analysis of production processes and efficiency; tracking of products by analyzing telematics-/movement-data. |
| **Distribution** | Improved inventory management; route optimization and capacity planning; sales forecast; tracking of shipped goods. |
| **Usage** | Global complaint-management for in-time identification of problems; spare-parts management by collecting product data to predict maintenance. |

Table 15: Examples of Big Data applications along the value creation process (Kleindienst 2017, p. 54)

For manufacturing across various industries, the task force responsible for Big Data at the society of German engineers detailed out 48 use cases in their status report (VDI/VDE-Gesellschaft Mess- und Automatisierungstechnik 2016b). Independent from the application, there is a need for "better tools with more automation to facilitate the exploration" of Big Data (Stanton 2016, p. 161). Stakeholders across sectors demand solutions for data integration; data curation;

handling of data-in-motion; advanced analytics; advanced visualization; user experience and usability; and data protection and privacy technologies (BDVA Big Data Value Association 2016, p. 21). Cybersecurity and data protection has been found to be the biggest barrier to the adoption of Big Data (Schäfer et al. 2012, p. 48). Another issue is that "managers don´t understand or trust Big Data-based models" (Barton, Court 2012, p. 6). This is often due to their "black box" nature. Mayer-Schönberger and Cukier argue: "The basis of an algorithm's predictions may often be far too intricate for most people to understand" (Mayer-Schönberger, Cukier 2013, p. 178). A central element for Big Data is secure repositories that can handle both structured and unstructured data called data lakes (Perry 2016, p. 10). But as Gilchrist rightly points out "Creating data lakes will not automatically facilitate business intelligence. If you do not know the correct question to ask of the data, how you can expect a sensible answer?" (Gilchrist 2016, p. 56). "Data has become a new factor of production, in the same way as hard assets and human capital. Having the right technological basis and organizational structure to exploit data is essential" (Cavanillas et al. 2016, p. 4). The European Big Data roadmap therefore focuses next to technology on business, policy and societal aspects (Becker et al. 2016, p. 286). To conclude, for Lindstrom, the focus on Big Data instead of small data is a sign of insecurity of managers (Lindstrom 2016, p. 76) and Marr states: "the reality is that most business are already data rich, but insight poor" (Marr 2015, p. 19).

## 3.5 Advanced Analytics

"Advanced analytics is likely to become a decisive competitive asset in many industries" (Barton, Court 2012, p. 5). Already today large-scale machine learning and other algorithms for real-time analytics are being used in industry (Domingue et al. 2016, p. 67). In 2020, 56% of the analytics are expected to be advanced, that is predictive or prescriptive analytics (Markkanen 2015, p. 4).

**Definitions**

**Analysis vs. Analytics**. Frequently these terms are confounded or used interchangeably in the context of data investigation. According to Lanquillon and Mallow, an analysis is a systematic investigation of a cause, a process to draw information and resulting insights out of data. Analytics is about the art of doing data analyses. It involves methods, tools and technologies supporting the analysis process and its results (Lanquillon, Mallow 2015a, p. 55).

**Simple vs. Advanced.** Lanquillon and Mallow also discuss what makes analytics „advanced" and conclude that advanced analytics are future oriented variants of predictive and prescriptive analytics using complex methods from statistics, data mining and machine learning. Which in return means that descriptive and diagnostic analytics variants focusing on the past belong to simple or traditional analytics (Lanquillon, Mallow 2015a, p. 62).

**Offline vs. Online.** Off-line validation is the sensitivity analysis of schedules against the uncertainties whereas on-line relates to anticipatory recognition of deviations, proactive analysis of the possible actions (Váncza et al. 2011, p. 807). Off-line also refers to processing a batch of historic data whereas on-line means streaming data and real-time processing.

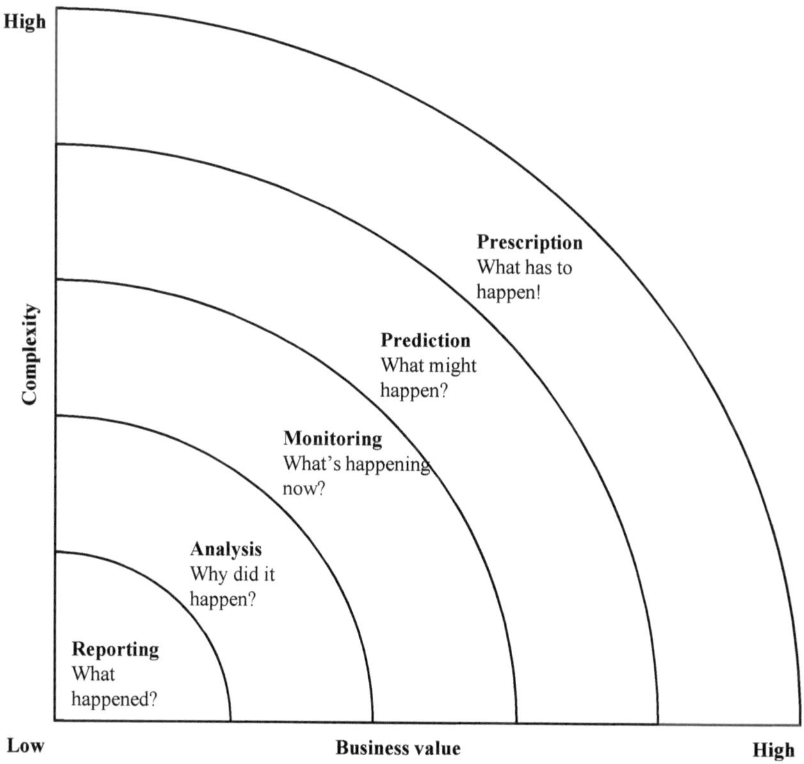


Figure 21: The spectrum of BI technologies (Eckerson 2007, p. 5)

**Business analytics** is the "capability of business systems and processes to use algorithms and statistics to derive meaning and insight from data, such as for decision making, planning and analysis" (APICS Suppy Chain Council 2015, p. 55).

According to Franks, descriptive analytics "summarize and describe what happened in the past", predictive analytics "predict what will happen in the future" and prescriptive analytics "determine actions to take to make the future happen" (Franks 2014, p. 5). As part of this research prescriptive analytics for operational control and maximum profitability are sought. Figure 21 illustrates the rising complexity from description through classical reporting, analysis and monitoring to prediction and prescription. Gandomi and Haider emphasize "that predictive analytics, which deals mostly with structured data, overshadows other forms of analytics applied to unstructured data, which constitutes 95% of Big Data" (Gandomi, Haider 2015, p. 143). Davenport sees three eras of analytics, Table 16, whereas analytics 3.0 integrates the best of Big Data and traditional analytics resulting in fast and impactful insights (Davenport 2014a, p. 197).

| **Analytics 1.0**<br>Traditional Analytics | **Analytics 2.0**<br>Big Data | **Analytics 3.0**<br>Fast Business Impact for the Data Economy |
|---|---|---|
| • Primarily descriptive analytics and reporting<br>• Internally sourced, relatively small, structured data<br>• "Backroom" teams of analysts<br>• Internal decision support | • Complex, large, unstructured data sources<br>• New analytical and computational capabilities<br>• "Data scientists" emerge<br>• Online firms create data-based products and services | • A seamless blend of traditional analytics and Big Data<br>• Analytics integral to running the business; strategic asset<br>• Rapid and agile insight delivery<br>• Analytical tools available at point of decision<br>• Cultural evolution embeds analytics into decision and operational processes |

Table 16: Analytics 3.0: Fast business impact for the data economy (Franks 2014, p. 16)

Pure prescriptive analytics are also called operational analytics. Franks states: "Operational analytics is about embedding analytics within business processes and automating decisions so that thousands or millions of decisions every day are made by analytics processes without any human intervention" (Franks 2014, xvi). Analytics of "physical-first" assets in factories, that don't necessarily generate digital data, are considerably different from "digital-first" devices, such IT hardware and their software application (Markkanen 2015, p. 3). Industry analytics spans various functional domains and time horizons, e.g., machine time horizon, operation time horizon, and planning time horizon (Diab et al. 2017, p. 9). They are applied to discover operational and behavioral patterns, perform accurate predictions quickly, and prescribe actions with confidence (Diab et al. 2017, p. 10). Aggarwal and Manual emphasize that "Big Data analytics should be driven by business needs, not technology". According to their research, companies need to address four important requirements to gain strategic value from analytics: "(1) a solid anchor to business value, (2) a pragmatic approach to IT, (3) attracting scarce talent, and (4) getting insights to the front line" (Aggarwal, Manuel 2016, p. 1). Similarly, Henke et al., point out that on top of a proper foundation in technological infrastructure and organizational governance, data analytics depends on relevant data and purposeful use cases (Henke et al. 2016b, p. 4). "Ultimately, it is the derived information (not the raw data) and how it can be acted on that determines what kinds of analytics are deployed" (Diab et al. 2017, p. 3).

**Algorithms**

Analytics cover a wide spectrum of applications with a variety of different algorithms and techniques, ranging from online analytical processing (OLAP) within structured query language (SQL) analytics to non-linear optimization, Figure 22.

| SQL analytics | Descriptive Analytics | Data Mining | Predictive Analytics | Simulation | Optimization |
|---|---|---|---|---|---|
| ▪ Count<br>▪ Mean<br>▪ OLAP | ▪ Univariate distribution<br>▪ Central tendency<br>▪ Dispersion | ▪ Association rules<br>▪ Clustering<br>▪ Feature extraction | ▪ Classification<br>▪ Regression<br>▪ Forecasting<br>▪ Spatial<br>▪ Machine learning<br>▪ Text analytics | ▪ Monte Carlo<br>▪ Agent-based modeling<br>▪ Discrete event modeling | ▪ Linear optimization<br>▪ Non-linear optimization |

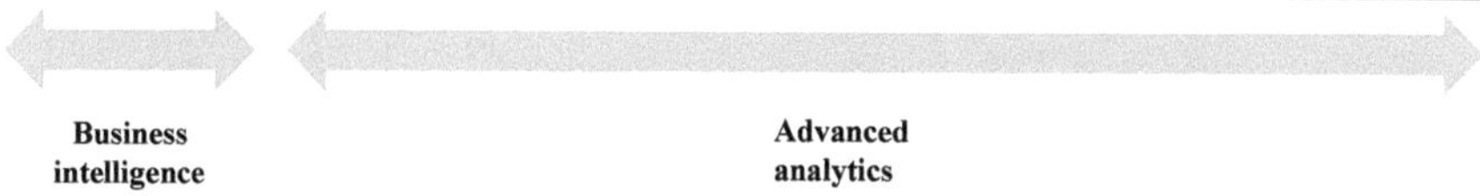


Figure 22: Analytics spectrum (Minelli et al. 2013, p. 14)

Optimization algorithms can be categorized into two types: (1) traditional, deterministic algorithms with specific rules; and (2) non-traditional, stochastic algorithms (Rao 2011, p. 4):

> 1. Traditional optimization algorithms: these are deterministic algorithms with specific rules for moving from one solution to the other. […] The examples of these algorithms include non-linear programming, geometric programming, quadratic programming, dynamic programming, etc. However, the optimization problems related to manufacturing are usually complex in nature and characterized by mixed continuous–discrete variables and discontinuous and non-convex design spaces. Hence, the traditional optimization methods fail to give global optimum solution, as they are usually trapped at the local optimum.
> 2. Non-traditional optimization algorithms: these algorithms are stochastic in nature, with probabilistic transition rules […] mainly based on biological, molecular, or neurological […] evolution and/or social behavior of species. […] Examples of these algorithms include simulated annealing, genetic algorithm, particle swarm optimization, artificial bee colony, shuffled frog leaping, harmony search, etc.

Artificial neural networks (ANN) belong to the second category and are "information-processing systems whose structure and function are motivated by the cognitive processes and organizational structure of neurobiological systems" (Corsten, May 1996, p. 67). Artificial neural networks aim build on desirable characteristics of the human brain, such as massive parallelism, distributed computation, learning and generalization ability, fault tolerance, and inherent contextual information processing (Jain, Mao 1996, p. 31).

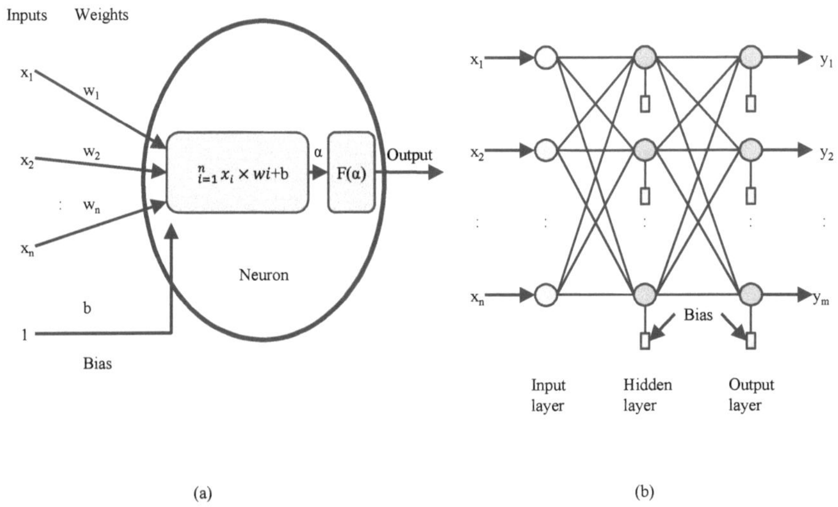


Figure 23: (a) Individual processing element, (b) structure of a feed-forward neural network (Agachi 2006, p. 39)

According to Jain and Mao, two major types of ANN can be distinguished: (1) feed-forward networks, Figure 23; and (2) recurrent (or feedback) networks. The latter are dynamic learning systems that adapt both the network architecture and the connection weights. In general there is supervised learning, i.e., outputs or correction for each input pattern is given; and unsupervised learning that is discovering the underlying structure, patterns and correlations between them without a teacher (Jain, Mao 1996, pp. 34–35).In 1996 Corsten and May pointed out that ANN "have potential in supporting the steering and control of production processes" (Corsten, May 1996, p. 74). Meanwhile, according to Schmidhuber, ANN have attracted wide-spread attention as they have won competitions and outperformed other machine learning methods (Schmidhuber 2015, p. 86).

**The Analytics Workflow**

In order to conduct analytics, we can look at the data value chain, Figure 24, spanning from data acquisition to data usage.

| **Data acquisition** | **Data analysis** | **Data curation** | **Data storage** | **Data usage** |
|---|---|---|---|---|
| ▪ Structured data<br>▪ Unstructured data<br>▪ Event processing<br>▪ Sensor networks<br>▪ Protocols<br>▪ Real-time<br>▪ Data streams<br>▪ Multimodality | ▪ Stream mining<br>▪ Semantic analysis<br>▪ Machine learning<br>▪ Information extraction<br>▪ Linked data<br>▪ Data discovery<br>▪ 'Whole world' semantics<br>▪ Ecosystems<br>▪ Community data analysis<br>▪ Cross-sectorial data analysis | ▪ Data quality<br>▪ Trust/Prove-nance<br>▪ Annotation<br>▪ Data validation<br>▪ Human-Data Interaction<br>▪ Top-down/ Bottom-up<br>▪ Community/ Crowd<br>▪ Human computation<br>▪ Curation at scale<br>▪ Incentivisation<br>▪ Automation<br>▪ Interoperability | ▪ In-Memory DBs<br>▪ NoSQL DBs<br>▪ NewSQL DBs<br>▪ Cloud storage<br>▪ Query Interfaces<br>▪ Scalability and performance<br>▪ Data Models<br>▪ Consistency, Availability, Partition-tolerance<br>▪ Security and privacy<br>▪ Standardization | ▪ Decision support<br>▪ Prediction<br>▪ In-use analytics<br>▪ Simulation<br>▪ Exploration<br>▪ Visualisation<br>▪ Modeling<br>▪ Control<br>▪ Domain-specific usage |

Figure 24: Data value chain (Curry et al. 2016, p. 18)

Processes for extracting insights from Big Data, according to Gandomi and Haider, consists of data management, i.e., acquisition and recording, extraction, cleaning and annotation, integration, aggregation and representation; and analytics, i.e., modelling and analysis, and finally interpretation (Gandomi, Haider 2015, p. 141). Davenport emphasizes that even before looking at the data value chain, it is critical to define the business problem to be solved. Furthermore he emphasizes the need to really act on results at the end of the process. The six steps for analytics-based decision making for Davenport are (1) recognize the problem or question, (2) review previous findings, (3) model the solution and select the variables, (4) collect the data, (5) analyze the data, and (6) present and act on the results (Davenport 2013, p. 4). The International Controller Association proposes a similar process for business analytics: (1) business understanding, (2) data understanding, (3) data preparation, (4) modelling, (5) evaluation, and (6) deployment (ICV - Internationaler Controller Verein 2016, pp. 51–52). Franks states that "determining the best way to implement an analytics process can be tough. [...Companies should] focus on finding the best approach from the many that can work" and offers a generic approach in Figure 25 (Franks 2014, p. 172).

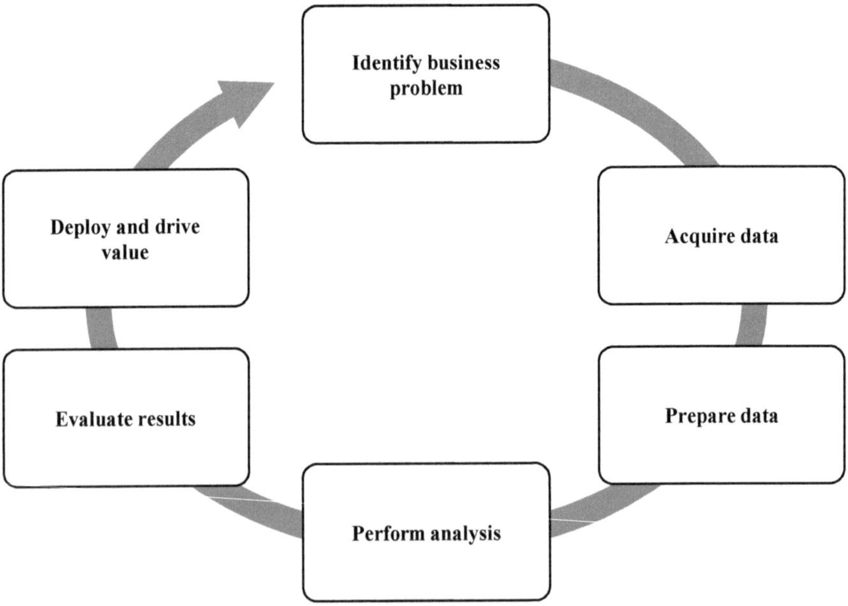


Figure 25: Generic analytics process flow (Franks 2014, p. 179)

### Increasing Requirements

With increasing data velocity and precision the requirements regarding analytics increase and lead to self-learning models that operate with limited supervision based on strong meta data and structure (Walker 2015, p. 54). Furthermore, data quality is essential for rapid and automated operational analytics (Franks 2014, p. 27), however, there are many additional requirements, as summarized in Table 17.

| | |
|---|---|
| **Correctness** | Industrial analytics must have a higher level of accuracy in its analytic results. Any system that interprets and acts on the results must have safeguards against undesirable and unintended physical consequence. |
| **Timing** | Industrial Analytics must satisfy certain hard deadline and synchronization requirements. Near instantaneous analytic results delivered within a deterministic time window are required for reliable and high quality actions in industrial operations. |
| **Safety** | When applying Industrial Analytics, and interpreting and acting on the result, strong safety requirements must be in place safeguarding the wellbeing of the workers, users and the environment. |
| **Contextualized** | The analysis of data within an industrial system is never done without the context in which the activity and observations occur. One cannot construct meaning unless a full understanding of the process that is being executed and the states of all the equipment and its peripherals are considered to derive the true meaning of the data and create actionable information. |
| **Causal-oriented** | Industrial operations deal with the physical world and industrial analytics needs to be validated with domain-specific subject matter expertise to model the complex and causal relationships in the data. The combination of first principles, e.g. physical modeling, along with other data science statistical and machine learning capabilities, is required in many industrial use cases in order to provide accurate analytics results. |
| **Distributed** | Many complex industrial systems have hierarchical tiers distributed across geographic areas. Each of these subsystems may have unique analytic requirements to support their operations. Therefore, industrial analytics must be tailored to meet the local requirements of the subsystems it supports. The requirements on timing (avoiding long latency) and resilience (avoiding widespread outage of service because of faults in the network or in a centralized system) require a distributed pattern of industrial analytics in that the analytic will be implemented close to the source of data it analyzes and to the target where its analytic outcome is needed. |

| | |
|---|---|
| **Streaming** | Industrial Analytics can be continuous or batch processes. Because of continuous execution in industrial systems, a large proportion of industrial analytics will be streaming in nature, performing analysis of live data and providing continuous flow of analytics results in support of the operations. Traditional batch-oriented analytics will still be performed either for building or improving analytic models, or for human decision-making. |
| **Automatic** | In order for the industrial analytics to support continuous operations, the analysis of streaming data and the application of analytic outcomes must be automatic, dynamic and continuous. As the technologies in industrial analytics advance, improvements in analytic modeling e.g., through learning may also be automatic. |
| **Semantics** | Analytical systems require data that has meaning and context. Unstructured data, when reported without attribution to the source and the component or system it represents, makes deriving value complex since it requires the analytics to guess or infer the meaning. Inference unnecessary adds significant uncertainty into the system. Most data can be properly attributed at the source, and if this information is communicated, it can significantly increase the success and accuracy of the analytical systems. |

Table 17: Industrial analytics requirements (Diab et al. 2017, p. 11)

### Analytics Professionals and Culture

"Making analytics operational is not a technology issue for most organizations" (Franks 2014, p. 143). "In the end, it all comes down to people" and therefore three outcomes are desired: (1) organizational alignment, (2) executive endorsement and sponsorship, and (3) investing in analytical human capital (Minelli et al. 2013, p. 125). "The value of analytics professionals is now widely accepted" (Franks 2014, p. 234). Table 18 gives an overview of the technical capabilities required for industrial analytics.

| | |
|---|---|
| **Visualize** | Display and manage data readings and analytics results using a common framework |
| **Explore** | Perform ad-hoc experiments with historical data |
| **Design** | Automation of the data analytics stages; data quality, data mining, and business intelligence algorithm composition |
| **Orchestrate** | Delegate work requests over a cluster of computing resources, and collect and aggregate intermediate and final results |
| **Connect** | Exchange data and work requests between components using a common framework |
| **Cleanse** | Merge data set form different data sources based on suitable criteria; remove irrelevant data and clean noise from data |

| | |
|---|---|
| **Compute** | Perform computation of statistical, first principle and machine learning model analytical calculations, including live analysis on streaming data, batch or ad hoc data mining and operation and business intelligence analysis |
| **Validate** | Ensure analytics results when applied in the context of the application and environment will not harm people or property. This function should be independent from the core analytics processing and act as a governor |
| **Apply** | Apply analytics results to various subsystems, including the automation systems (e.g. adjusting control parameter or models), operations and business processes, increasingly automatically or as information aiding human decision-making |
| **Store** | Archive and reproduce measured and calculated data streams, especially time-series sequences |
| **Manage** | Manage the information model, including data sources, computing resources and data analytics metadata |
| **Supervise** | Manage system reliability by ensuring processes are started and maintained, and that computer resources are not exhausted |

Table 18: Industrial analytics capabilities (Diab et al. 2017, p. 13)

Even though there are a lot of technical skills required in the role of a data scientist, equally important competencies are social (team work, communication, conflict management, leadership), economic (business model innovation, business case evaluation, project management and controlling), and legal (data protection, ethics) (Meir-Huber, Köhler 2014, p. 34). A holistic definition of the data scientist role is provided in Table 19.

| **Data scientist** | | | | |
|---|---|---|---|---|
| **Big Data business developer** | **Big Data technologist** | **Big Data analyst** | **Big Data developer** | **Big Data artist** |
| Identification, evaluation and implementation of innovative business models | Development and provision of scaleable Big Data infrastructure and storage | Innovative linkage of data using machine learning, statistics and mathematics | Scalable programming, machine learning and data management | Visualization of data, graphic design, communication and psychology |

Table 19: The roles of data scientists (Meir-Huber, Köhler 2014, p. 35)

Next to analytics professionals and organization, it is important to create a culture of fact based decision making through embedded analytics in business processes

(Davenport 2014a, p. 146). An analytics culture includes knowing "what is possible using predictive analytics and what is not", to "value data", to "be 'data driven'", and to "have buy-in from the 'front line' who must act upon the decisions that result from using predictive analytics to predict behaviors" (Finlay 2014, p. 42). Establishing new cultural norms and organizational behaviors requires commitment (Ransbotham et al. 2016, p. 4). This also includes knowledge management to avoid knowledge getting lost when experts leave the company (Schank et al. 2010, p. 208).

**Current State, Challenges and Opportunities**

Analytics is "the engine driving value-creation in IIoT" (Diab et al. 2017, p. 15). But only 20-30% of the estimated potential has been captured in manufacturing with major barriers being leadership skeptical of impact and siloed data in legacy IT systems (Henke et al. 2016a, p. 10). There are several technical requirements, Table 20, across various industrial sectors to make Big Data analytics work (Becker et al. 2016, p. 275).

| Urgent requirements | Very important requirements | Important requirements |
|---|---|---|
| • Data security and privacy<br>• Data sharing<br>• Data integration<br>• Real-time insights | • Data quality<br>• Data management engineering<br>• Real-time data transmission<br>• Deep data analytics<br>• Pattern discovery<br>• Modelling and simulation<br>• Natural language analytics | • Data improvement<br>• Data enrichment<br>• Data visualization & user experience<br>• Usage analytics<br>• Predictive analytics<br>• Descriptive analytics |

Table 20: Cross-sectorial requirements for Big Data research (Becker et al. 2016, p. 275)

Dogan et al. mention benefits of advanced computing power and analytical tools in operations, two of them are: "producing more realistic and detailed models, coping with missing and substandard data, and enabling complex methods and algorithms"; and "securing quicker proof of value—meaning, they can more rapidly build momentum behind larger transformation efforts requiring process, behavior, technology and organizational change" (Dogan et al. 2015, p. 42). Furthermore, advanced analytics can be effectively combined with lean management to identify operational inefficiencies quicker, uncover new waste, support problem solving and the identification of solutions (Dhawan et al. 2014, p. 1). "As a large percentage of industrial companies have not incorporated machine data in their analytics process for decision support and intelligent operations, industrial analytics and IIoT offer a great opportunity to drive the next round of value creation" (Diab et al. 2017, p. 15).

### 3.6 Summary: Impact of Digitization on Manufacturing

Digitization presents a significant economic opportunity for society and industry. Industry 4.0, the fourth industrial revolution based on cyber-physical systems, originated in Germany, but currently similar initiatives are ongoing in the USA, China and other countries. Productivity increases come from improved asset utilization, resource management and operations optimization based on real-time monitoring and control. This is of particular relevance in process industries with their high capital intensity, time constraints and given that a lot of data is already captured. While the value of digital transformations is clear to companies in general, they need help with how to implement improved operational processes and manage the required change on the people side. Industry 4.0 covers several dimensions and the smart factory, smart operations and data-driven services are the most relevant ones for this work. Smart factories aim for self-x properties, i.e., self-awareness leading to predictive maintenance or self-organization to autonomously optimize productivity by reducing waste. Smart operations build on real-time data provided by the Industrial Internet of Things, as its backbone. The IIoT provides visibility on any "thing", any "place" at any "time". The underlying technologies, such as sensors, actors, internet and communication technologies are at different maturity levels but making significant progress. One of the biggest trends is the convergence of operational technology (OT), such as automation and advanced process controls, with information technology (IT) including advanced analytics and Big Data. One of the key sources of value comes from improved decision making to increase operational efficiency based on data. Big Data can include both structured and unstructured data as well as internal and external data which is collected in data lakes. However, companies don´t seek big but smart data that is relevant, accurate and sometimes small. Analytics and Big Data must be driven by business needs not technology. Advanced analytics go beyond descriptive analytics into prediction and prescription. The success of analytics depends not only on algorithms and the analytics workflow, but crucially on people. New roles such as the one of the data scientist have emerged complementing the required functional, IT and change management expertise with analytics skills. Advanced analytics is considered complementary to operations improvement approaches such as lean management, which can be an advantage as many industrial companies do not yet utilize Big Data analytics in operational decision making.

| **Learning** | **Delimitations** | **Requirements** |
|---|---|---|
| • Significant economic opportunity<br>• Productivity increases from real-time control and improved asset/resource utilization<br>• Process industries already have a lot of data<br>• Many industrial companies have not yet fully exploited data analytics for operational improvement<br>• Digital transformation requires an improvement process ("how"), as it is not only about technology but also people<br>• A combination of functional, IT, change management and analytics skills required<br>• Smart factories shall be autonomous and self-organizing<br>• The convergence of OT and IT brings advanced process control and advanced analytics together<br>• The value from data comes from improved decision making based on predictive and prescriptive analytics performed online, i.e., in real-time based on streamed data<br>• This is a complex topic for industrial companies requiring an approach for implementation, complementary to operations improvement philosophies such as lean | INCLUDES<br>• Big Data capabilities, e.g., streaming of data, data lakes and advanced (predictive and prescriptive) analytics<br>EXCLUDES<br>• Hardware, equipment upgrades with new technologies, e.g. sensors, communication, etc. | • Consolidate data from various data sources with consistent time stamps<br>• Use of predictive and prescriptive analytics<br>• Link analytics and advanced process control<br>• Develop an implementation approach consistent with existing operations improvement methodologies |

Table 21: Summary of conclusions from digitization perspective

# 4 Management Perspective: Performance Opportunities with Decision Support Systems

In this chapter a perspective of management is given. Section 4.1 starts with decision making followed by performance measures (section 4.2) as basis for fact-based decisions. Section 4.3 acovers performance measurement and management systems, section 4.4 decision support systems and a summary of performance opportunities with decision-support systems in covered in section 4.5.

## 4.1 Decision Making

To start with, the prime task of the leadership teams of industrial companies is to manage ecoanomic performance by taking appropriate decisions to achieve their objectives (Drucker 1966, p. 7). According to Christensen and Hemmer, the key objective for managers of a firm is to find the output– input combination that results in the maximal profit (Christensen, Hemmer 2006, p. 565). Typically managers make decisions using a cost–benefit approach that considers technical and behavioral aspects (Horngren et al. 2015, p. 35). Industrial management combines techno-economics and leadership aspects. Techno-economics is fact based, rational and aims to improve efficiencies and economics. Leadership is about people, life and human purpose (Wohinz 2011, p. 45). "Management is primarily a human activity that should focus on encouraging individuals to do their jobs better" (Horngren et al. 2015, p. 35). In business, customers take a central role as they define value by the utility of goods and services to them, which is expressed by their willingness to pay (Drucker, Maciariello 2008). The human nature of business makes management essential. According to Ackoff, managers will always be needed, even with progress in management models, algorithms, and computers, as new or different problems continuously arise (Ackoff 1978, p. 200). In 1963 Gutenberg stated that all important enterprise decisions are made in an atmosphere of uncertainty (Gutenberg 1963, p. 8). Managers in manufacturing are frequently confronted with a large spectrum of different decision to be made, e.g., product design, material selection, manufacturing process, plant layout, flexible manufacturing, product end-of-life scenario, and environmentally conscious manufacturing programs (Rao 2013, pp. 2–3). In order to help managers make decisions significant attention is given to data. According to Vercellis enterprises


M. Hammer, *Management Approach for Resource-Productive Operations*, Industrial Management, https://doi.org/10.1007/978-3-658-22939-9_4

gain competitive advantages if they are able to make faster and better decisions by turning data into information and knowledge (Vercellis 2009, XIV).

**Definitions**

A decision is basically a "choice made between alternative courses of action"[14]. Decision-making is defined in the Oxford dictionary as: "The action or process of making decisions, especially important ones"[15]. In decision-making theory, the term is being used more broadly and includes in general all acts of selecting one of several alternative choices of action (Laux et al. 2012, p. 3).

**Types of Decisions**

Decisions in a business context can be viewed as strategic, tactical or operational and vary by value-at-stake and frequency (Taylor 2012, p. 78). Trade-off decisions are frequently required due to conflicting strategic goals such as low costs through high asset utilization or high customer service through rapid response (Wildemann 2010, p. 26). Depending on the predictability of the future, decisions need to be made: (1) under certainty, (2) under risk, (3) under uncertainty, or (4) under conflict (Hitomi 1996, p. 39). Rumsfeld framed this as:

> "there are known knowns; these are things we know we know. We also know there are known unknowns; that is to say we know there are some things we do not know. But there are also unknown unknowns -- the ones we don't know we don't know" (Rumsfeld 2002).

**Human Decision Making**

While we tend to think that humans make intelligent conscious decisions based on the laws of logic, the reality is that decision making is largely an unconscious activity (Gigerenzer 2007, p. 3; Schank et al. 2010, p. 11). Kahneman et al. found that humans are heavily biased decision makers relying on heuristics and making judgement errors, for example, for probabilities of events (Kahneman et al. 1982, p. 18). Next to biases there is also the chance variability of judgements which Kahneman et al. more recently termed "noise" (Kahneman et al. 2016, p. 38). Making decisions takes varying degrees of cognitive effort depending on the type of decision (Novatsis, Wilkinson 2016, p. 139), as shown in Figure 26. Human decision makers struggle with an overload of information and choice leading to decision fatigue (Tompkins 2016, p. 41). Replacing human judgement with algorithms offers a solution with positive results (Kahneman et al. 2016, p. 44).

---

14 http://www.businessdictionary.com/definition/decision.html, last accessed 23.08.2017

15 https://en.oxforddictionaries.com/definition/us/decision-making, last accessed 10.03.2017

This is one of the main reasons for the emergence of decision support systems and sources of value from Big Data analytics.

Moving from right to left involves:

- Less mental effort
- Less influenced by stress
- Quicker

| **Recognition-primed decisions** | | **Rule-based decisions** | | **Choice decisions** | | **Creative decisions** | |
|---|---|---|---|---|---|---|---|
| **Positive** | **Negative** | **Positive** | **Negative** | **Positive** | **Negative** | **Positive** | **Negative** |
| ▪ Very fast<br>▪ Requires little conscious thought<br>▪ Can provide a satisfactory, workable option<br>▪ Is useful in routine situations<br>▪ Reasonably resistant to stress | ▪ Requires that the user be experienced<br>▪ May be difficult to justify<br>▪ Can encourage looking only for evidence to support one's mode, rather than considering evidence that may not support that model (confirmation bias) | ▪ Good for novices<br>▪ Can be rapid, if rule has been learned<br>▪ Gives a course of action that has been determined by experts<br>▪ Easy to justify as "following prescribed procedures"<br>▪ Not necessary to understand the reason for each step | ▪ Can be time consuming if manual has to be consulted<br>▪ Cannot find written rule or procedure<br>▪ If interrupted it is easy to miss a step<br>▪ Rule may be out of date or inaccurate<br>▪ Map cause skill decay<br>▪ Map not understand the reason for each step<br>▪ The wrong procedure may be selected | ▪ Fully compares alternative courses of action<br>▪ Can be justified<br>▪ More likely to produce an optimal solution<br>▪ Techniques available | ▪ Requires time<br>▪ Not suited to noisy distracting environments<br>▪ Can be affected by stress<br>▪ May produce cognitive overload and "stall" decision maker | ▪ Produces solution for unfamiliar problem<br>▪ May invent new solution | ▪ Time consuming<br>▪ Untested solution<br>▪ Difficult in noise and distraction<br>▪ Difficult under stress<br>▪ May be difficult to justify |

Moving from left to right involves:

- More mental effort
- More influenced by stress
- Takes a long time

Figure 26: Main types of decision making and cognitive effort (Novatsis, Wilkinson 2016, p. 139)

**Fact Based Decision Making**

In the context of Big Data and its influence on management McAfee, Byrnjolfsson state boldly: "Data-driven decisions are better decisions – it´s as simple as that" (McAfee, Brynjolfsson 2010, p. 63). In manufacturing, shop floor data is an important source of insights for decision makers (Almeida, Azevedo 2016, p. 126). However the data needs to be processed to become value adding information for decision making, leading to actions and improvement of performance (Hitomi 1996, p. 412). In Figure 27, Horngren et al, lay out a 5-step fact-based decision making process.

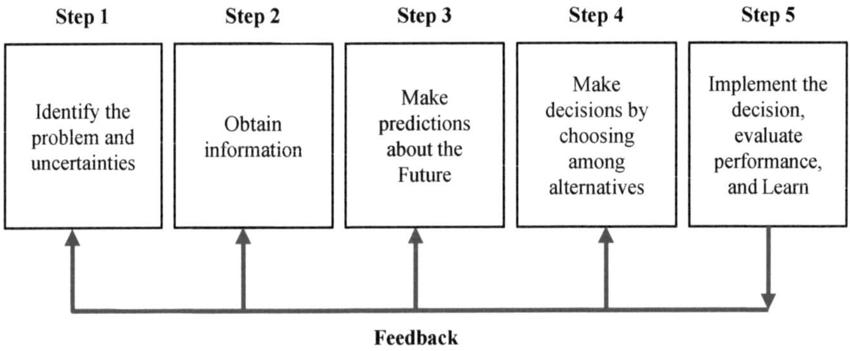


Figure 27: Five-step decision making process (Horngren et al. 2015, p. 472)

As mentioned before, managers typically apply a cost-benefit logic in decision making (Horngren et al. 2015, p. 35) and aim to take proactive decisions based on a small set of performance indicators representing the status quo of their companies (Almeida, Azevedo 2016, p. 127).

## Levels of Decision Making

The information characteristics and performance measures for fact-based decision making depend upon the organization level, Figure 28.

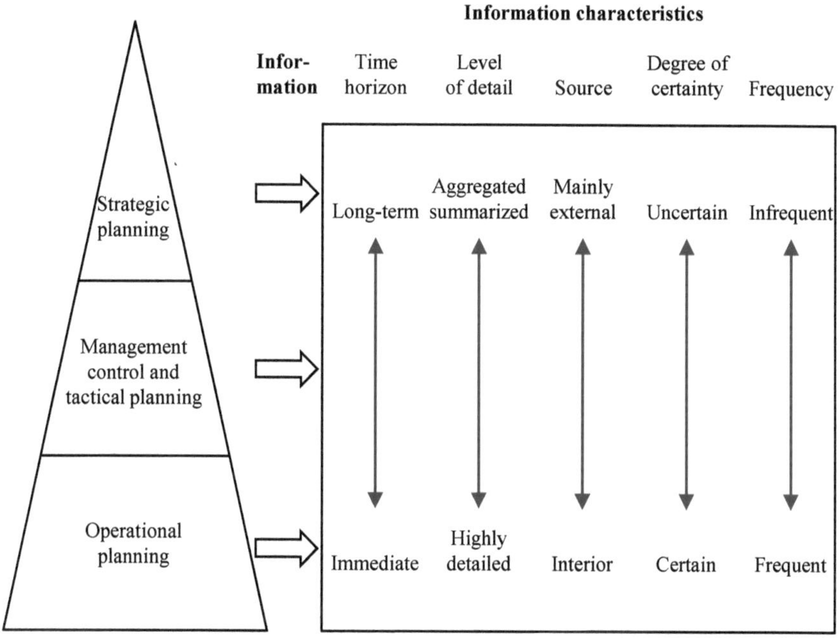


Figure 28: Information characteristics for managerial decisions (Curtis, Cobham 2005, p. 10)

Back in 1965 Anthony investigated specific characteristics of management and operational control, Table 22.

| Characteristic | Management Control | Operational Control |
|---|---|---|
| Focus of activity | • Whole operation | • Single task or transaction |
| Judgement | • Relatively much; subjective decisions | • Relatively little; reliance on rules |
| Nature of structure | • Psychological | • Rational |
| Nature of information | • Integrated; financial data throughout; approximations acceptable; future and historical | • Tailormade to the operation; often non-financial; precise; often in real time |
| Persons primarily involved | • Management | • Supervisors (or none) |
| Mental activity | • Administrative; persuasive | • Follow directions (or none) |
| Source discipline | • Social physchology | • Economics; physical sciences |
| Time horizon | • Weeks, months, years | • Day-to-day |
| Type of costs | • Managed | • Engineered |

Table 22: Some distinctions between management control and operational control (Anthony 1965, p. 93)

Management control chooses operating rules for elements of an organization and the prioritization for operating rules in order to maximize the overall objective function (Arrow 1964, p. 397). "Operations control focuses on specific tasks [... and] is essentially objective" (Anthony 1965, iii) . There is a general consensus that, only by linking strategic and operational performance, it is possible to improve the overall organizational performance. Despite the fact that strategy and operations are two different and sometimes not associated perspectives, when they are properly aligned the plant is more likely to achieve specific performance goals (Almeida, Azevedo 2016, p. 133). The profit per hour approach links both the operational control and the management control levels.

## Current State, Challenges and Opportunities

In order to make better rational and real-time decisions on operations level, what is needed is data, the right performance measures, and decision support systems. But as per Minelli et al, a future decision culture with humans will need to include traits such as agility to cope with continuous transformation of people, process, and technology; multi-disciplinary talent with business, math, and technology skills; and the ability to build synergistic ecosystems and partnerships (Minelli et al. 2013, pp. 127–128). A holistic strategy in the information age includes the technical portfolio, capabilities and people (Benzi 2017, p. 109).

## 4.2 Performance Measures

"When you can measure what you are speaking about, and express it in numbers, you know something about it..." (Thomson 1889, p. 73). This chapter focuses on defining measures of performance, their characteristics and linkage to outcomes. It also aims to discuss some of the aspects Neely et al. 1995, p. 108 brought up, e.g.: "Should measures focus on processes, the outputs of processes, or both?"; "Is time the fundamental measure of manufacturing performance?"; or "How can measures which do not encourage short-termism be designed?"

**Definitions**

The performance of a company is directly related to value creation, which is discussed first. The term **value** can be defined from three perspective according to the Business dictionary[16]:

> 1. Accounting: The monetary worth of an asset, business entity, good sold, service rendered, or liability or obligation acquired.
> 2. Economics: The worth of all the benefits and rights arising from ownership. Two types of economic value are (1) the utility of a good or service, and (2) power of a good or service to command other goods, services, or money, in voluntary exchange.
> 3. Marketing: The extent to which a good or service is perceived by its customer to meet his or her needs or wants, measured by customer's willingness to pay for it. It commonly depends more on the customer's perception of the worth of the product than on its intrinsic value.

Therefore, **value creation** is both subjective, determined by the realized amount of value by individual, organization, or society; and relative, comparing the use value with the exchange value. An important condition is that at the time of the exchange, the monetary amount must exceed the producer's costs (Lepak et al. 2007, p. 182).

The **performance** of a production system, according to Aldinger, is defined as 1) the result of a transformation process, 2) the work required, and 3) the potential capabilities to perform a transformation (Aldinger 2009, p. 50). In the definition of Lebas, performance is case and decision-maker specific: "performance is about deploying and managing well the components of the causal model(s) that lead to the timely attainment of stated objectives within constraints specific to the firm and to the situation" (Lebas 1995, p. 29).

A **performance measure** as per Neely et al is „a metric used to quantify the efficiency and/or effectiveness of an action [...] either in terms of the actual

16 http://www.businessdictionary.com/definition/value.html, last accessed 05.07.2017

efficiency and/or effectiveness of an action, or in terms of the end result of that action" (Neely et al. 1995, p. 80).

In industry, the term key performance indicator (KPI) is widely used and refers to "A financial or nonfinancial measure that is used to define and assess progress towards specific organizational goals and typically is tied to an organization´s strategy and business stakeholders "(Pittman, Atwater 2016, p. 95). An important high-level financial metric is the return on invested capital (ROIC), which will be discussed as part of this chapter.

**Characteristics of Performance Measures**

In general performance indicators can be absolute measures condensed through summation or aggregation when needed, or relative numbers expressed as ratios, indices or being weighted (Gladen 2003, p. 13). Next to requirements such as reliability, accuracy, comparability, continuity and relevance, two specific distinctions are worth detailing further: leading and lagging, financial and non-financial metrics.

**Leading and Lagging Indicators**

Brignall et al framed the thinking about leading and lagging indicators by allocating performance dimensions into their results and determinants framework (Table 23), which distinguishes the two conceptually different categories: (1) 'ends' or 'results', i.e., lagging indicators; and (2) 'means' or 'determinants', i.e., leading indicators (Brignall et al. 1991, p. 34). Organizational goals, typically linked to lagging indicators should be SMART, which is defined by Pitman and Atwater as "specific, measurable, achievable/attainable, relevant/realistic, and timely" (Pittman, Atwater 2016, p. 174). KPIs serve not only to understand the status of operational performance, but also help in discussing deviations from target and solving problems. Ackhoff distinguishes reactive, retrospectively oriented problem solving from proactive, prospectively oriented problem solving (Ackoff 1978, p. 26). In line with this, the focus of companies needs to be put on (1) aligning and measuring lagging indicators representing the organizations goals, e.g., profit maximization; (2) determining current performance based on data, e.g., as part of our discussion profit per hour; and (3) solving problems and proactively influencing leading indicators, i.e., also profit per hour, that influences the lagging result of cumulative profit at the end of a time period, e.g., a fiscal year.

| | Dimensions of performance | Types of measure |
|---|---|---|
| Results | Competitiveness | • Relative market share and position Sales growth<br>• Measures of the customer base |
| | Financial performance | • Profitability<br>• Liquidity<br>• Capital structure<br>• Market ratios |
| Determinants | Quality of service | • Reliability<br>• Responsiveness<br>• Aesthetics/appearance<br>• Cleanliness/tidiness<br>• Comfort<br>• Friendliness<br>• Communication<br>• Courtesy<br>• Competence<br>• Access<br>• Availability<br>• Security |
| | Flexibility | • Volume flexibility<br>• Delivery speed flexibility<br>• Specification flexibility |
| | Resource utilization | • Productivity<br>• Efficiency |
| | Innovation | • Performance of the innovation process<br>• Performance of individual innovations |

Table 23: Results and determinants - performance measures across six dimensions (Brignall et al. 1991, p. 36)

**Financial and Non-Financial Metrics**

In manufacturing performance measures do not only relate to financial metrics such as cost, but also to non-financial metrics related to quality, time or flexibility, as shown in Table 24. The combination of non-financial and financial measures provides an integrative perspective of performance (Yadav, Sagar 2013, p. 951).

| Quality | Flexibility | Cost | Time |
|---|---|---|---|
| Q1: Performance<br>Q2: Features<br>Q3: Reliability<br>Q4: Conformance<br>Q5: Technical durability<br>Q6: Serviceability<br>Q7: Aesthetics<br>Q8: Perceived quality<br>Q9: Humanity<br>Q10: Value | F1: Material quality<br>F2: Output quality<br>F3: New product<br>F4: Modify product<br>F5: Deliverability<br>F6: Volume<br>F7: Mix<br>F8: Resource mix | C1: Manufacturing cost<br>C2: Value added<br>C3: Selling price<br>C4: Running cost<br>C5: Service cost | T1: Manufacturing lead time<br>T2: Rate of production introduction<br>T3: Delivery lead time<br>T4: Due-date performance<br>T5: Frequency of delivery |

Table 24: Multiple dimensions of quality, time, cost and flexibility (Neely et al. 1995, p. 83)

Origins go back to the *Tableau de Bord* (managerial dashboard or instrument panel) which was developed in the early 1960s in France (Lebas 1994, p. 471). It consists of non-financial variables that help steer physical and human assets during daily operations to achieve the company′s financial goals (Lebas 1994, p. 481). The thought of providing managers with a comprehensive integrated view was taken forward with the invention of the balanced scorecard (BSC) by Kaplan and Norton in the 1990s. The BSC combines operational measures on customer satisfaction, innovation, continuous improvement, internal efficiencies with financial measures (Kaplan, Norton 1992, p. 71). A current study reconfirms that strategic decision makers should measure business performance in terms of financial as well as operational indicators (Vij, Bedi 2016). Profit per hour presents both a financial and operational metric.

**Management Accounting**

The work in this document relates to management accounting, which differs from financial/cost accounting in several ways. As per Mowen, financial accounting is externally focused, backward looking and must comply with externally defined reporting rules. Management accounting, on the other hand, is internally focused, emphasizes the future and aims to provide information for decision-making (Mowen et al. 2013, p. 7). In this context, cost are classified into relevant and irrelevant costs. According to Drury, "relevant costs are future costs that differ between alternatives"; and "irrelevant costs consist of sunk costs, allocated costs and future costs that do not differ between alternatives" (Drury 2012, p. 195).

When the cost of already purchased resources do not vary between the choice of alternative options, they are referred to as sunk cost (Drury 2012, p. 33). Allocated costs deal with indirect, not product related costs, also called overhead (Zimmerman 2011, p. 47). Cost assignment approaches for overhead can follow a standard, normal or actual costing system (Mowen et al. 2013, p. 435). Only variable costs are considered within the measurement of profit per hour, that is to say, only costs which "increase in direct proportion to increases in activity output", opposed to fixed costs (Mowen et al. 2013, p. 92). As per Drury, there is "a move towards the widespread adoption of shortrun variable costing techniques" (Drury 2012, p. 216) that includes throughput costing and Theory of Constraints, which will be both discussed in chapter 4.2.2. In the oil & gas industry, for example, variable costs are mainly energy costs, non-energy utility costs, and process material costs while personnel, maintenance, property and other costs are treated as fixed (Hey 2017, p. 327). In process industries, such as oil refining, process costing is used instead of job-costing for distinct products (Horngren et al. 2015, pp. 130–131). Cooper and Kaplan claimed that if managers measure costs right, they make the right decisions (Cooper, Kaplan 1988, p. 96). There is a variety of different costing systems ranging from simplistic systems which are inexpensive to operate to highly sophisticated, expensive systems which employ cause-and-effect cost allocations (Drury 2012, p. 48). Horngren, points out several possible issues with cost data, e.g., the time period of the cost driver and cost do not match, the relationship between cost driver and cost changes due to modification of the process/introduction of new technology, fixed costs are allocated as if they are variable, data is missing or unreliable, and inflation (Horngren et al. 2015, pp. 416–417). Furthermore, the different transfer pricing policies for internal customers, i.e., market price, cost-based price, or negotiated prices, (Mowen et al. 2013, p. 539) affect the profit per hour concept.

### 4.2.1 Return on Invested Capital

"Companies that grow and earn a return on capital that exceeds their cost of capital create value" (Koller et al. 2015, p. 3). This had already been discussed end of the 19th century by Alfred Marshall in his book Principles of Economy (Marshall 1895, p. 142). Koller et al emphasize that growth merely increases value if the return on invested capital (ROIC) exceeds the cost of capital. Otherwise, growth actually decreases value (Koller et al. 2015, p. 17). Figure 29 summarizes relevant aspects in a value driver tree.

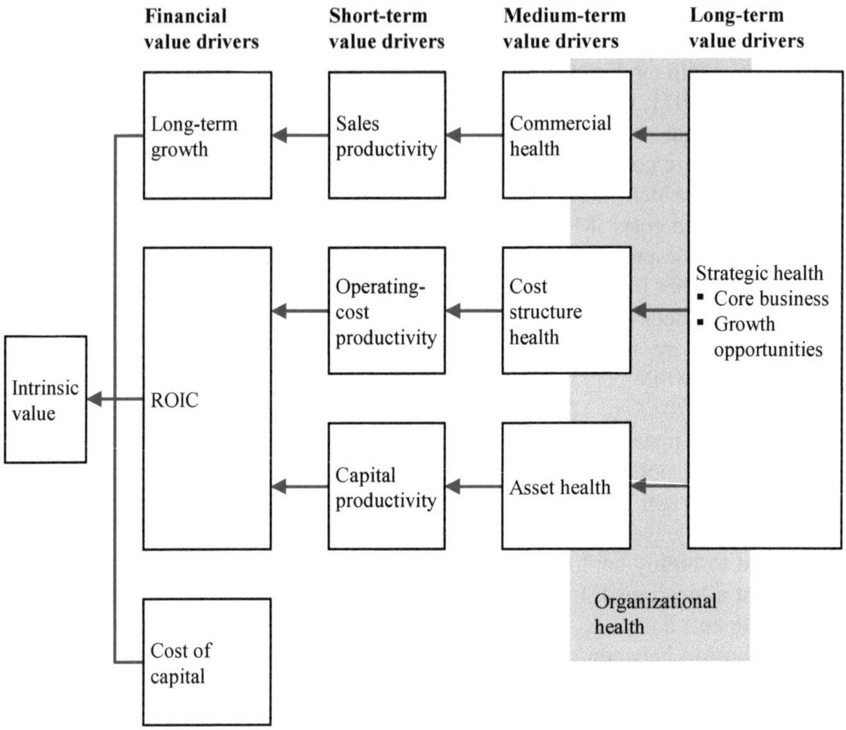


Figure 29: Value driver tree (Koller et al. 2015, p. 582)

Horngren et al highlight that the fact of ROIC being a single percentage integrating all the components of profitability such as revenues, costs, and investment makes it a very popular performance measure in business. Moreover, it can also be used for comparisons with rates of returns of alternative opportunities (Horngren et al. 2015, p. 900). The concept of return on invested capital[17] bringing together sales, earnings and total investment as shown in Figure 30 originated at the Du Pont company in the beginning of the 1900s (Chandler 1977, p. 446).

17 Throughout this document ROIC is used instead of ROI as ROI commonly refers to single investment decisions.

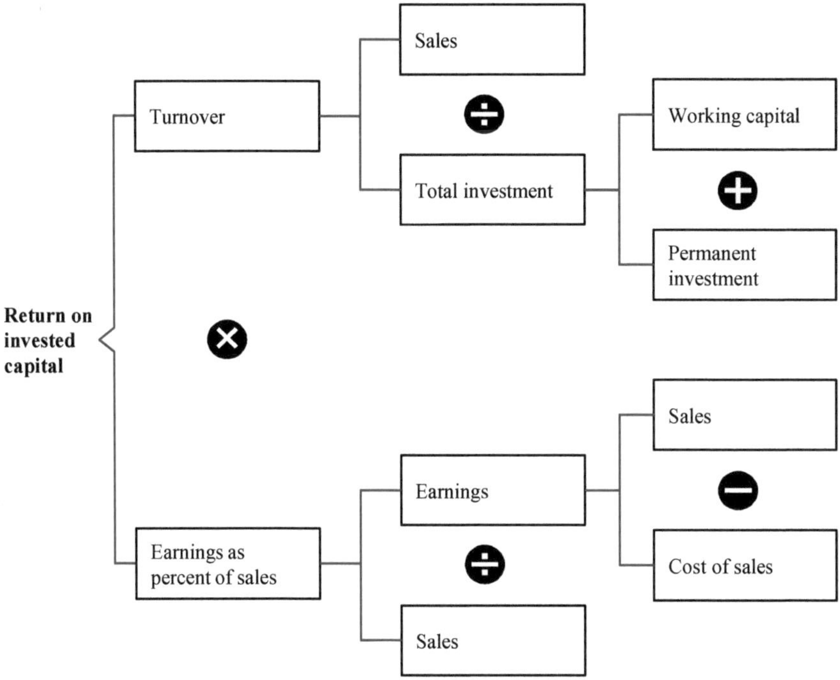


Figure 30: Du Pont equation (Davies 1950, p. 7; Chandler 1977, p. 447)

Visualizing the structure of a KPI tree, e.g., for ROIC, helps with assessing performance and finding reasons for low performance (Almeida, Azevedo 2016, p. 150). Typically a sensitivity analysis is used, which Pittman, Atwater 2016, p. 169 describe as "a technique for determining how much an expected outcome or result will change in response to a given change in an input variable". ROIC is usually expressed as a function, Equation 1, of earnings before interest, taxes and amortization (EBITA).

$$ROIC = (1 - Operating\ Cash\ Tax\ Rate) x \frac{EBITA}{Revenues} x \frac{Revenues}{Invested\ Capital}$$

Equation 1: ROIC calculation (Koller et al. 2015, p. 210)

Alternative performance measures such as return on equity (ROE) and economic profit are both a function of ROIC and can therefore be optimized through ROIC improvements. A drawback of ROE is that it can be influenced by the company's debt-to-equity ratio, i.e., replacing equity with debt, leading to higher risk for shareholders (Koller et al. 2015, p. 223).

Within the concept of ROIC four types of decisions can be taken to maximize shareholder value: (1) operative decisions influencing revenues, cost and profitability; (2) capital allocation decisions related to the overall invested capital; (3) financing decisions affecting cost of capital; and (4) investment into non-material potential such as innovation or human capital affecting share value as well as cost of capital (Groll 2003, p. 101). Related to this, Epstein and Lee promoted the calculation of the "return on action" as part of their Action-Profit-Linkage (APL) model. They used the same logic as for the sensitivity analysis of ROIC, namely, identifying causal linkages between managerial actions and their effects on profitability (Epstein, Lee 2000, p. 59). When reviewed, in 2013, Yadav and Sagar found however, that the practical application of APL is not widely available (Yadav, Sagar 2013, p. 958). This could indicate an opportunity for further consideration. In general, the objective of a firm is to find the output–input combination that results in the maximal profit (Christensen, Hemmer 2006, p. 565). The focus of further discussion in later chapters of this thesis will be operative decisions. It can be said that ROIC is a suitable, high-level, financial metric for operations improvement. The use of value trees helps to disaggregate ROIC to derive actionable areas of opportunity.

### 4.2.2 Time-Based Performance Measures

"If time be of all things the most precious, wasting time must be [...] the greatest prodigality [...] Lost time is never found again" (Benjamin Franklin, William Temple Franklin 1818, p. 249). That is why time is a competitive element and important driver of strategy (Horngren et al. 2015, p. 768). Time based competitors focus on reducing engineering time in R&D, throughput time in operations, and order processing lead time in sales and marketing (Azzone et al. 1991, p. 83). The value added is a function of time (Westkämper, Decker 2006) and can manifest itself in two ways: (1) higher cash inflows, e.g., through increases in market share and (2) lower cash outflows through improvements in efficiency (Azzone et al. 1991, p. 79). Horngren defines a time driver as "any factor that causes a change in the speed of an activity when the factor changes", for example, capacity constraints or bottlenecks (Horngren et al. 2015, p. 769). Galloway and Waldron coined the term throughput accounting (TA), a time-based costing system based on three concepts (Galloway, Waldron 1988b, p. 35):

1. Manufacturing units are an integrated whole whose operating costs in the short term are largely predetermined. It is more useful and infinitely simpler to consider the entire cost, excluding material, as fixed and to call the cost the "total factory cost".
2. For all businesses, profit is a function of the time taken to respond to the needs of the market. This in turn means that profitability is inversely proportional to the level of inventory in the system, since the response time is itself a function of all inventory.
3. [It is] the rate at which a product contributes money that determines relative product profitability. And [it is the rate at which a product contributes money compared to] the rate at which the factory spends it that determines absolute profitability.

Based on the above concepts and their belief that contribution should be measured in terms of the rate at which money is received rather than as an absolute, Galloway, Waldron 1988a, p. 34, defined the following three ratios (Equation 2, Equation 3, Equation 4).

$$Return\ per\ factory\ hour = \frac{Sales\ price - Material\ cost}{Time\ on\ the\ key\ resource}$$

Equation 2: Return per factory hour (Galloway, Waldron 1988a, p. 34)

$$Cost\ per\ factory\ hour = \frac{Total\ factory\ cost}{Total\ time\ available\ on\ the\ key\ resource}$$

Equation 3: Cost per factory hour (Galloway, Waldron 1988a, p. 34)

$$TA\ ratio = \frac{Return\ per\ factory\ hour}{Cost\ per\ factory\ hour}$$

Equation 4: Throughput accounting (TA) ratio (Galloway, Waldron 1988a, p. 34)

A more recent definition of throughput accounting can be found in the dictionary of the American Production and Inventory Control Society (APICS) (Pittman, Atwater 2016, p. 188):

> "A management accounting method based on the belief that because every system has a constraint that limits global performance, the most effective way to evaluate the impact that any proposed action will have on the system as a whole is to look at the

expected changes in the global measures of throughput, inventory, and operating expense".

The notion of constraint in this definition involves time and is also the focal point of monetary operational and global performance measures within the Theory of Constraints (TOC) (Rahman 1998, p. 342), further elaborated in chapter 5.4:

- Throughput: the rate at which the system generates money through sales (sold output minus totally variable cost)
- Inventory: all the money invested in things the system intends to sell
- Operating expense: all the money the system spends in turning inventory into throughput.
- Net profit: an absolute measurement in dollars [or any other currency] expressed as total throughput minus operating expense.
- Return on investment: a relative measurement which equals Net profit divided by the inventory.

Two of the main criticisms of TOC and TA are: (1) They are short-term decision tools, and (2) operating expenses are sometimes regarded as fixed, which would make TOC and TA in these cases the same as variable costing. Nevertheless, "TA is an important development in modern accounting that allows managers to understand the contribution of constrained resources to overall profitability [...and allows for] better analytical decisions" (Freeman 2007, p. 6). The use of time-based accounting methods with a metric such as return (profit) per factory hour seems of actual relevance, given the push to respond in agile ways to external volatility and to use lean principles for instance to minimize inventory.

**A Closer Look at Profit per Hour**

In the area of manufacturing optimization there are three basic philosophies that can be employed: (1) maximum-production rate or minimum-time, (2) minimum-cost, and (3) maximum-profit-rate. Optimizing for profit rate is recommend in the case of constraint capacities in a given time interval (Hitomi 1996, p. 154) and influences both revenues and cost, while the first and second strategy, have a clear bias to revenue and cost respectively. Another word for profit rate would be profit velocity, a term adopted by Rothschild in 1998. He argues that time-based economics and the analysis of profit velocity helps make better decisions for product mix, pricing and target customers (Rothschild 1998, pp. 233–234). Rothschild founded a company called Profit Velocity Solutions, which filed a patent application for a "Computer-Aided System for Improving Returns on

Assets (ROA)" in 2015. Figure 31 shows a graphic representation of ROA for different products and their respective profit per unit and units per asset-hour (Rothschild et al. 2015, p. 3). This is an example of bringing operations and management control levels together in discrete industries.

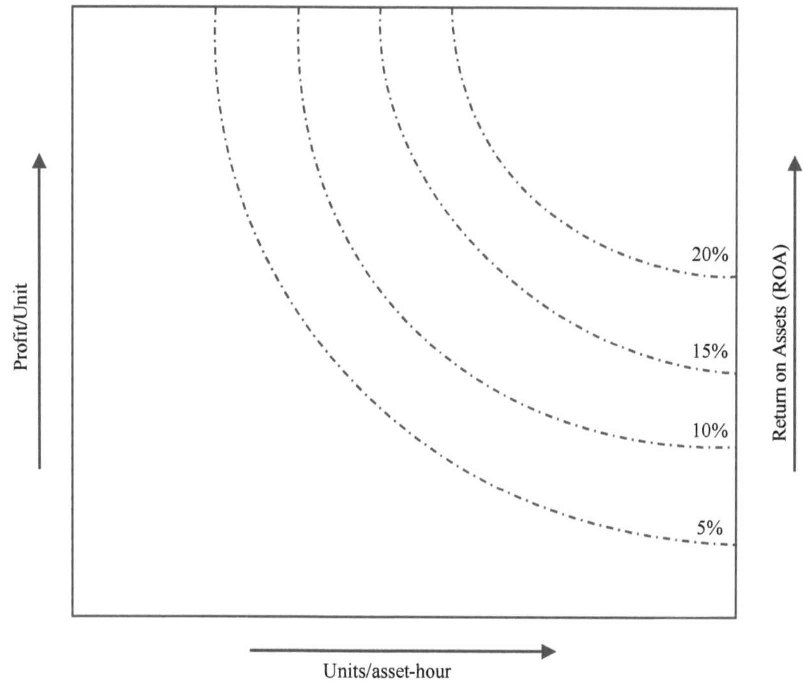


Figure 31: Matrix p/unit, unit/h, ROA (Rothschild et al. 2015, vii)

In the context of process industries, Anderson et al discussed the benefits of advanced process controls to help operate production plants closer to the overall optimum defined by profit per hour (Anderson et al. 1994, p. 82). The optimum in real time optimization is constrained by plant operating conditions involving process variables like temperatures, pressures, flow rates, yield or viscosity; capacities of the plant, its equipment and storage; and economic factors such raw material costs or product margins (Seborg et al. 2004, p. 512). Given the large number of factors involved and the complexity in industries such as pharmaceuticals, chemicals, and mining, nowadays advanced analytics are applied to help (Auschitzky et al. 2014, p. 1). Profit per hour has also been defined one of five core beliefs for unlocking industrial resource productivity (Hammer, Somers

2016, IX). As the time scale varies across different industrial management systems and reporting cycles (Rakar et al. 2004, p. 1), it is worth noting that "per hour" in this discussion is a placeholder for a short time-based metric. Finally, on the topic of time horizons, Horngren warns, that "managers could take actions that cause short-run increases in these measures but that conflict with the long-run interest of the company" (Horngren et al. 2015, p. 906). Koller et al. have a similar view that the often debated focus on shareholder value is not a problem, but short-termism is (Koller et al. 2015, p. 4).

### 4.2.3 Current State, Challenges and Opportunities

The discussion in this chapter aimed to understand the status quo, the importance of performance measure and critical factors to consider. Accepting the profit objective of commercial firms´ high level financial KPIs such as ROIC and their disaggregation help to understand the sensitivities of actions measured as leading indicators on the outcome expressed by lagging indicators. The answer to Neely´s questions at the beginning of this chapter "Should measures focus on processes, the outputs of processes, or both?" would therefore be both. Modeling the linkages between actions and profits continues to be challenging. While Christensen, Hemmer 2006, p. 563 see demand for simplification of the complex cost models, Buschbacher 2016, p. 41 see the solution in algorithm-based, dynamic KPIs based on Big Data analytics going forward. Neely et al. 1995, p. 109, also concluded that future KPIs would be predictive measures for the future based on past data. As there is always a bottleneck in production and process industries many already operate 24/7, the answer to "Is time the fundamental measure of manufacturing performance?" has to be yes. Time based metrics such as profit per hour and time-based accounting methods exist but don´t seem to be widely adopted yet. Their focus on variable cost is meaningful from the angle that fixed cost can be either considered as "sunk cost" or are not adjustable in the short-term. The final challenge of short-termism, the push of investors and mangers for quarterly results remains. However, a recent article gave evidence that "managing for the long term pays off' (Barton et al. 2017).

## 4.3 Performance Measurement and Management Systems

Performance measurement and management (PMM) systems play a critical role for managers. In a global survey conducted by the Business Application Research Center in 2009, more than 80% of companies responded that they see the need to improve their performance management processes (Bange et al. 2009, p. 5). Another recent study by Möller et al. investigated 196 German and Swiss companies regarding their focus on performance management systems. The researchers found that the financial concept of ROIC prevails as the most common instrument (77%), followed by other functional concepts such as Total Quality Management (51%) or Six Sigma (28%). Overarching, multi-dimensional performance management systems are less frequently used or unknown, with the exception of the balanced scorecard (37%) (Möller et al. 2014, p. 436).

**Definitions**

According to Neely et al, performance measurement can be defined as "the process of quantifying the efficiency and effectiveness of action" (Neely et al. 1995, p. 80). A performance management system is a "system for collecting, measuring, and comparing a measure to a standard for a specific criterion for an operation, item, good, service, business, etc. A performance measurement system consists of a criterion, a standard, and a measure" (Pittman, Atwater 2016, p. 132). Anthony described performance management using the term "management control" as "the process by which managers assure that resources are obtained and used effectively and efficiently in the accomplishment of the organization´s objectives" (Anthony 1965, p. 27). A more recent definition is offered by Horngren et al.: "A management control system is a means of gathering and using information to aid and coordinate the planning and control decisions throughout an organization and to guide the behavior of its managers and other employees" (Horngren et al. 2015, p. 864). Already in 1969 Skinner laid out a comprehensive management process linking industry factors, company strategy with manufacturing policies, and performance dimensions such as productivity, service, quality (Skinner 1969, p. 8). It is crucial to understand, that competitive advantages cannot be obtained just by measuring performance (Schläfke et al. 2012, p. 115). It requires process improvement, the implementation of changes and management of performance through practices and people (Bourne 2008, p. 68). The notion of a control loop that includes both measurement and corrective action is important (Bititci et al. 2000, p. 702). Performance management is about closing the loop as depicted in Figure 32 (Neely et al. 1995, p. 107). Controlling requires information about the current state, e.g., through the means of a scorecard; information about deviations from targets to direct attention; and problem solving and execution of counter measures (Obermaier 2016, p. 301).

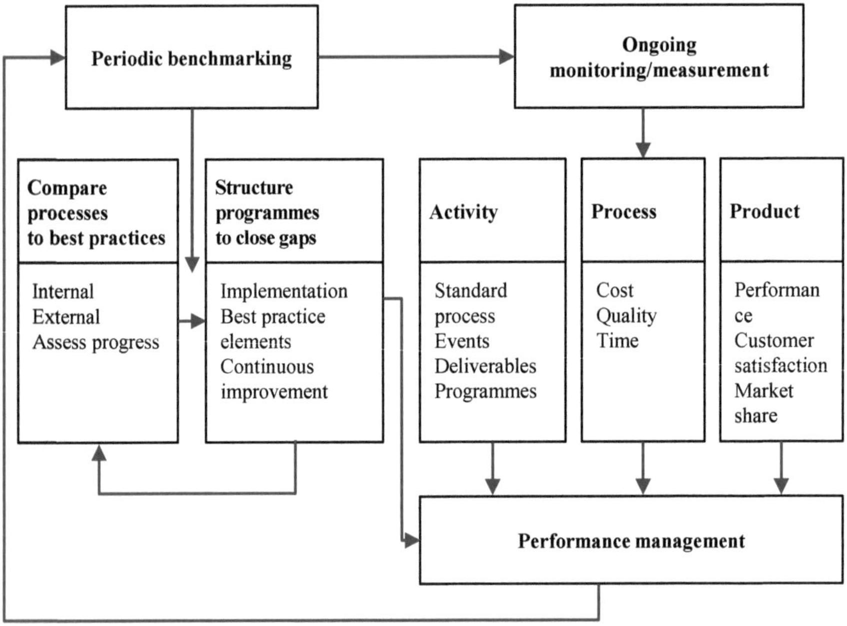


Figure 32: Closed loop performance management (Neely et al. 1995, p. 107)

## Approaches, Critique and Trends

Yadav and Sagar reviewed the evolution of PMM approaches, Figure 33, and their extensions such as the balanced scorecard, performance pyramid, performance prism, the EFQM excellence model, Kanji´s business scorecard, "system dynamics based" balanced score card (BSC); holistic approaches like integrated dynamic performance measurement systems or the holistic performance management framework; and context-specific PMM frameworks, e.g., process-based frameworks (input-process-output-outcome framework) or financial performance drivers (economic value added) (Yadav, Sagar 2013, pp. 963–964). While the focus on financial measures continues to be highly criticized in general (Almeida, Azevedo 2016, p. 130), there are also other important aspects for current PMM systems that are shown in Figure 34 (Kleindienst 2016, p. 3). Yadav and Sagar see the biggest research need in developing effective PMM systems, that are holistic, integrated and dynamic to support companies in volatile and competitive business conditions (Yadav, Sagar 2013).

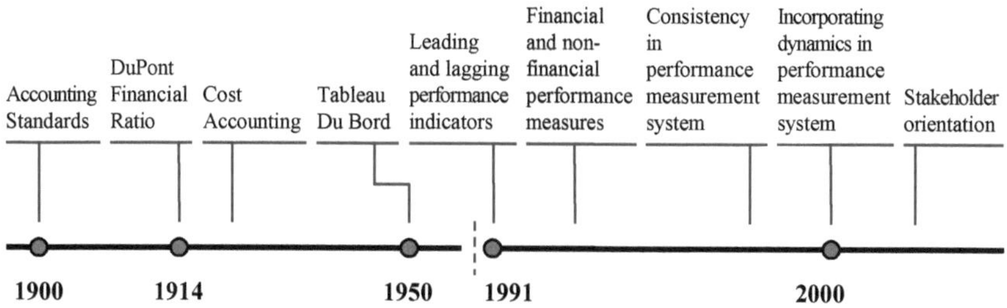


Figure 33: Evolution and trends for performance measurement and management (adapted from Yadav, Sagar 2013, p. 950, 956, 962)

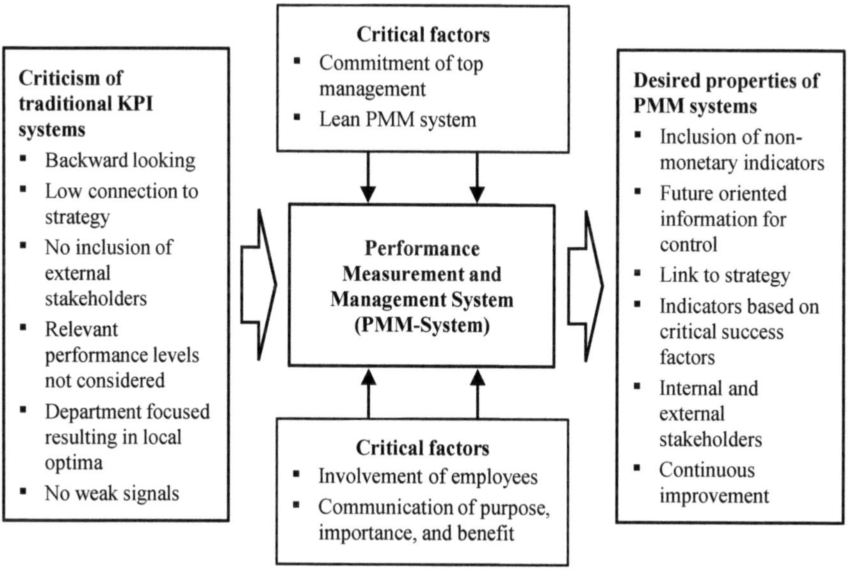


Figure 34: Criticism, factors and properties of PMM systems (Kleindienst 2016, p. 3)

According to Bititci, such a dynamic PMM system would consist of (1) a monitoring system of the external business environment; (2) a monitoring system of internal performance and environment; (3) a review system combining both internal and external information, comparing the current situation with set objectives, and deriving priorities; and (4) an internal deployment system for execution of actions (Bititci et al. 2000, p. 696). In order to quantify the positive effects of improvement actions a baseline and defined policy is required. The Efficiency Valuation Organization (EVO) publishes the International Performance Measurement and Verification Protocol (IPMVP), in which measurement and verification is defined as "the process of using measurement to reliably determine actual savings" (EVO - Efficiency Valuation Organization 2012, p. 4). Savings as well as other performance trends are typically visualized in dashboard, Figure 35 provides an example.

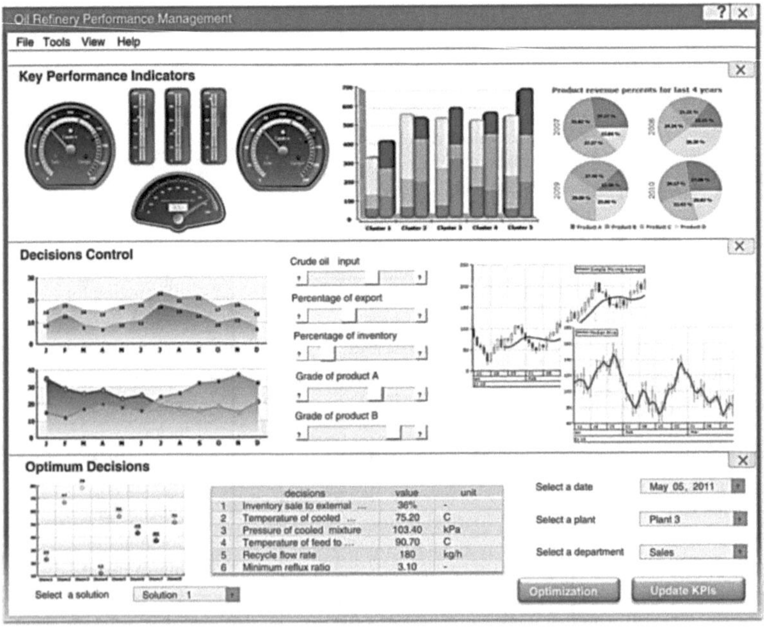


Figure 35: Dashboard for oil refinery (Hu et al. 2012, p. 734)

The current trend of digitization, with more internal/external data and complementing analytics competences, will lead to major changes in management control processes, e.g., (1) from reactive-analytical to proactive-prognostic control, (2) quantitative value driver models, (3) more frequent, agile optimization and control cycles based on real-time data, (4) automated analytics based control, (5) integrated cross-functional, cross-enterprise control (Kieninger et al. 2015, p. 10).

**Current State, Challenges and Opportunities**

For managers to control their companies, both performance measurement and management is required. Although a variety of approaches exist, challenges remain. The convergence of strategic and operational performance measurement is facilitated through the drive for integrated systems. Through digitalization real time performance measurement on both levels becomes possible. This will allow for dynamic management control, closing the loop between measurement, decision and action, and result in the increased agility of companies.

## 4.4 Decision Support Systems

Capturing strategic and operational business opportunities increasingly depends on decision support systems and analytical tools (Schläfke et al. 2012, p. 111). The area of business intelligence (BI), Big Data, and analytics is attracting significant interest in business and academia (Chen et al. 2012, p. 1165). Information becomes a strategic resource with considerable consequences for companies and their decision making processes (Seufert et al. 2014, p. 18). In the time of Big Data, "decisions may often be made not by humans but by machines" (Mayer-Schönberger, Cukier 2013, p. 16).

**Definitions**

A decision support system is a "computer system designed to assist managers in selecting and evaluating courses of action by providing a logical (usually quantitative) analysis of relevant factors" (Pittman, Atwater 2016, p. 46). Business intelligence is the "the capability to gather, sort, classify and maintain data and knowledge for the purpose of improving competitive positioning and business management" (APICS Suppy Chain Council 2015, p. 55).

**Approaches, Critique and Trends**

The first related systems were termed "management information systems (MIS) back in the 1960s (Lanquillon, Mallow 2015b, p. 257). They feature an "integrated approach for providing interpreted and relevant data that can help managers make decisions. This information can reflect the progress or lack of progress made in achieving major objectives" (Pittman, Atwater 2016, p. 104). Several other terms have been adopted since, Table 25.

| Term | Time frame | Specific meaning |
|---|---|---|
| Decision support | 1970–1985 | Use of data analysis to support decision making |
| Executive support | 1980–1990 | Focus on data analysis for decisions by senior executives |
| Online analytical processing (OLAP) | 1990–2000 | Software for analyzing multidimensional data tables |
| Business intelligence | 1989–2005 | Tools to support data-driven decisions, with emphasis on reporting |
| Analytics | 2005–2010 | Focus on statistical and mathematical analysis for decisions |
| Big Data | 2010–present | Focus on very large, unstructured, fast-moving data |

Table 25: Terminology for using and analyzing data (Davenport 2014a, p. 10)

BI is criticized for being backward-looking, whereas Big Data is forward-looking through predictive or even prescriptive analytics suggesting a specific course of action. However, this distinction appears artificial and not meaningful as both are ultimately aiming to gain insights to support decisions (Lanquillon, Mallow 2015b, p. 258). Omri views BI analytics as a specialization of Big Data-Analytics focusing on structured data instead of unstructured, inconsistent sets of data (Omri 2015, p. 105). Integrated decision support, according to Clark and Dostal, represents the highest maturity level in performance management (Clark, Dostal 2013, p. 6). Performance management analytics (PMAs) is "the extensive use of data and analytical methods to understand relevant business dynamics, to effectively control key performance drivers, and to actively increase organizational performance" (Schläfke et al. 2012, p. 111). In 1978, Ackhoff illustrated the interplay of decision making systems, Figure 36, in the larger context.

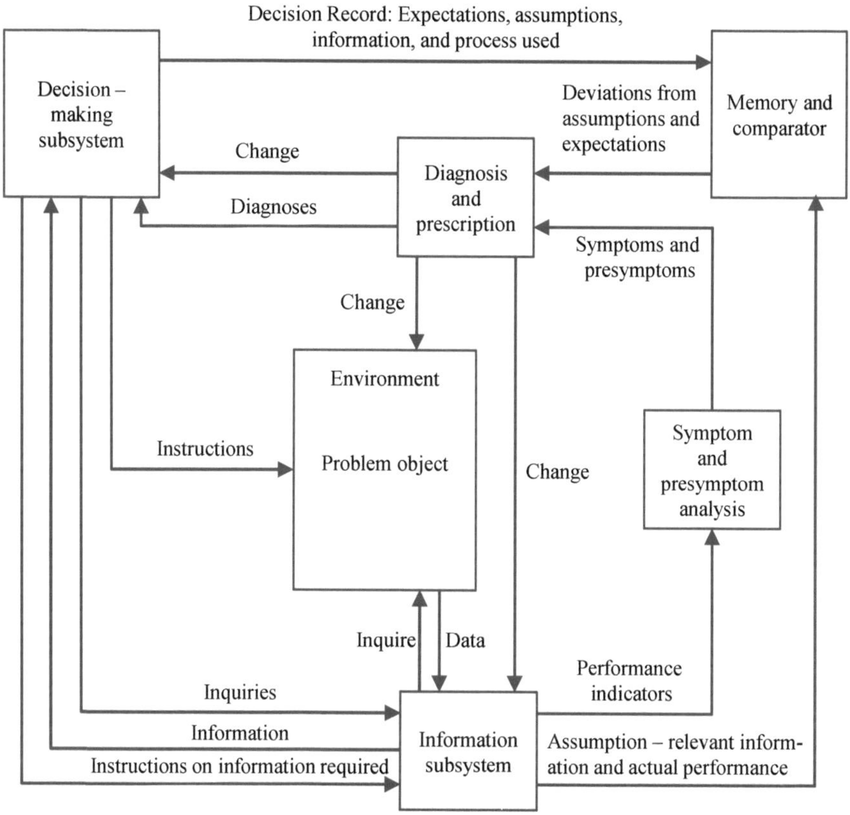


Figure 36: Diagrammatic representation of a problem-solving system (Ackoff 1978, p. 191)

Taylor provides four principles in respect to decision management systems: "(1) begin with the decision in mind, (2) be transparent and agile, (3) be predictive, not reactive, (4) test, learn, and continually improve" (Taylor 2012, p. 76). Furthermore, in the context of the overall decision lifecycle spanning from strategy definition to execution, automation is a relevant aspect (Taylor 2012, p. 82). Automation can help tackle various types of latencies, Figure 37, including analysis latency or decision latency. For Iafrate, efficient organization applying a combination of effective systems and tools with proper decision KPIs can develop into a "zero latency" organization (Iafrate 2014, p. 26).

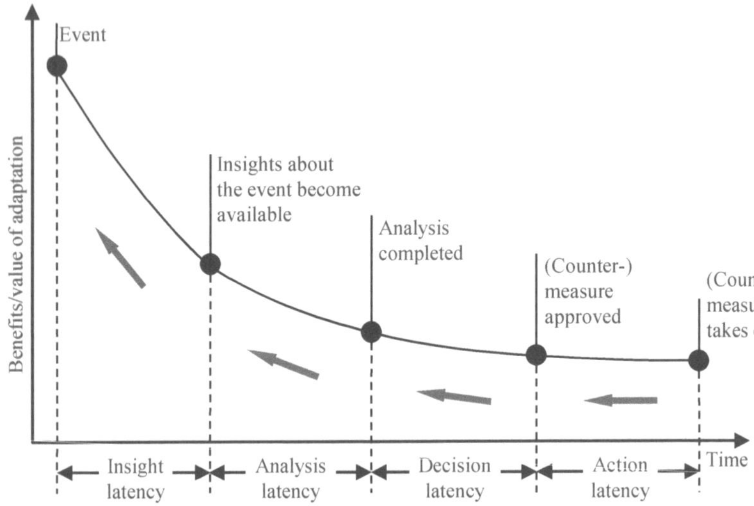


Figure 37: Corporate adaptation (decision making/latency) (Schuh et al. 2017, p. 11)

**Current State, Challenges and Opportunities**

Decision support systems have come a long way, been known under various names, and are becoming of particular relevance with the increasing degree of digitization. Advantages include quicker, fact based decisions reducing the latency between events and actions. The integration of top floor and shop floor (Kleinemeier 2014, pp. 575–576), also dubbed „Controlling 4.0“ (Obermaier 2016, p. 301) enables opportunities on many fronts, including gains in resource productivity and efficiency (Kagermann et al. 2013, p. 7). Related research activities include self-optimizing decision-making in production control (Schuh et al. 2013, p. 443) or artificial intelligence (AI). According to a study on technology tipping point from the World Economic Forum, 45% of respondents expect an AI machine to become a member of the corporate board of directors by 2025 (World Economic Forum 2015, p. 21).

## 4.5 Summary: Performance Opportunities with Decision-Support Systems

Decision making is the primary task of corporate managers. Human decision making, however, is flawed and biased. Fact-based decisions can best be taken by machines or by managers guided by decision support systems. Performance measures embrace financial and non-financial aspects and indicators can be leading or lagging. Performance can be defined in different ways, but in this work focuses on financial performance expressed by the return on invested capital. ROIC can be disaggregated into value drivers for further analysis of operational efficiencies. This way the management and operational control levels are linked, i.e., potential gains in resource productivity and efficiency from the shop floor translate into financial results on the top floor. Time based metrics are of particular importance for profit maximization of constrained operations, common in continuous process industries. Profit per hour has been used infrequently and with the focus on product mix decisions within planning. Within techno-economics systems, performance measurement and management systems have evolved over time and aim to close the loop between measurement, decisions and actions. Technology also helps to reduce decision making latency. Using the profit rate as a leading operational target control parameter presents an opportunity to maximize the lagging, future total returns of invested capital.

| Learning | Delimitations | Requirements |
|---|---|---|
| • Human decision making is biased and flawed<br>• Performance measures and decision support systems help managers make data driven decisions<br>• Performance measurement and management systems aim to be dynamic closing the loop between measurement, decision and action<br>• Performance measures include financial, non-financial and leading/lagging indicators<br>• Management and operational control are distinguished levels that can be linked through a value driver tree for ROIC<br>• Profit rate not commonly used as a leading operations target parameter<br>• Technology and digitization can help reduce decision making latency and compute profit rate in real-time using advanced analytics | INCLUDES<br>• Time-based profit optimization<br>• Dynamic, closed-loop performance management<br>• Operations orientation (internal focus) considering external factors and overall strategic objectives<br>• Target group are decision makers in a manufacturing site, e.g., plant managers, process engineers and operators<br>EXCLUDES<br>• Capital and financing aspects, e.g., debt/equity optimization | • Profit orientation with the goal of maximizing ROIC<br>• Profit rate as leading operational KPI<br>• Linking operations level with management level through value driver tree<br>• Decision support, e.g., cockpit or closed loop automatic decision making |

Table 26: Summary of conclusions from management perspective

# 5 Operations Perspective: Achieving Resource-Productive Operations

This chapter gives a perspective on resource-productive operations (section 5.1), operations improvement methods (section 5.2), advanced process control (section 5.3) and a summary of how to achieve resource-productive operations in section 5.4.

## 5.1 Resource-Productive Operations

Operations management in the context of production covers a wide spectrum of factors, such as technological, managerial and methodological factors, shown in Figure 38. Industrial resource productivity, according to Hammer and Somers, is a priority across manufacturing sectors due to trends on both the supply side, e.g. resource scarcity, and the demand side, e.g. growth in resource demand. Resource-productive manufacturers aim to optimize variable costs for materials, energy or water while taking the operational requirements such as throughput and quality into account (Hammer, Somers 2016, p. 49).

When it comes to resources, the "Limits of growth report" from 1972 identified five critical factors: (1) population, (2) agricultural production, (3) natural resources, (4) industrial production, and (5) pollution (Meadows et al. 1972, pp. 11–12). More recently, in 2016, Stuchety et al explained that the significant economic growth over the past 30 years, when measured by GDP, has been driven largely by depleting natural capital (Stuchtey et al. 2016, p. 21) and to illustrate this point they cite the Global Footprint Network[18] "in 2015, we used a full 1.6 planets with most rich countries using between two and five times more than their share" (Stuchtey et al. 2016, p. 12).

18 Global Footprint Network: *Earth Overshoot Day:* Press Release, Oakland, CA, USA, July 12, 2016 http://www.overshootday.org/newsroom/press-release-english/, last accessed 12.05.2017


M. Hammer, *Management Approach for Resource-Productive Operations*,
Industrial Management, https://doi.org/10.1007/978-3-658-22939-9_5

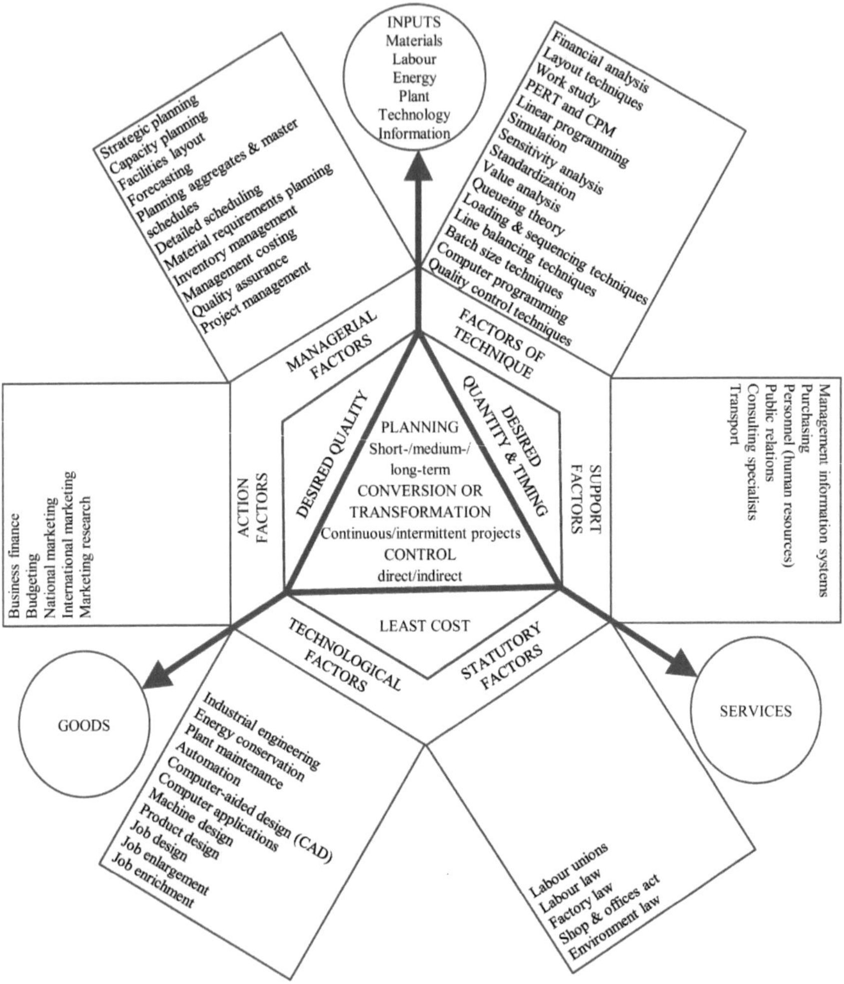


Figure 38: The scope of production and operations management (Steyn 1989, p. 12)

Manufacturing industry is one of the root causes in this global dilemma (Rao 2011, p. 339) and accounts for 25.9% of all energy consumption in Europe[19], and 32% in the US in 2015[20]. At the same time, improving industrial operations through the application of manufacturing philosophies such as lean or Six Sigma is a critical enabler to achieve operational excellence supporting the highest levels of resource productivity. In manufacturing, materials represent the largest cost factor, at over 70% on average (United Nations Industrial Development Organization 2015, p. 192). Lacy and Rutqvist see four distinct forms of waste:

> "(1) **Wasted resources** are materials and energy that cannot be continually regenerated, but instead are consumed and forever gone when used. (2) Products with **wasted lifecycles** have artificially short working lives or are disposed of even if there is still demand for them from other users. (3) Products with **wasted capability** sit idle unnecessarily; for instance, cars typically sit unused for 90 percent of their lives. (4) **Wasted embedded values** are components, materials, and energy that are not recovered from disposed products and put back into use" (Lacy, Rutqvist 2015, xvii).

For McDonough and Braungart, however, "the very concept of waste does not exist" and in 2002 they proposed a shift in product life-cycle thinking from "Cradle-to-Grave" to "Cradle-to-Cradle". This requires designing fundamentally different products and systems aiming to close the material cycles in the biosphere and technosphere (McDonough, Braungart 2002, p. 104).

**Definitions**

In the following the key elements of "Resource-Productive Operations" are reviewed. Pittman, Atwater define **resource** as: "anything that adds value to a good or a service in its creation, production, or delivery", which includes materials, energy, direct and indirect labor, equipment and facilities, information, and capital. **Resource management** in this context is seen as "an emerging field of study emphasizing the systems perspective, encompassing both product and process life cycles, and focusing on the integration of organizational resources toward the effective realization of organizational goals" (Pittman, Atwater 2016, p. 159-160). **Productivity** is an overall measure of the ability to effectively (efficiently and economically) convert resources into goods or services. In short, a ratio of output over input. This also applies to information systems, for turning raw data into information (Hitomi 1996, p. 15; Pittman, Atwater 2016, p. 146).

---

19 Eurostat Statistics Explained: *Consumption of Energy*, http://ec.europa.eu/eurostat/statistics-explained/index.php/Consumption_of_energy, last accessed 02.12.2016

20 U.S. Energy Information Administration (eia): *Monthly Energy Review* – November 2016, https://www.eia.gov/totalenergy/data/monthly/pdf/mer.pdf, last accessed 04.12.2016

Efficiency in operational management and aims to comply with the principle of rationality. On the one hand there is the minimum principle that is to minimize the resources needed to achieve a certain production output. On the other hand the maximum principle refers to maximize the production output at a given resource input, also known as **resource productivity**. This includes material productivity, energy productivity and also labor productivity which in general belong to the category of factor productivity (Ramsauer 2013b, p. 9). We speak of **total productivity** when all resources are included in an overall measure of a firm. Productivity can be physical productivity expressed in units or **value productivity** measured in monetary values (Hitomi 1996, p. 17). Maximum value productivity expressed in the ROIC is the objective of the majority of companies outside of the non-profit sector.

### Trade-Offs

In order to maximize total productivity invariably trade-offs need to be considered. Trade-off decisions exist whenever there are at least 2 different courses of actions with unequal outcomes in terms of effectiveness and value (Ackoff 1978, p. 12).

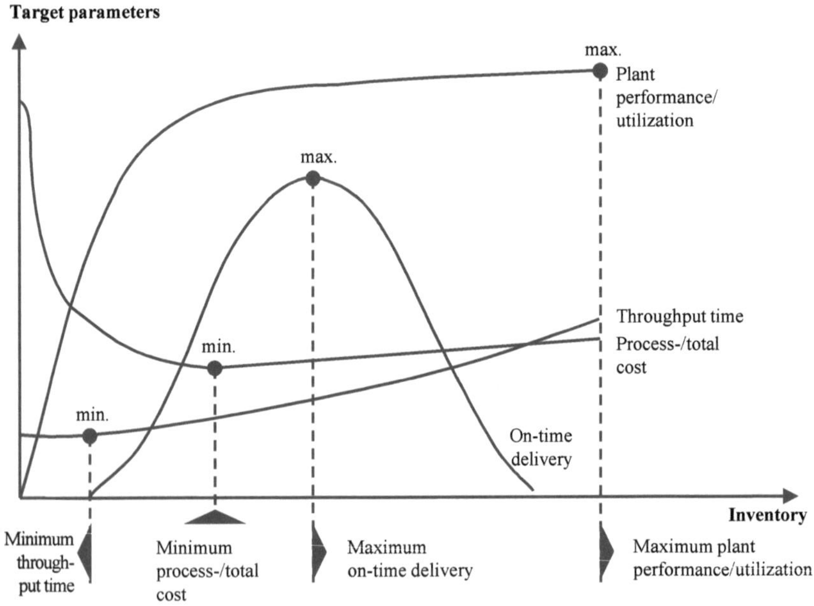


Figure 39: Positioning within the core goals of production management (Schuh, Schmidt 2014, p. 22)

Figure 39 shows an example of conflicting targets, e.g., maximization of utilization vs. delivery performance vs. optimal cost. In trade-off theory, "the improvement in one aspect of operations performance comes at the expense of deterioration in another aspect of performance, [and is] now substantially modified to include the possibility that in the long term different aspects of operations performance can be improved simultaneously" (Slack et al. 2010, p. 668). According to Adam, situations of conflicting targets frequently lead to the inability to make corporate decisions. Especially when the objectives, behaviors and policies of different functions and business units cannot be aligned to an overall target priority. As a consequence, even if all functions do their best in their area, the performance of the total system will be insufficient (Adam 1997, p. 29). In order to identify the optimal decision in such a case of multiple relevant evaluation aspects, Adam suggests a value synthesis to derive a single-dimensional target function such as profit maximization (Adam et al. 1998, p. 3). However, this is a complex undertaking, and "Complex problems seldom have simple solutions [...] that involve manipulating only one causal variable" (Ackoff 1978, p. 118). On top of this, Skinner points out that trade-off decisions have to be made continuously and include competitive and strategic elements (Skinner 1969, p. 6). Table 27 shows examples of important trade-off decisions in manufacturing.

| **Decision area** | **Decision** | **Alternatives** |
|---|---|---|
| Plant and equipment | • Span of process<br>• Plant size<br>• Plant location<br>• Investment decisions<br>• Choice of equipment<br>• Kind of tooling | • Make or buy<br>• One big plant or several smaller ones<br>• Locate near markets or locate near materials<br>• Invest mainly in buildings or equipment or inventories or research<br>• General-purpose or special-purpose equipment<br>• Temporary, minimum tooling or "production tooling" |
| Production planning and control | • Frequency of inventory taking<br>• Inventory size<br>• Degree of inventory control<br>• What to control<br>• Quality control<br>• Use of standards | • Few or many breaks in production for buffer stocks<br>• High inventory or a lower inventory<br>• Control in great detail or in lesser detail<br>• Controls designed to minimize machine downtime or labor cost or time in process, or to maximize output of particular products or material usage<br>• High reliability and quality or low costs<br>• Formal or informal or none at all |

| | | |
|---|---|---|
| Labor and staffing | • Job specialization<br>• Supervision<br>• Wage system<br>• Supervision<br>• Industrial engineers | • Highly specialized or not highly specialized<br>• Technically trained first-line supervisors or nontechnically trained supervisors<br>• Many job grades or few job grades; incentive wages or hourly wages<br>• Close supervision or loose supervision<br>• Many or few such personnel |
| Product Design/ Engineering | • Size of product line<br>• Design stability<br>• Technological risk<br>• Engineering<br>• Use of manufacturing engineering | • Many customer specials or few specials or none at all<br>• Frozen design or many engineering change orders<br>• Use of new processes unproven by competitors or follow-the-leader policy<br>• Complete packaged design or design-as-you-go approach<br>• Few or many manufacturing engineers |
| Organization and Management | • Kind of organization<br>• Executive use of time<br>• Degree of risk assumed<br>• Use of staff<br>• Executive style | • Functional or product focus or geographical or other<br>• High involvement in investment or production planning or cost control or quality control or quality control or other activities<br>• Decisions based on much or little information<br>• Large or small staff group<br>• Much or little involvement in detail; authorization or nondirective style; much or little contact with organization |

Table 27: Trade-off decisions in manufacturing - "you can´t have it both ways" (Skinner 1969, p. 7)

**Theoretical Limits**

We live in a world of constraints and limits. A constraint is "Any element or factor that prevents a system from achieving a higher level of performance with respect to its goal" (Pittman, Atwater 2016, p. 33). Definitions for "limit" according to the Oxford and Cambridge dictionaries vary from "A point or level beyond which something does not or may not extend or pass"[21] to "the greatest amount, number, or level of something that is either possible or allowed"[22]. A theoretical limit, as used in this work, is an absolute limit given by nature and laws of physics. Examples would be the limitation of 24 hours per day or the law of conversation

21 https://en.oxforddictionaries.com/definition/limit, last accessed 12.05.2017
22 http://dictionary.cambridge.org/dictionary/english/limit, last accessed 12.05.2017

of energy stating that the total energy of an isolated system remains constant and can only be transformed. In industrial manufacturing processes, different forms of energy are being used and present theoretical limits for optimization (Kals 2015, p. 22; Kreitlein et al. 2016, pp. 50–54):

- Chemical energy: All materials contain chemical energy which can be transformed, e.g., by combustion into other energy forms. Each chemical reaction needs at least the necessary activation energy to start this transformation process. This activation energy is identical to the theoretical limit.
- Electric and magnetic energy: Electric as well as magnetic energy is used in industry in various applications. Concerning the transformation of electric to other forms of energy the degree of efficiency is subject to certain limitations.
- Mechanical energy: Subcategories of mechanical energy are kinetic energy; potential, elevation, or position energy; wave energy; elastic energy or sound energy.
- Thermal energy: Physically every item with a temperature above absolute zero (-273.15°C) contains thermal energy. An addition of thermal energy expresses itself in a higher internal energy of the system, and to achieve this higher level of internal energy a certain activation energy is, at least, required.

The traditional approach to resource efficiency starts with understanding the current state and subsequent bottom-up brainstorming. A more aggressive approach is to start with the theoretical limit instead, Figure 40. Theoretical limit thinking is compatible with the Overall Equipment Effectiveness (OEE), a commonly used operations KPI, which is a time based metric helping to understand the gap between actual and ideal performance. Stamatis uses the term total effective equipment performance (TEEP) when the basis of consideration is the theoretical limit of calendar hours, that is, 24 hours per day, 365 days per year (Stamatis 2010, p. 22). An application of theoretical limit thinking to raw material consumption of a chemicals company found "that up to 30 percent of its raw-material inputs were wasted" (Hammer et al. 2014, p. 2). Theoretical limits present an important point of orientation for optimization. Or as Ackoff states: "Our ability to solve problems is thereby limited by our conception of what is feasible" (Ackoff 1978, p. 25).

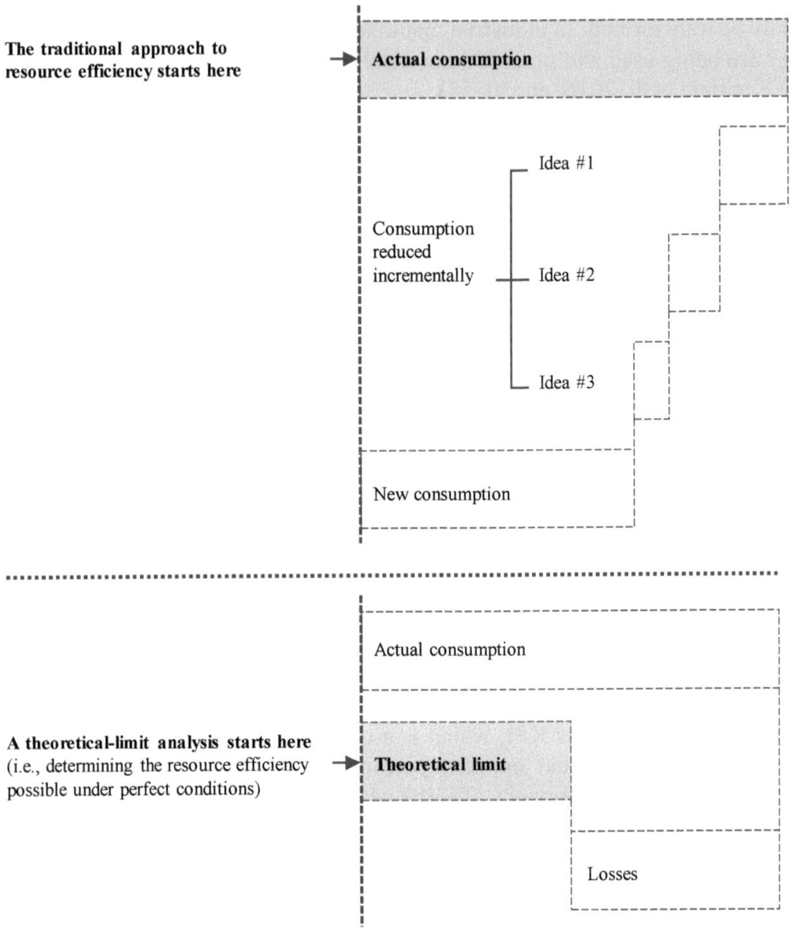


Figure 40: Analyzing the theoretical limit exposes unseen losses (Hammer, Somers 2015, p. 16)

**Loss Thinking**

Considering the gap between current performance and theoretical limits, a lot of improvement opportunity appears. Two examples by Allwood illustrate this: (1) a typical car operates inefficiently at around 10 times the theoretical limit, and (2) the best available technology to extract pure aluminum and iron from their oxides uses over double the absolute theoretical minima calculated by Gibbs (Allwood et al. 2012, pp. 102–103). Losses can be illustrated by using a loss bridge diagram, as in Figure 41.

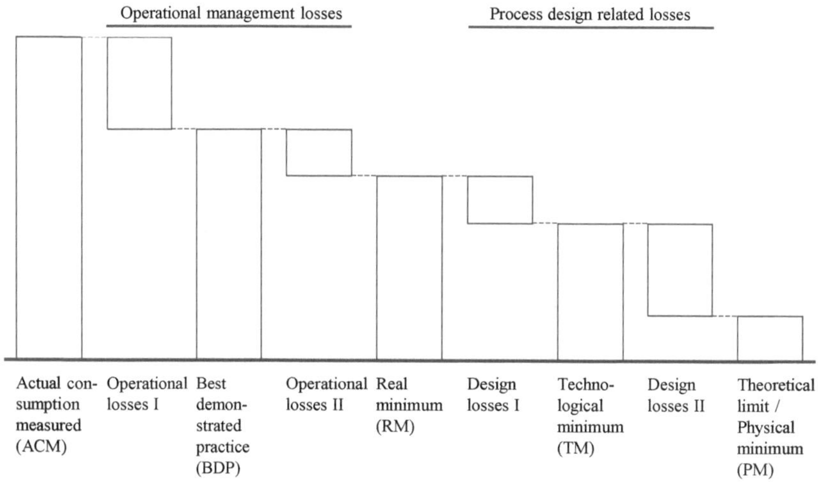


Figure 41: Resource-productive operations loss bridge (Hammer et al. 2017a, p. 7)

The overall gap between actual resource consumption measured and theoretical limit is broken down into operational management losses and process design related losses. For example, improving process control (e.g., operator procedures, equipment settings) helps to reach Best Demonstrated Practice (BDP), the lowest documented, historical resource use for the current system design. But it is obvious even BDP is not the real minimum as further operational losses exist. Process design losses, on the other hand, relate to equipment related losses (design losses I) and technology driven limitations (design losses II). In general, it is worth noting that losses are additive.

Three documented cases exemplify loss thinking further:

(1) A company for solid/liquid and dust filtration solutions went through a holistic process optimization effort tackling a variety of different losses such as material losses (e.g., filter media, auxiliary materials), losses during start-

up/shutdown and overdosing. This was achieved through (a) operational management solutions such as standardization of cutting patterns and the reduction of product variety, along with (b) process design improvements, e.g., automation of dosing and cleaning, as well as installing a new geothermal power plant with heat recovery and photovoltaics (Schmidt et al. 2017, pp. 74–77).

(2) A passenger bus manufacturer could achieve a reduction of 28% in energy demand in the period of 2011 to 2015 through the development and application of a "best practice guide" for energy management to reduce operational losses (Schmidt et al. 2017, 238–241).

(3) In a move to tackle process design losses and adhering to Good Manufacturing Practice (GMP), a producer of printing ink, decided to implement a computer based raw material dosing system. With this measure they could eliminate losses related to human interventions (e.g. dosing errors, lack of accuracy) and reduce raw material losses by 8-10 tons per year (Schmidt et al. 2017, pp. 106–109).

**Current State, Challenges and Opportunities**

Given the challenges outlined in chapter 2 and there is a clear need for industrial resource productivity, be it externally driven by supply shortages, demand growth and competition; or internally driven by profitability objectives. Five core beliefs guide the journey to industrial resource productivity, Table 28.

| **Think lean** | **Think Limits** | **Think profit per hour** | **Think holistic** | **Think circular** |
|---|---|---|---|---|
| Build resource productivity improvements on top of traditional lean thinking as lean and green are highly synergetic and use the same fundamentals | Stretch your aspirations by using the theoretical limit concept fostering creative thinking and delivering break-through impact | Prioritize profit as the main factor for final decisions understanding the relationships between throughput, yield, energy, and the environment | Involve the whole organization to sustain change reinforcing the benefits from technical improvements by improving and tailoring management systems, mindsets and behaviors | Move from finite supply chains to supply circles boosting business opportunities and competitive advantages by optimizing across product and service lifecycles |

Table 28: Five core beliefs to unlock industrial resource productivity (Hammer, Somers 2016, p. 34)

A multitude of trade-offs have to be considered because factors such as throughput, quality, energy are all interrelated. Taking the theoretical limit for guidance and using loss bridges helps to determine the magnitude of losses and specific areas for improvement. Process improvement embraces all "activities designed to identify and eliminate causes of poor quality, process variation, and non-value-added activities" (Pittman, Atwater 2016, p. 141) and entails both continuous and breakthrough improvement.

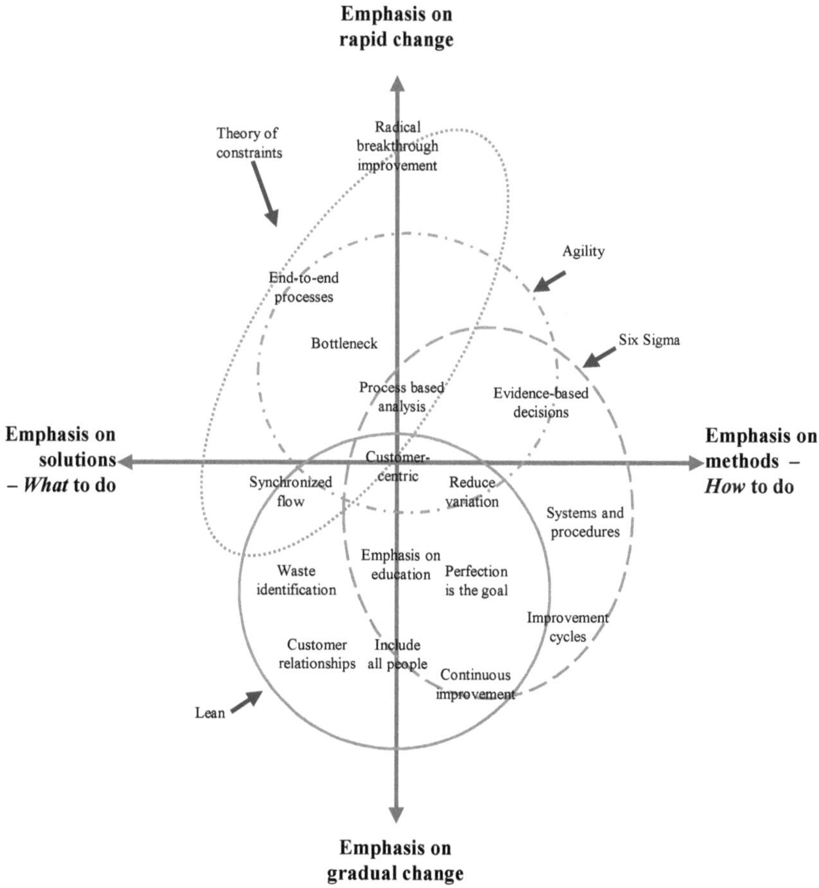


Figure 42: The approaches on the two dimensions of improvement (Slack et al. 2010, p. 558)

According to Slack continuous improvement: “assumes many, relatively small, incremental, improvements in performance [and] stress[es] the momentum of improvement rather than the rate of improvement” while breakthrough improvement “implies major and dramatic change in the way an operation works [...and is] also known as innovation based improvement” (Slack et al. 2010, p. 659). Process innovation is usually driven either by engineering or as Davenport points out by the “information technology function” (Davenport 1993, p. 7). Most of the improvement approaches go back to the formal discipline of industrial engineering (Burton 2011, p. 32) and while their principles are not new, their benefits are still well recognized (Chatterjee 2016, xv). Burton stresses that companies should integrate the best of the various improvement methodologies, shown in Figure 42, such as Lean and Six Sigma or enabling IT, into their own approach and that they should deemphasize the discussion around particular tools as they “are a means, not an end” (Burton 2011, p. 27). In the following sections the four approaches: lean, six sigma, the theory of constraints and agility will be reviewed.

## 5.2 Lean

Lean manufacturing is one of the most common and well established operations improvement methodologies. Womack, Jones and Rood, the authors of the book “The Machine that Changed the World” concluded in 1990 that “Lean production is a superior way for humans to make things” and recommended its adoption as quickly as possible. The reasons for their powerful statement were the two main benefits of lean. First, lean production supplies better products in a greater variety. Secondly, lean production provides more fulfilling and challenging work tasks for employees (Womack et al. 1990, p. 119). Ever-better quality, quicker response, greater flexibility, and higher value are also frequently referred to as golden goals of lean (Schonberger 2008, p. 48). Lean is applicable across industries leading to competitive advantage through operations transformation (Drew et al. 2004, p. 1). Due to their capital intensity, the benefits of lean in process industries can be even higher than in discrete manufacturing (Floyd 2010, pp. xv–xvi).

**Definition**

The term “lean production” was invented as part of the International Motor Vehicle Program by researcher John Krafcik. "Lean" means using “less of everything compared with mass production”, i.e., shorter product development and production lead times, lower capital investment and inventory levels, less human effort and defects (Womack et al. 1990, p. 13). Lean can be defined as a systematic approach built out of principles, practices, tools and techniques that help tackle waste, variability and inflexibility in order to meet the requirements of customers and shareholders, i.e., a combination of cost, quality, delivery and safety objectives (Drew et al. 2004, p. 15). Further descriptors of a lean production system include: "a consistent way of thinking", "a total management philosophy", "focus on total customer satisfaction", "an environment of teamwork and improvement", "a never-ending search for a better way" (Liker 2004, p. 297).

**Focus on Waste Reduction**

Lean production is based on the Toyota Production System (TPS) and goes back to the 1950s and Eiji Toyoda and Taiichi Ohno (Womack et al. 1990, pp. 30–31). At that time, post-World-war II, Toyota´s primary objective was to be as efficient as possible by relentlessly eliminating waste in production. Taichi Ohno summarized this concept in a later interview: "All we are doing is looking at the timeline from the moment the customer gives us an order to the point when we collect the cash. And we are reducing that time line by removing non-valued-added wastes." The principle of waste reduction and respect for humanity form the fundament of the Toyota Production System and were previously passed on from Sakichi and Kiichiro Toyoda (Ohno 1988, xiii-ix). TPS starts with internal or external customers and their definition of value. This allows for the observation of any kind of process, be it in manufacturing or in the service sector, and separation of value adding from non-value adding steps (Liker 2004, p. 27). Originally, seven types of waste were distinguished by Taichi Ohno: (1) Waste of overproduction, (2) Waste of time on hand (waiting), (3) Waste in transportation, (4) Waste of processing itself, (5) Waste of stock on hand (inventory), (6) Waste of movement, (7) Waste of making defective products (Ohno 1988, p. 20). Another common type of waste in literature is (8) Unused employee creativity (Liker 2004, pp. 28–29). Many more, not so obvious, forms can be found, e.g., getting customers to buy what they don't want or need, automating wasteful processes, excessive analyses/ costing/reporting (Schonberger 2008, pp. 48–49). Compression thinking takes it even further by "considering how nature sees waste in order to reach well beyond waste as only a customer might see it" (Hall 2010, pp. 92–93). Heinen and Wulf state that the principles of lean manufacturing are a perfectly suitable basis for an energy and environment oriented production strategy (Heinen, Wulf 2011, p. 504). Several independent studies confirmed that lean and green are highly synergistic. Dües concluded: "The research findings indicate that a Lean environment serves as a catalyst to facilitate Green implementation. The integration of Lean and Green practices will bring benefits to companies and introducing Green as the new Lean is no longer a strong and unsupported statement. It is rather undeniable that the ultimate Lean will be Green" (Dües et al. 2013, p. 99). Hallam, Conteras found positive evidence that "lean is pushing green outcomes through operational waste reduction" (Hallam, Contreras 2016, p. 2179). Fercoq has also confirmed the convergence of Lean and Green management in his quantitative research. Specifically, waste reduction techniques are considered one of the main areas of the overlap between Lean and Green (Fercoq et al. 2016, p. 567). Hammer and Somers provide a specific overview of the translation of the lean types of waste to resource productivity and complement the classic lean waste categories with two additional, resource-productivity specific sources of waste: (1) Inefficient equipment, for example, legacy motors and pumps that are much less efficient than similar equipment designed more recently; (2) Failure to fully integrate systems and to take advantage of available energies across processes. For example, a product is heated with steam during production and then chilled with cooling water for storage (Hammer, Somers 2016, p. 53) or using excess process heat of a refinery for city district heating (Schmidt et al. 2017, pp. 254–257).

**Lean Production Systems**

The Toyota production system serves as the blueprint for the implementation of lean production systems. Beyond specific tools and techniques, the success of TPS and lean rests on people´s mindset and behaviors. "Toyota's ability to align these intangible factors with its operating system is probably the aspect of its success that is most often overlooked" (Drew et al. 2004, xv). "People benchmark Toyota's organizational innovations, not its technical ones" (Hall 2010, p. 77). The "Toyota Way" as described by Liker is comprised of 14 principles. Some of the most relevant ones selected are: base your management decisions on a long-term philosophy, even at the expense of short-term financial goals; the right process will produce the right results; continuously solving root problems drives organizational learning; and go & see for yourself to thoroughly understand the situation (genchi genbutsu) (Liker 2004, pp. 37–41). TPS is not only a system for production but much more than that. Taichi Ohno claimed: "I am confident it will reveal its strength as a management system adapted to today's era of global markets and high-level computerized information systems" (Ohno 1988, xv).

**Implementation Approach**

Before explaining the tactical steps for implementing a large-scale lean improvement program it is important to understand the five core principles of lean. As per Womack and Jones, these are: (1) precisely specify *value* by specific product, (2) identify the *value stream* for each product, (3) make value *flow* without interruptions, (4) let the customer *pull* value from the producer, and (5) pursue *perfection* (Womack, Jones 2003, p. 10). Lean is not project implementable in a short- or mid-term period (Liker 2004, p. 297). "Implementing lean is a journey" (Drew et al. 2004, p. 1) which is comprised of the following steps:

- A conscious decision to start based on a clear business need to transform operations. A high-level roadmap for the implementation journey taking potential risks into account (Drew et al. 2004, p. 81).
- Assessing the opportunity by using the customer perspective of value and developing a real sense of urgency (Drew et al. 2004, p. 93).
- Aligning the leadership team around the details of implementation and engaging the organization through a compelling 'change story' to communicate the desired end state, the path to get there, and measurable objectives linked to the business needs (Drew et al. 2004, p. 123).
- Demonstrating the benefits of lean for business and employees through a successful pilot implementation sustained by the line team (Drew et al. 2004, p. 147).
- Embedding change and scaling the lean program through the development of a continuous improvement culture (Drew et al. 2004, p. 169).

**Mindsets and Behaviors**

The mindset of lean companies is one of perfection, i.e., continually declining costs, zero defects, and endless product variety (Womack et al. 1990, pp. 13–14).

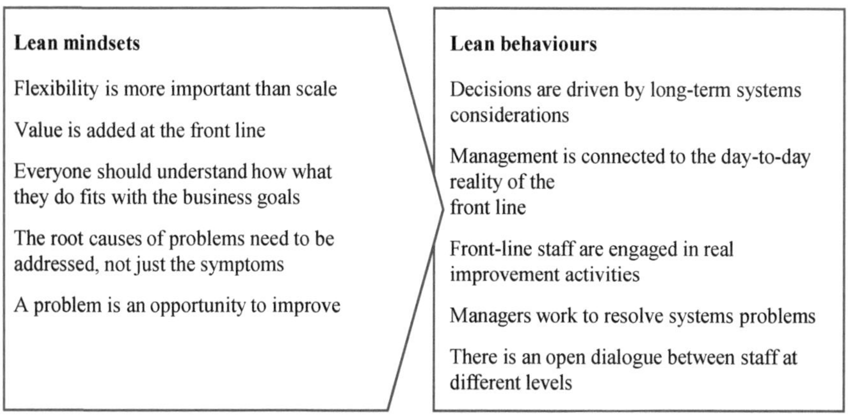


Figure 43: Lean mindsets and behaviors (Drew et al. 2004, p. 69)

Achieving world-class results requires transparency from suppliers to customers in order to find better ways to create value (Womack, Jones 2003, p. 26). Total employee involvement is another cornerstone for improvement. Empowered frontline operators, e.g., in process industries, deal autonomously with day-to-day process optimization, while engineers and managers concentrate their effort on larger, strategic improvement opportunities (Floyd 2010, pp. 9–10). Figure 43 shows examples of typical lean mindsets and behaviors.

**Current State, Challenges and Opportunities**

Lean is a methodology that is well known and adopted by many companies. It includes a combination of technical, managerial, and people aspects. The main focus is to relentlessly reduce waste, which is compatible with efforts to improve sustainability and resource productivity. The power of lean lies in the simplicity of its principles even if their implementation can be challenging and mostly depends on people. The combination of lean and green presents the fundament for achieving resource-productive operations. As part of this work, applying loss thinking, i.e., tackling profit losses is of particular relevance.

## 5.3 Six Sigma

The origins of Six Sigma go back to the late 1970s and Motorola and now it is considered a tactical strategy for business excellence being deployed by companies worldwide (Patela 2016, p. 1). There are many myths when it comes to Six Sigma, such as “Six Sigma is all about statistics” or ”Six Sigma works only in large organizations, requiring strong infrastructure and massive training”, and ”Six Sigma is not cost-effective”. However, when Kumar et al studied these pre-conceptions, they came to the conclusion, that Six Sigma is not a management “fad” but a “fit”. This is due to the impact of Six Sigma as an effective strategy leading to significant improvements in business performance in a wide range of organizations. What makes the difference is “the degree of discipline in the sequencing and use of tools, upper management active involvement, linkage to strategy, and measurement of results tied to the bottom line” (Kumar et al. 2008, p. 882).

**Definition**

There are multiple ways to define Six Sigma. A simple definition for Six Sigma is: “A methodology that furnishes tools for the improvement of business processes. The intent is to decrease process variation and improve product quality” (Pittman, Atwater 2016, p. 173). A more holistic definition would be: “Six Sigma is an organized, parallel-meso structure to reduce variation in organizational processes by using improvement specialists, a structured method, and performance metrics with the aim of achieving strategic objectives” (Schroeder et al. 2008, p. 540). The statistical meaning of Six Sigma is that the standard deviation of a normal distribution fits +/- six times between the upper and lower specification limits defined by the customer. This corresponds to a quality level of 99.9999998 % and with only 3.4 defects in a million Six Sigma is virtually defect-free (Patela 2016, p. 13; Lunau 2009, p. 9). Beyond the metric, as per Kubiak and Benbow, Six Sigma is built upon the philosophy that if you control the input of a process, you control the outputs. Furthermore; it is a methodology aiming to define, measure, analyze, improve, and control (DMAIC) processes by using a set of qualitative and quantitative tools and techniques (Kubiak, Benbow 2009, p. 7). Ultimately, the philosophy consists of a targeted translation of the voice of the customer into the language of the process to manufacturing goods and services with high quality to combine economics (efficiency) and customer satisfaction (effectiveness) (Töpfer 2004, p. 16).

**Focus on Variation**

The primary focus of Six Sigma is to reduce process variation to increase business performance through higher quality, reliability or customer service. "Variation is defined as an inevitable change in the output or result of a system (process) because all systems vary over time. Two major types of variations are (1) common, which is inherent in a system, and (2) special, which is caused by changes in the circumstances or environment" (Patela 2016, p. 2). The management of variation and use of statistical process control (SPC) goes back to W. Edwards and is well established (Schonberger 2008, p. 66). SPC includes assessing and improving the inherent process capability as well as subsequently operating the process without variation. SPC shifts the emphasis from lagging indicators (e.g., end of line quality inspection) towards leading indicators for controlling manufacturing processes (Floyd 2010, p. 154). The underlying mindset is to find a real solution for a real problem by turning it into a statistical problem with a statistical solution (Lunau 2009, p. 11). Based on this "statistical thinking" paradigm of action and learning based on process, variation and data, Six Sigma aims to improve processes and increase customer satisfaction (Kumar et al. 2008, p. 882).

**The DMAIC Cycle**

The five stage, iterative DMAIC improvement cycle is based on the philosophy that $Y = f(x)$, the process outcome (Y) is driven by the process inputs (X). The phases are defined as follows (Patela 2016, p. 4):

> **Define:** Determine the nature of the problem by understanding the project output *Y* and how to measure it.
> **Measure:** Collect data and facts to determine potential Xs and measure existing performance (Xs and Y).

**Analyze:** Study the information by determining *X–Y* relationships and, after verification, quantify important Xs to identify root causes of a problem.
**Improve:** Implement solutions to improve the process by optimize Xs to improve Y.
**Control:** Monitor and control the process, e.g., important Xs and the output *Y* over time, to ensure the solutions are sustained.

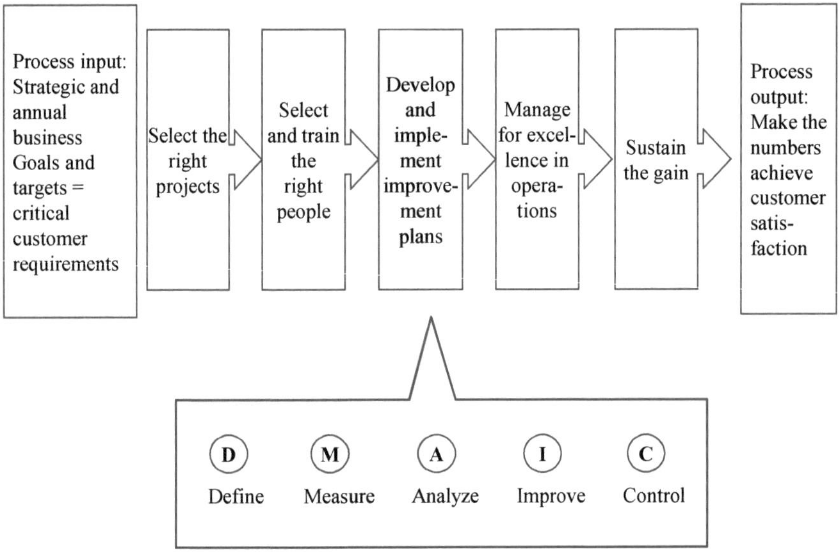


Figure 44: Generic Six Sigma process (Patela 2016, p. 5)

Six Sigma and its implementation process is considered the "engine" to achieve the desired Business Excellence Performance (Töpfer 2004, p. 16). Literature offers a wide variety of different implementation processes. A generic approach is offered by Patela in Figure 44. Töpfer highlights 7 steps for implementing Six Sigma: (1) Understanding the project-oriented, specific direction/requirements and capacity of Six Sigma; (2) Involving company leadership and gaining commitment of managers; (3) Establishing a Six Sigma organization and recruiting staff; (4) Qualifying Six Sigma specialists (Champions, Master Black Belts, Green Belts and Yellow Belts); (5) Selecting suitable Six Sigma projects (in production, at suppliers, in R&D or at customers); (6) Analyzing the monetary results of Six Sigma; (7) Implementing project controlling and establishing knowledge management (Töpfer 2004, p. 19). Burton offers 10 accelerators of Six Sigma: **Strategic Leadership and Vision** (1) Reset deployment leadership, strategy, and vision; **Deployment Planning** (2) Develop a robust implementation plan, (3) Provide customized education and development, (4) Communicate, communicate, communicate, (5) Launch with the best in mind; **Execution** (6) Provide strong extensive mentoring support, (7) DMAIC the deployment process regularly, (8) Accelerate individual project paths, (9) Complete the C in DMAIC 10. Practice concurrent continuous deployment (Burton 2011, p. 80). Furthermore, the DMAIC cycle is not only consistent with the PDCA problem-solving steps defined by Deming, but it also integrates specific tools, Table 29, into each step of the method (Schroeder et al. 2008, p. 542).

| | **Tools** | **Mission** |
|---|---|---|
| **Define** | • Project Charter<br>• SIPOC<br>• CTQ Matrix<br>• Stakeholder Analysis | • The project is defined<br>• Current state and target state are depicted and the process to be improved is marked off<br>• Customer and business requirements are clearly defined |
| **Measure** | • Measurement Matrix<br>• Operational Definition<br>• Measurement System Analysis<br>• Sample Size and Strategy<br>• Charts and Diagrams<br>• Quality Key Figures | • The starting situation is captured<br>• Key figures and an operational definition are developed, the measurement system analysis is completed, and the data collected |
| **Analyze** | • Cause Effect Diagram<br>• FMEA<br>• Process Analysis<br>• Value Stream Map<br>• Hypothesis Tests<br>• Regression<br>• DOE | • The causes for the problem are identified<br>• All possible causes are collected and summarized into the decisive key figures through process and data analysis |
| **Improve** | • Brainstorming<br>• "Must" Criteria<br>• Effort-Benefit Matrix<br>• Criteria-based Selection<br>• Piloting<br>• Roll out Planning | • The solution is implemented<br>• Possible solutions are generated on the basis of core causes, systematically selected, and prepared for implementation |
| **Control** | • Documentation<br>• Procedural Instructions<br>• Control and Run Charts<br>• Reaction Plan and Process<br>• Management Diagrams | • The sustainability of the result is secured<br>• The implemented solutions are documented and will be monitored using key figures<br>• A reaction plan secures prompt intervention |

Table 29: Six Sigma tools per phase (Lunau 2009, p. 12)

**Philosophy of Fact-Based Decision Making**

Six Sigma is a business strategy, a "way of life", aiming to close the gap between actual and target performance through analysis of root causes, problem solving and objective decision making (Kumar et al. 2008, p. 890). This requires a shift in mindset of people from fire fighting, i.e., solving problems as they occur, to a proactive process improvement based on facts (Kumar et al. 2008, p. 882). The saying "In God we trust, all others bring data'' emphasizes the notion of data-based problem exploration and decision-making (Schroeder et al. 2008, p. 543). The key success factor in implementing Lean Six Sigma is the behavior of people (Burton 2011, p. 80).

**Current State, Challenges and Opportunities**

Pyzdek boldly states: "Six Sigma is different. It demands results" (Pyzdek 2011, xii). Several independent studies by academics and practitioners investigated the link between Six Sigma adoption and organizational performance. The results do not only confirm causal relations that Six Sigma management activities exert positive effects on corporate competitiveness, but also that in many cases the gains in bottom-line benefits and customer-oriented management are significant (Choi et al. 2012, p. 546; Braunscheidel et al. 2011, p. 447; Kumar et al. 2008, p. 887). These measurable financial benefits are verified by the finance department of companies adopting Six Sigma (Schroeder et al. 2008, p. 542). Another investigation showed also substantial synergies between Six Sigma and performance management cockpits, e.g., based on the Balanced Scorecard (BSC) methodology. Furthermore, self-evaluation concepts such as the model of the European foundation of Quality Management (EFQM) help to verify performance improvements. Overall, there are clear causal synergies/complementarities with the continuous improvement process in general (Töpfer 2004, p. 16).

> "Lean-Six Sigma is a fact- based, data-driven philosophy of improvement that values defect prevention over defect detection. It drives customer satisfaction and bottom-line results by reducing variation, waste, and cycle time, while promoting the use of work standardization and flow, thereby creating a competitive advantage. It applies anywhere variation and waste exist, and every employee should be involved" (Kubiak, Benbow 2009, p. 9).

The structured DMAIC approach and people focused implementation process seems a strong fundament for a methodology to be developed as part of this thesis. A combination of Lean and Six Sigma and other improvement concepts is most suitably evidenced by integrated efforts in industry. The focus on process control will be further enabled by digitization. Kumar states that "Six Sigma matches well to knowledge-based information society" (Kumar et al. 2008, p. 888). One criticism is that Six Sigma efforts are handled as projects. Schonberger mentions the irony of improvement activities, such as Six Sigma initiatives or Kaizen events, being treated as discontinuous projects instead of ongoing continuous improvement journeys (Schonberger 2008, p. 50).

## 5.4 Theory of Constraints

As already mentioned, it is important to understand the boundaries of a system and the limits for optimization. In this respect, one popular improvement methodology has to be mentioned, the Theory of constraints (TOC). TOC goes back to the book "The Goal – A Process of Ongoing Improvement" which was first published in 1984 (Goldratt, Cox 2004). The improvement goal for most business organizations is long-term profitability (Jackson, Low 1993, p. 41). Rahman summarized the concept of the TOC stating that "every system must have at least once constraint. If it were not true, then a real system such as a profit making organization would make unlimited profit" and furthermore that "The existence of constraints represents opportunities for improvement" (Rahman 1998, p. 337).

**Definitions**
A constraint is characterized as "anything that limits a system from achieving higher performance versus its goal" (Goldratt 1988, p. 453). Two types can be distinguished: (1) physical constraints (e.g., process capacity) and (2) non-physical constraints (e.g., market demand, supplier reliability, or performance targets) (Jackson, Low 1993, p. 41). Constraint management is defined as: "The practice of managing resources and organization in accordance with the theory of constraints (TOC) principles" (Pittman, Atwater 2016, p. 33). TOC includes three different aspects: (1) a "logistics paradigm", (2) a thinking process, and (3) new performance measures (Rahman 1998, p. 337).

**The "Logistics" Paradigm of TOC**
Two of the main elements under the logistics paradigm are the five focusing steps of ongoing improvement and the drum-buffer-rope manufacturing execution methodology.

- The five focusing steps of on-going improvement are: (1) identify the system's constraints; (2) decide how to exploit the system's constraints; (3) subordinate everything else to the above decision; (4) elevate the system's constraints; and (5) if in the previous steps a constraint has been broken, go back to step one, but do not allow inertia to cause a system constraint (Goldratt 1990, p. 8).

- Drum–buffer–rope (DBR) manufacturing execution methodology: (D) the drum is the physical constraint of the plant to produce more. The rest of the plant follows the beat of the drum making sure that the drum has work and that anything the drum has processed does not get wasted. (B) the buffer protects the drum from the effects of disruptions in non-constraint resources and has time as unit of measure. Buffer management is the use of these time buffers as an information system to manage and improve throughput. (R) the rope refers to the work order release to the shop floor at exactly one "buffer time" before they are due, thus avoiding too-high work-in-process in the system (Panizzolo 2017, p. 158).

**TOC Performance Measures and Thinking Process**

Another aspect of TOC are new performance measurements impacting cost-accounting systems, as discussed as part of chapter 4.2. TOC performance measures, i.e., throughput, inventory and operating expense link operational decisions to organizational profit (Pittman, Atwater 2016, p. 189). Furthermore, TOC entails a thinking process, a generic approach for investigating, analyzing, and solving complex problems following three steps (1) find "what to change", (2) clarify "to what to change to", and (3) "how to cause the change" (Goldratt 1990, p. 8). "TOC is built on the realization that every complex environment/ system is based on inherent simplicity and the best way to manage, control and improve the system is by capitalizing on this inherent simplicity. That's why the constraints are the leverage points" (Goldratt, Cox 2004, p. 360). The review suggests that there is an unmet need for studies exploring how TOC methods can be applied not just in problem situations, but in situations which are problematic in a positive rather than negative sense (Kim et al. 2008, pp. 173–174).

**Current State, Challenges and Opportunities**

A recent study investigated the impact of TOC practices on the performance of manufacturing plants, by looking at five indicators: manufacturing cost, due-date performance, lead-time, inventory level, and cycle time. The results confirm a positive influence of practices such as the drum–buffer–rope methodology on several of the above performance indicators. However, it also concludes that the results and adoption vary by country and high manufacturing performance can also be achieved by other means (Panizzolo 2017, p. 168). Contributions of constraint management include providing a clear focus for the organization as well as emphasizing "generation of contribution margin through sales to improve profits rather than through cost reduction". One of the key challenges of this approach is an unstable environment, e.g., changes in demand and mix) causing the bottleneck to shift (Jackson, Low 1993, p. 46). The TOC contributes significantly with its focus on improving bottlenecks, which has positive effects on both the cost and revenue side. It is also relevant in the context of the maximum profit rate objective discussed in chapter 3.

## 5.5 Agility

In a context of turbulence resulting in frequent changes in production and shorter product life cycles, agility is a deciding competitive prerequisite and is invaluable (Sull 2010, p.1; Abele, Reinhart 2011, p. 122). Agility offers companies the chance to differentiate themselves from competition; to react quicker than competitors to short term market opportunities; to remain cost-effective in declining market conditions; and to continuously adapt to changing customer requirements (Luczak 2017, p. 18). Agility, in the end, works like an insurance policy for companies, with differing price points for varying levels of coverage against uncertainty. The question for companies many times is: "What is the optimal insurance point, without being over nor underinsured" (Ramsauer et al. 2017, pp. 7–8).

**Definitions**

There are many definitions, for example: "The ability to quickly, plan, source, make, and deliver to adapt and respond to changes in the competitive environment" (Pittman, Atwater 2016, p. 6). Frequently, these definitions are reactive in character. Another more pro-active view on agility is defined by Schurig et al. 2014, p. 957, and Luczak 2017, p. 19: "Agility in manufacturing is the capability of a production company to proactively prepare for uncertainties and to react quickly to changes in order to optimize the economic situation of a company, measured by profitability, by using the entire production network". Sull differentiates three types of agility: (1) strategic agility to benefit from game-changing opportunities, (2) portfolio agility to be able to shift resources between different business areas, and (3) operational agility to maximize opportunities within a business (Sull 2010, p. 2). Agility goes well beyond other concepts such as changeability, re-configurability, flexibility and adaptability when looked at from a product and production point of view (Schuh, Schmidt 2014, p. 19). Schurig also confirms that agility differs from other existing concepts such as flexibility, resilience or enterprise risk management. In short, flexibility helps to cope with minor changes in production, while the other two are more strategically relevant topics. Resilience aims to increase the robustness of companies in the face of external shocks. Enterprise risk management focuses on significant business risks, even with low probability. Agility on the other hand specifically includes opportunities for economic optimization and shares the short-term responsiveness to external changes with the concept of flexibility. As a result, agility is a systematic approach incorporating both strategic and operative angles to quickly react to volatility (Schurig 2017, p. 92).

**How Agility Works**

The capacity for a company to change their market or production performance depends on a number of internal and external factors, Figure 45. The internal analyses reveal the available degrees of freedom and thus the constraints for change, while the external world defines the change drivers and desired amount of change (Wiendahl, Hernández 2002, p. 135).

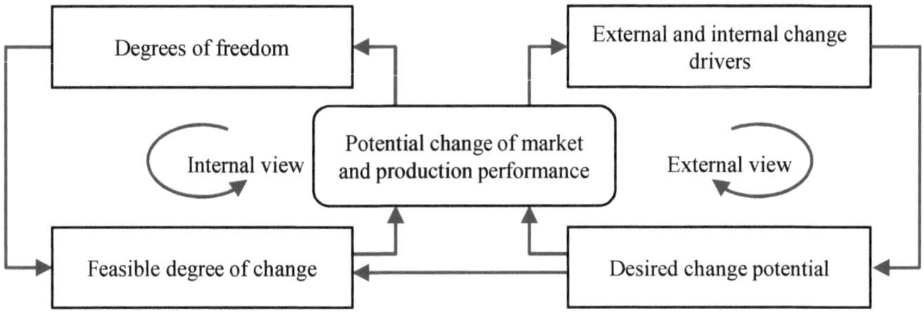


Figure 45: Dynamic of change capacity (Wiendahl, Hernández 2002, p. 135)

The need for action related to uncertainty is determined by the probability of occurrence, the potential consequences and the capacity to react (Kremsmayr 2017, pp. 62–63). To understand the mechanics of agility, Figure 46, shows a scenario with a change in demand for purpose of illustration. To begin with, the overall time line is comprised of (1) the reaction time, (2) realization time and (3) effective time. The reaction time can be further broken down into: perception time to realize a change is happening; the sense-making time to process the situation and possible range of actions; the decision time to select counter measures; and the planning time to prepare the implementation specific response measures (Hernández Morales 2003, p. 49). The reaction time, and in particular the perception and sense-making times can be reduced through the installation of an early warning system (Aschenbrücker et al. 2014, p. 6). This would require the definition of appropriate leading indicators and the implementation of an efficient monitoring and control system as pointed out by Heldmann et al. In the next step, the realization time is defined by the time it takes for an agility measure to be implemented and reach its full intensity. Finally, the duration that a measure is sustained at its intensity is reflected in the effective time. The selection of industry-specific agility levers have an effect on realization time, effective time and measure intensity (Heldmann et al. 2015, pp. 36–37).

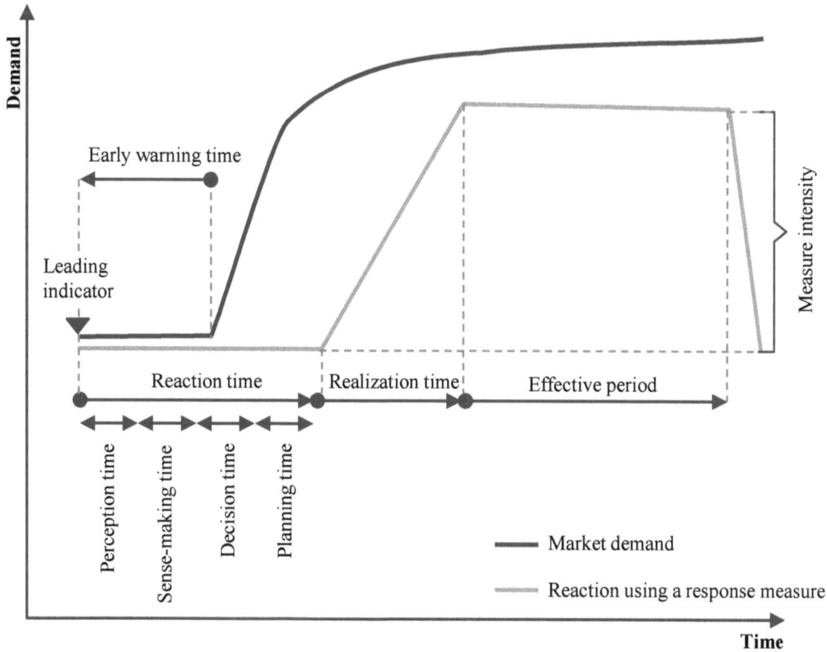


Figure 46: Mechanics of change (Rabitsch 2016, p. 95)

**Agility Monitoring**

As part of volatility management, Schimank et al found that the ability to anticipate, adapt and be resilient are closely linked to the efficient use of controlling instruments on different corporate levels. However, in their survey they found vast differences in the use and maturity of tools such as scenario analysis (Schimank et al. 2015, p. 42). Simulation models typically combine external influences depicted in scenarios with internal variables of the production system to optimize key performance indicators (Albrecht et al. 2013, p. 142). Monitoring systems, which are a critical element to better understand uncertain business environments go beyond scenario analysis. Monitoring systems require selecting and placing sensors to capture a wide variety of inputs, broadly speaking, they capture both quantitative data as well as qualitative information. Two types of monitoring can be distinguished: (1) information based monitoring typically used for strategic control, and (2) signal based monitoring for operations control. The first requires extensive decision relevant information to be interpreted by managers or experts. The latter is based on measurable information allowing defining automatic decision rules focusing on early warning to support operations and strategic control (Heldmann 2017, pp. 163–164).

**Current State, Challenges and Opportunities**

Some of the most common misconceptions about agility are: "agility and efficiency are a contradiction", "agility is expensive", and "agility is a purely defensive strategy". Deubel worked through these qualitative statements and found positive, quantitative evidence of the advantages of agility expressed in finance metrics such as break-even level and return-on-sales (Deubel 2017, 103–109). Agile companies have the advantage to prepare themselves to operate at more than one operating point. Some of them can be less efficient than the optimal lean state, but the change between these points is easy and possible with less effort. As the future is hardly predictable agile companies have competitive advantages in comparison to lean only companies. A hypothesis from a practitioner´s view by Diederichs is: “While lean companies are not automatically agile, they most likely are able to master agility better compared with companies that are less successfully leveraging lean tools” (Schurig 2017, p. 97). Another study of the lean, agile, resilient and green paradigm in supply chain management by Carvalho et al. concluded that all four serve the same overall purpose of satisfying customer needs at the lowest possible cost just from different angles: lean from a waste minimization; agile from rapid response to market changes, resilient from efficient response to disturbances; and green supply environmental impact minimization (Carvalho et al. 2011, p. 174). Technological progress through digitization allows for increased transparency and better decision making and real-time optimization in production (Pointner 2017, p. 230). Agility is a prerequisite in a VUCA world and is not going to go away. A critical enabler for agility will be the monitoring of external and internal Big Data. There is a need for time based, short interval KPIs for process control on an operational level.

## 5.6 Advanced Process Control

Process control and optimizing operating parameters is a critical success factor in manufacturing (Rao 2011, p. 3), in particular in process industries where it originated. Process control developed from local measurement devices to central control rooms and more recently to computer based, plant wide on-line control

(Agachi 2006, p. 1). In a context of increased environmental turbulence companies get benefits from their capability to realize a high level of performance by managing day-to-day activities; to continuously improve; and to implement discontinuous, radical changes (Bartezzaghi 1999, p. 247). McMillan affirms: "As plants are pushed beyond nameplate, it is increasingly obvious that the importance of process control has grown to the point where it is the single biggest leverage point for increasing manufacturing capacity and efficiency" (Svrcek et al. 2014, xiii). Reducing process variability, a shared goal with Six Sigma, through ongoing process control leads to safer operations; more sustainable manufacturing/reduced environmental impact, i.e. lower energy use and less waste; improved bottom line returns, e.g., from increased output; efficiency gains, i.e., higher yields; quality gains; and agility gains (Anderson et al. 1994, p. 81; Brisk 2004, pp. 10–11). Improved process control helps in two ways: (1) to reduce process variability and (2) to shift the average (Seborg et al. 2004, p. 10). Process control paired with the aspect of automated decision making for optimization is commonly regarded as "the most effective means of generating the highest profit from plants, while responding to marketplace variations with minimal capital investment" (Agachi 2006, p. 11). Optimization results can either be displayed to plant operators (advisory mode) in order to make better decisions or directly sent to controllers (closed-loop mode) (Marlin et al. 1991, p. 75). Automation within process control systems, if appropriately used, is an effective way to achieve safe and efficient operations (Edmonds, Wilkinson 2016, p. 23).

**Definitions**

**Process control** is defined as: "Activities involved in ensuring a process is predictable, stable, and consistently operating at the target level of performance with only normal variation[23]. The act of process control involves "the monitoring of instrumentation attached to equipment (valves, meters, mixers, liquid, temperature, time, etc.) from a control room to ensure that a high-quality product is being produced to specification" (Pittman, Atwater 2016, p. 140). Typically this is done with a control system, which is "a combination of elements which act together in order to bring a measured and controlled variable to a certain, specific, desired value or trajectory termed the 'set/point of reference'" (Agachi 2006, p. 2). Elements of modern process control systems are: field instrumentation with interface to the control system; computer-based systems for data processing and display of information; control algorithms to provide the logic for manipulating control variables; and control room operators (Li et al. 2011, pp. 894–895).

---

23 http://www.businessdictionary.com/definition/process-control.html, last accessed 16.08.2017

**Optimization** is "the use of specific methods to determine the most cost-effective and efficient solution to a problem" such as the operation of plants through the use of quantitative tools for industrial decision making (Edgar et al. 2001, p. 4). Ackoff articulated in 1978 that ultimately the outcome of solving a problem [such as process control and optimization] depends on the choice of controllable [manipulable] variables by the decision maker considering constraints, and uncontrollable variables [disturbances] (Ackoff 1978, pp. 11–12). Figure 47 shows that next to the input variables there are also the output variables which are determined by the system.

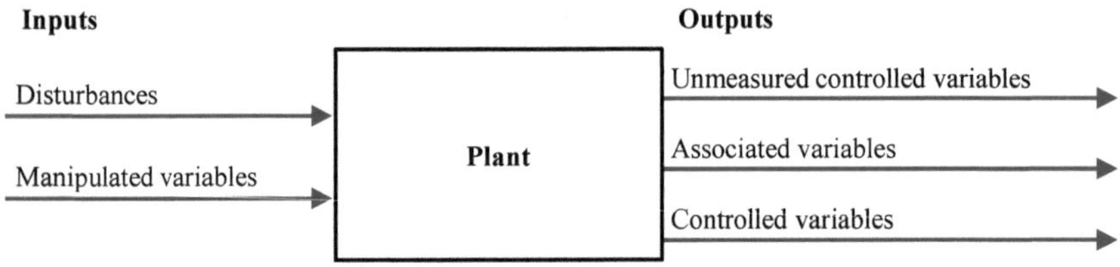


Figure 47: Definition of input and output variables considered for control system design (Agachi 2006, p. 2)

Agachi distinguishes measured and unmeasured controlled variables as well as associated variables, which need to stay within certain bounds (Agachi 2006, p. 2). "The formulation of objective functions is one of the crucial steps in the application of optimization to a practical problem" (Edgar et al. 2001, p. 84). Parameters can be categorized as continuous or discrete, Table 30. Continuous variables such as temperature, pressure, or flow are uninterrupted as time proceeds and can take on any value within a certain range. Discrete variables can only take on specific values, such as open/closed (2 position valve) or on/off (motor without variable frequency drive) (Groover 2001, p. 82).

| Comparison factor | Continuous control in process industries | Discrete control in discrete manufacturing industries |
|---|---|---|
| Typical measures of product output | Weight measures, liquid volume measures, solid volume measures | Number of parts, number of products |
| Typical quality measures | Consistency, concentration of solution, absence of contaminants, conformance to specification | Dimensions, surface finish, appearance, absence of defects, product reliability |
| Typical variables and parameters | Temperature, volume flow rate, pressure | Position, velocity, acceleration, force |
| Typical sensors | Flow meters, thermocouples, pressure sensors | Limit switches, photoelectric sensors, strain gages, piezoelectric sensors |
| Typical actuators | Valves, heaters, pumps | Switches, motors, pistons |
| Typical process time constants | Seconds, minutes, hours | Less than a second |

Table 30: Comparison between continuous and discrete control (Groover 2001, pp. 62–63)

**Automation** in production systems can be differentiated between the automation of the physical manufacturing system in the factory and the computerization of information in the manufacturing support systems. However, in modern production systems these two aspects integrate (Groover 2001, p. 9). Thus, "automation means the replacement of both human physical and mental activities by machines" (Hitomi 1996, p. 343). Nof distinguishes four elements of automation in Figure 48.

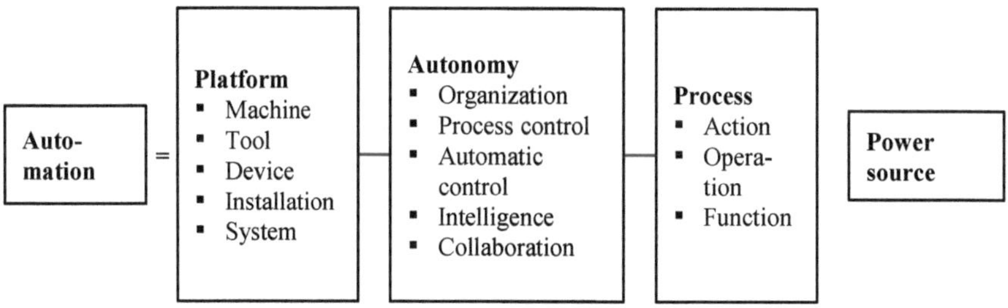


Figure 48: Automation formalism (Nof 2009a, p. 14)

A high level of automation is a common feature in process control system in process industries. They continuously monitor process variables and control equipment, which is especially critical in the area of safety, e.g., avoiding overfilling a vessel, over pressurize, etc. However, a potential disadvantage of "engineering out the human through automation" is the loss of situational awareness and motivation of operators (Edmonds, Wilkinson 2016, pp. 15–16). On the other hand, even highly skilled operators struggle to select optimal settings for complex, stochastic processes with a high number of variables (Rao 2011, p. 3). "The poor performance of human operators in the control room is now being seen as one of the key reasons why [...] process control systems fail to deliver their full potential" (Li et al. 2011, p. 894). Thus, automation and the application of suitable optimization algorithms continue to seem the most effective solution (Rao 2011, p. 3).

**Levels of Control**

Five levels of automation and control are generally distinguished in a company, Figure 49. Activities range from the device or field level up to the enterprise level, serve different functions and occur at widely different frequencies. Information is exchanged between all levels and coordinated to make the plant operation as profitable as possible (Groover 2001, pp. 76–77; Seborg et al. 2004, p. 11; Abel et al. 2008, pp. 23–24). Similar levels are used by the International Society of Automation (ISA) in their ISA-88 and ISA-95 standards. The ISA discusses the level of ERP (Enterprise Resource Planning) systems with a focus on financial and logistic activities, which is supported by the level of MES (manufacturing execution system) activities related to production management, followed by the lower levels of process control.[24] On top of this there can be a further layer dealing with multi-enterprise networks (Nof 2009a, p. 25). According to Shobrys and White, applications for the different levels have been developed as independent point solutions with varying models, algorithms, users and process owners, e.g., planning in the headquarters, scheduling at the plant, and process control by engineering departments. There is a need for integration and *"Clearly they have to work together"* (Shobrys, White 2002, p. 149). The focus of this work is the real-time optimization, and multivariable and constraint control levels with an hourly frequency.

24 https://isa-95.com/technical-isa-88-and-isa-95/, last accessed 18.05.2017

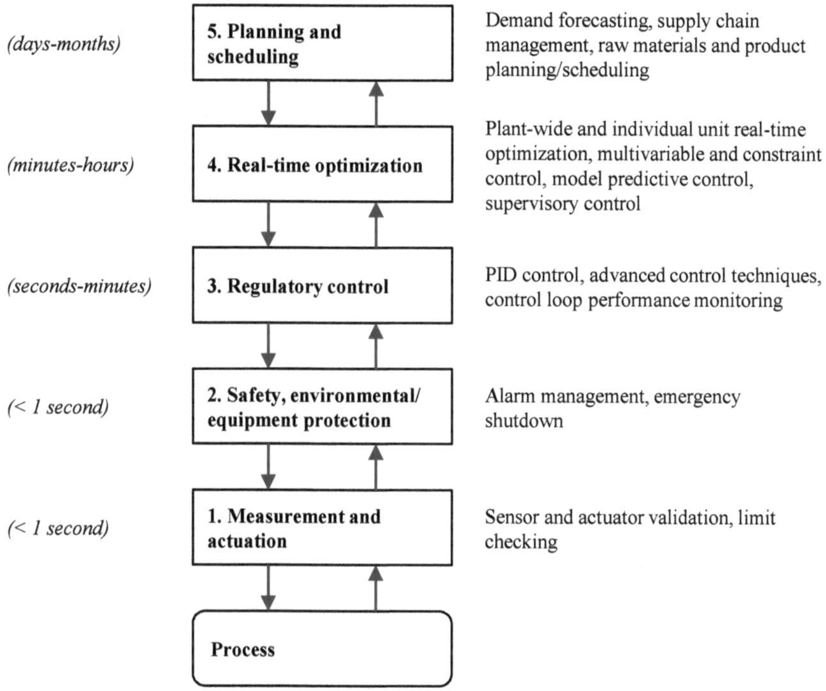


Figure 49: Five levels of process control and optimization in manufacturing (adapted from Seborg et al. 2004, p. 511)

**Open vs. Closed Loop**

An important distinction in process control is between open loop and closed loop operation. In the first case, the recommendations are brought to the attention of a human operator for action, whereas in the second case, process control adjustments are directly executed by computer systems (Bellman 1964, p. 186). The elements of a closed loop control system or feedback control system are shown in Figure 50.

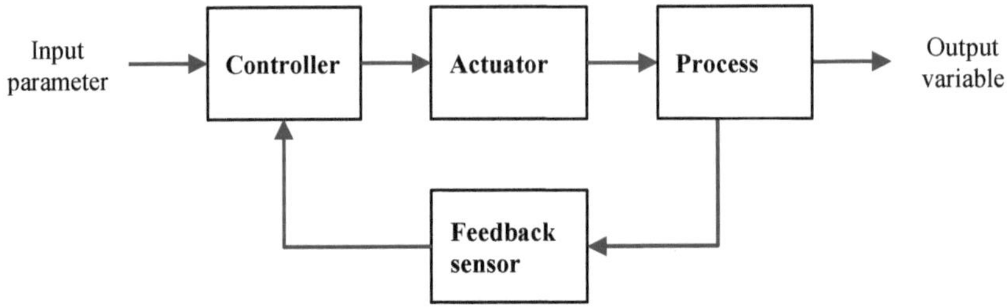


Figure 50: Feedback control system (Groover 2001, p. 70)

**Advanced Process Control (APC)**

Advanced Process Control (APC) is particularly relevant for companies with high raw material or energy costs, tight product specification, or limited production capacity (Anderson et al. 1994, p. 81). In the 1980s, Cutler and Perry quantified the value of real-time optimization and control with 6-10% of the value added by the process. Half (3-5%) coming from eliminating the variability introduced by operators and the other half through process optimization, i.e., selecting correct constraints and on-line optimization (Cutler, Perry 1983, p. 667). Joint industry-university studies in the 1990s showed benefits of applying APC in the range of 1.4-6% of operating costs and 1% in extra revenue (Marlin et al. 1991, p. 79; Anderson et al. 1994, p. 78). The benefits were confirmed also a decade later through many successfully applications (Brisk 2004, p. 10) and widely recognized in academia and industry (Agachi 2006, p. 24). Advanced process control extends beyond traditional process control in several ways, as also illustrated in Figure 51. It reaches higher levels of control, i.e., handling constraints, while aiming for online optimization to maximize economic benefits. APC is able to deal with nonlinear dynamic processes that include multivariable interactions between controlled parameters, high variation and uncertainty, and include online control (Anderson et al. 1994, p. 79; Agachi 2006, p. 24; Svrcek et al. 2014, p. 245). Furthermore, it differs from other methods such as SPC which is a monitoring strategy to help investigate if a process stays within normal behavior. APC, however, is a complementary control strategy for taking corrective actions in case of deviations from the setpoint (Seborg et al. 2004, p. 582). Typical benefits of an APC application, Figure 52, range from 3% to 5% of operating cost, whereas the source of the benefits come approx. 1/3 from more capacity, 1/3 from improved control/stability, and 1/3 from other factors such as lower energy requirements or higher recovery (Canney 2003, p. 50).

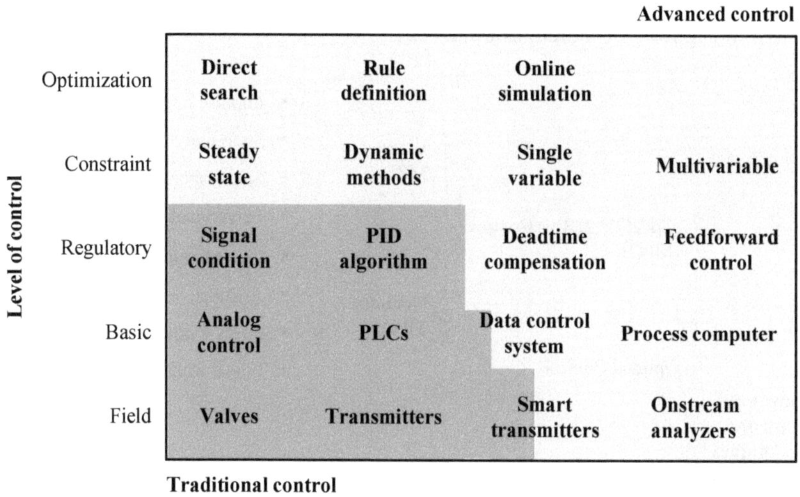


Figure 51: Process control: advanced vs. traditional (Anderson et al. 1994, p. 79)

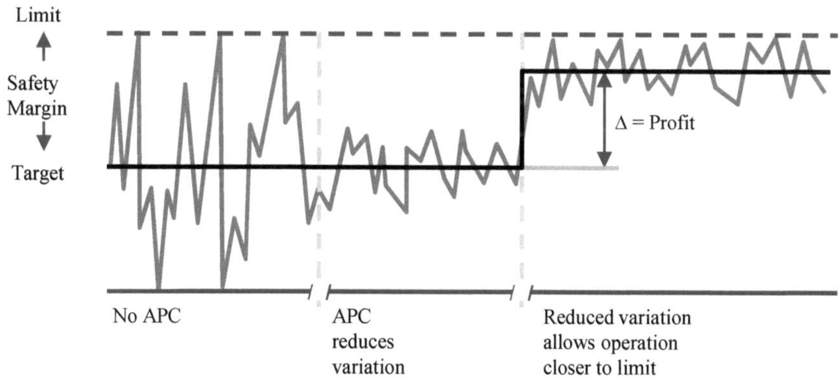


Figure 52: Economic benefit given by the use of advanced process control (APC) (Agachi 2006, p. 24)

Advanced control techniques in general can be classified into several groups as shown in Figure 53 (Agachi 2006, p. 12).

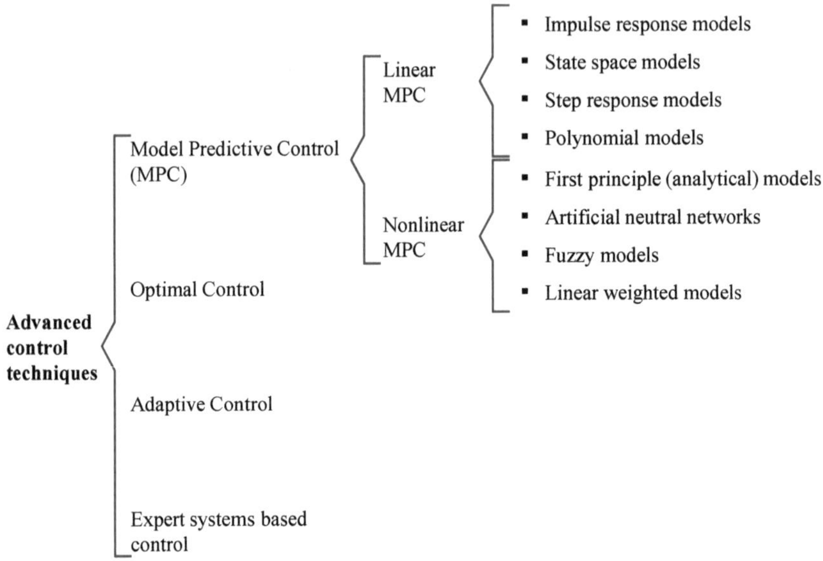


Figure 53: Classification of advanced control techniques (Agachi 2006, p. 12)

Nowadays "APC has become synonymous with model predictive control (MPC)" (Svrcek et al. 2014, p. 245). MPC techniques go back to the 1970s and a wide variety of related algorithms have been deployed across the world (Svrcek et al. 2014, p. 248). Brisk estimated more than 6,000 installations of MPC up to 2005 (Brisk 2005, p. 39), but MPC has not yet penetrated all sectors, as per Figure 54, which shows an approximate distribution of the number of MPC applications versus the degree of process nonlinearity (Agachi 2006, p. 26).

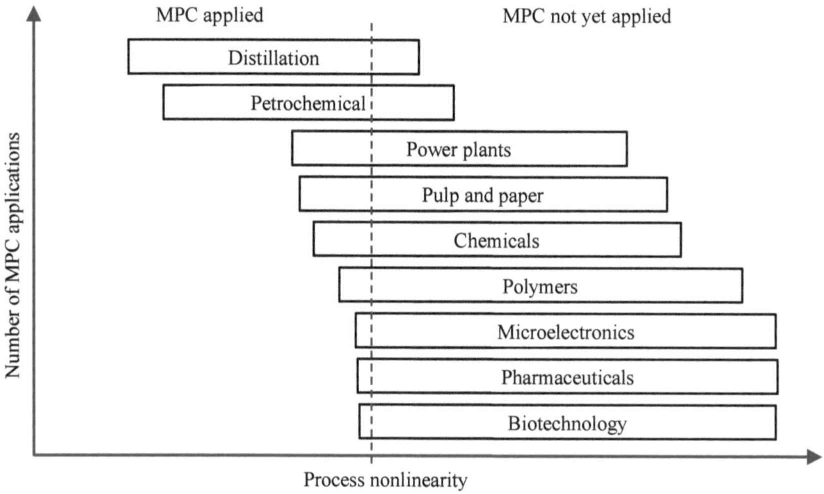


Figure 54: Distribution of MPC application versus the degree of process nonlinearity (Agachi 2006, p. 25)

MPC, Figure 55, is the most common advanced control method used in industry. It is a class of multivariable computer control algorithms that utilize an explicit process model to predict the future plant behavior and to derive an appropriate control action to get the output as close as possible to the target value (Qin, Badgwell 2003, p. 733; Svrcek et al. 2014, p. 246). MPC offers several advantages, e.g., it captures both dynamic and static interactions between inputs, outputs and disturbances; constraints are reflected systematically; control and optimization are coordinated; and predictions help with the early warning of problems (Seborg et al. 2004, p. 535). The two main disadvantages of MPC are: (1) the significant amount of time required to develop an analytical model of complex processes with good accuracy, and (2) the computation effort to optimize these large scale processes (Agachi 2006, p. 37).

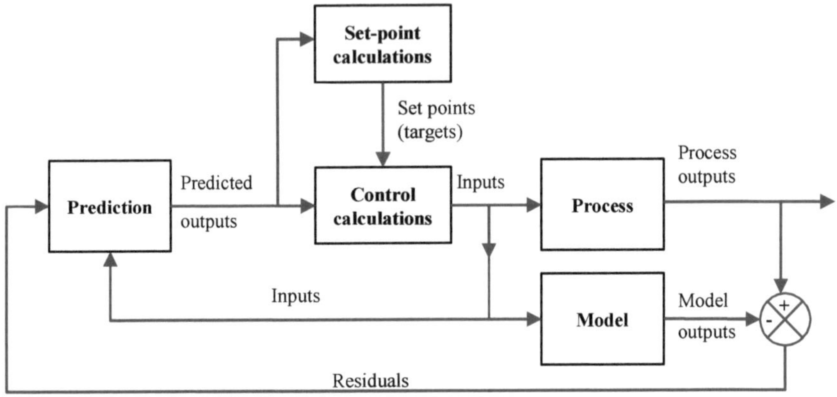


Figure 55: Block diagram for model predictive control (Seborg et al. 2004, p. 535)

**Real-Time Optimization (RTO)**

In the mid to late 1980s, the combination of MPC technology with increased capabilities in computer processing and equation modeling, resulted in the first attempt at real-time optimization of a steady-state process (Darby et al. 2011, pp. 874–875). Cutler and Perry pointed out that "real time optimization with multivariable control is required to maximize profits" (Cutler, Perry 1983, p. 663). Therefore the optimization of set points requires both an economic model with a financial objective, i.e., profit per hour, and an operating model consisting of a steady-state process model and constraints (Seborg et al. 2004, p. 515). The extensions of RTO and MPC to the planning and scheduling layer is seen as a promising research direction (Darby et al. 2011, p. 882).

**Current State, Challenges and Opportunities**

Advanced Process control and systems theory have existed for a while in process industries, historically driven by waves of automation. Control models need to trade off local against global optima, short against long-term optimization, profit against process KPI maximization. Process industries, according to Anderson, have not fully exploited the benefits of process control, but there is increasing management awareness of its potential returns and wider availability of modern control systems and techniques. This will help companies to improve their operations and maximize the returns on their assets (Anderson 1996, p. 3). An ongoing concern is the continuous measurement of economic benefits and the cost/benefit calculation of combined APC and RTO systems (Bauer, Craig 2008, p. 12). For Canney it is clear that the economic benefits of APC systems are achieved in the long-term through the combination of skills and an implementation methodology. “APC is not a commodity” and is critical to business success (Canney 2005, p. 58).

**Data**

Measurement accuracy and data consistency are highly relevant topics for control instrumentation and important prerequisites for optimization (Seborg et al. 2004, p. 222). And even before that, the basic availability of measurement devices providing relevant data is crucial. Ackoff stated: “We are more likely to be wrong in what we accept without evidence, no matter how obvious it may be, than in what we accept with evidence, no matter how doubtful it may be.” Therefore turning uncontrolled variables into measured/controlled variables helps to release constraints on the actions available to decision makers. Lack of control of variables usually turns out to be a lack of knowledge and understanding of it (Ackoff 1978, p. 100). The same is true for physical constraints such as compressor loads, column loadings or critical pressure. The quality of real time data is crucial for the correct identification of constraints and for the optimizer to know the status of the plant relative to physical system limits. Only then can the process control system suggest a realizable optimal mode of operation (Cutler, Perry 1983, p. 665).

**Modelling**

Next to aspects of data for modelling, a challenge is the completeness of the model itself. The coverage of all variables including disturbances and constraints is an important prerequisite for the quality of the optimization of a target function (Taha 2007, p. 3). Building accurate mathematical models of real world processes and plants with all their details is a highly complicated undertaking involving complex equations, unknown functions and values – is hard to do (Bellman 1964, p. 186). This is even more true for advanced industrial plants with even more complexity. According to Terwiesch and Ganz, building and tuning models individually for every plant is still today very expensive and requires highly skilled experts. One solution would be reusing models across areas and industries (Terwiesch, Ganz 2009, p. 140). After building models their continuous update is of equal importance to avoid profitability losses due to degradation of APC performance, as shown in Figure 56 (Canney 2003, p. 49). Degradation is caused by changing external circumstances such as seasonality, product demands and internal reasons such as fouling of heat exchangers, wearing out of mechanical equipment or regeneration of catalysts. On-line computer systems help with realistic models through real-time updating (Cutler, Perry 1983, p. 665).

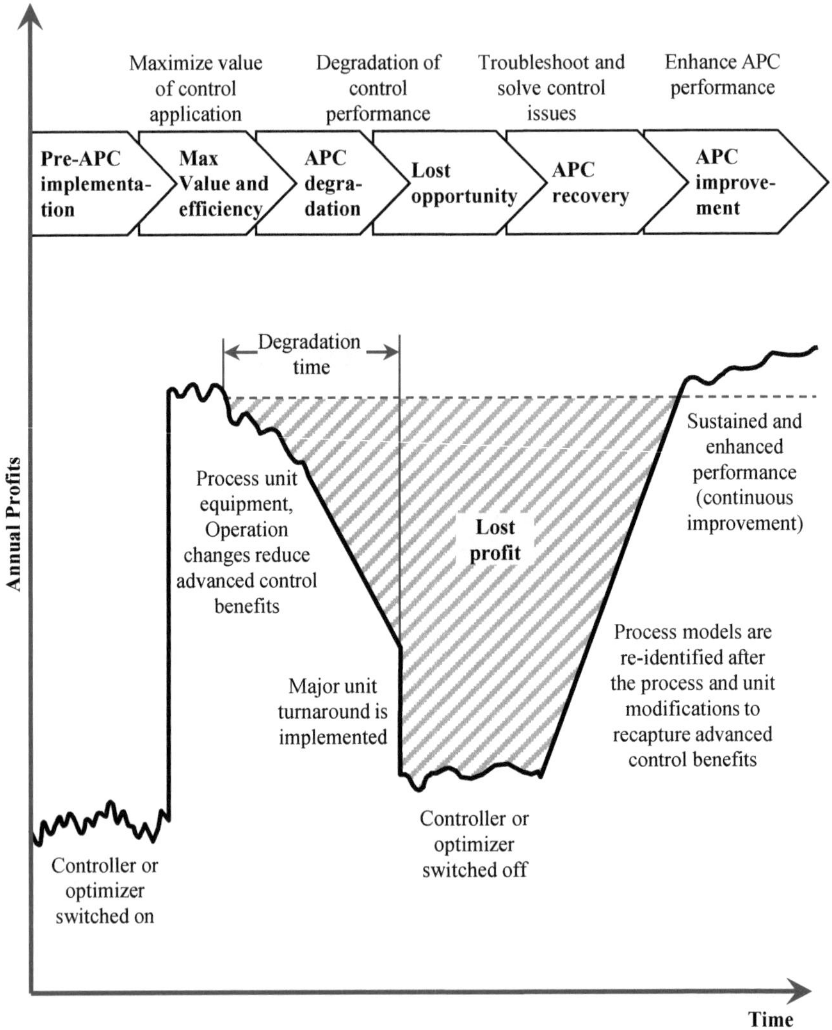


Figure 56: Sustaining APC value (Canney 2003, p. 49)

**Skills**

"Process control should not only be advanced: its basic performance should be advancing, not retreating" (Brisk 2005, p. 39). The success of this depends in the case of simple controls as well as advanced RTO control systems on skills and capabilities. Canney declares that "Most current APC projects are constrained by process and business expertise rather than limitation of computing hardware and custom software" (Canney 2003, p. 48).

**Global vs. Local Optimization Alignment**

From a business point of view, decisions on the control level cannot be made in isolation from other functions such as planning and scheduling. Many companies in process industries continue to struggle with maintaining consistency among all decisions with negative economic consequences (Shobrys, White 2002, p. 149). Cutler and Perry wrote "To really achieve true plant optimization, local and global optimization results must ultimately be consistent" (Cutler, Perry 1983, p. 667). The technology for this is available, but other factors such as organizational structure, aligned behaviors and a common global charter visible to all business areas are needed for effective integrated decision-making and overall optimization (Shobrys, White 2002, p. 159). "Our conceptions of what can be done in problematic situations are often limited by constraints attributed to technology. We frequently forget or overlook the fact that technology and its use are controllable" (Ackoff 1978, p. 71).

**Outlook**

The future of process industries might move closer to visions of producing quantities equal to the smallest product order sizes. The agile processing capability required for this must be offered by a responsive plant with well-performing control systems (Brisk 2005, p. 38). Artificial Intelligence-based control using methods such as genetic algorithms and neural networks (Nof 2009b, 628) will help to offset the main disadvantages of MPC: the high amount of time required to develop an analytical model of complex processes with good accuracy, and the computation effort to optimize these large scale processes. "The advantageous properties of neural networks, such as parallel computation, nonlinear mapping and learning capabilities, make them an alluring tool in many chemical engineering problems" (Agachi 2006, p. 37). There is an opportunity to extend MPC/RTO with advanced, non-linear, self-learning models as digital technologies converge. By complementing APC systems with advanced analytics, see Figure 57, the optimization of a wider range of manufacturing processes becomes possible (Feldmann et al. 2016, p. 3).

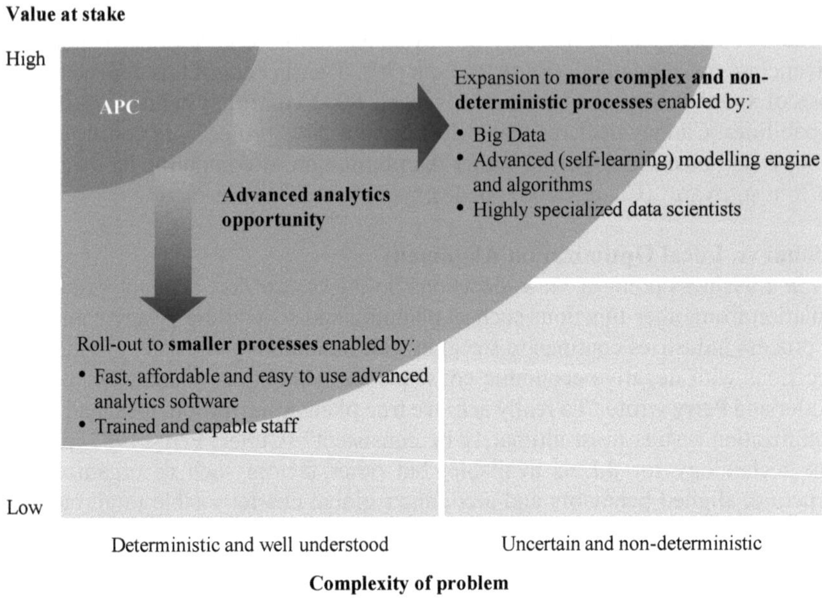


Figure 57: Advanced analytics goes beyond APC systems (Feldmann et al. 2016, p. 3)

## 5.7 Summary: Achieving Resource-Productive Operations

Industrial resource productivity is an important requirement across manufacturing sectors, in particular in the resource-intense process industries. To maximize productivity trade-off decisions between conflicting goals such as throughput, energy, yield and quality, have to be made on the basis of profit per hour. Furthermore, operations have to be constantly improved. Lean principles have proven to work well to reduce waste, i.e., inefficiencies in processes, and are synergistic with green management. Lean also puts a lot of emphasis on sustainable change which is based on peoples′ mindsets and behaviors. Understanding the limits of optimization and focusing on the bottleneck is an important contribution of the theory of constraints. Six Sigma is based on a well-known, standardized implementation methodology structured around the five phases define, measure, analyze, implement and control. A clear process methodology is essential in large scale operations transformation programs. In addition, Six Sigma focuses on the reduction of process variation, is often combined with lean, and has a strong emphasis on the financial impact of initiatives. Agility is one of the requirements to cope with increased external volatility. Agility links the internal, operational view with the external, market view. Agile shares a common vision with lean, which is to satisfy the customer needs at the lowest possible costs. Advanced process controls help companies to reduce variation in processes and increase the profit rate. This can be achieved through closed-loop, non-linear model predictive controllers, for example based on artificial neural networks. The integration of the various approaches, together with advanced analytics and process control technology provides an opportunity that process industries have not yet fully exploited.

| Learning | Delimitations | Requirements |
|---|---|---|
| • Industrial resource productivity is a priority in process industries and has not yet been fully optimized<br>• Trade-off decisions are required and can be based on profit per hour<br>• The theoretical limit provides the basis for quantifying and continuously eliminating losses<br>• There is a need for changing people's mindsets and behaviors and having a well-known, structured implementation methodology<br>• Agility is internal capability to cope with external volatility<br>• Advanced analytics offer additional profit opportunities and go beyond advanced process control systems | INCLUDES<br>• Maximizing industrial productivity of assets and resources in process industries<br>• Focus on bottleneck<br>• Loss thinking with reference to the theoretical limited<br>• Structured approach for operations improvement<br>• Closed loop, advanced process control enhanced by advanced analytics<br>EXCLUDES<br>• Agility monitoring of the external environment and handling of external influences, such as price and demand volatilities | • Structured implementation methodology<br>• Compatibility with a well-known improvement approach<br>• On-going process improvement through closed-loop process control<br>• Sustainability of results through the integration of technical, managerial, and people aspects |

Table 31: Summary of conclusions from operations perspective

# 6 Practice Perspective: Learning from Case Research in the Cement and Ammonia Industry

After the review of related literature, this chapter provides a practical perspective based on sanitized[25] examples from cement clinker production (section 6.1) and ammonia production (section 6.2). Section 6.3 summarizes the learning and requirements for the application of analytics in process industries.

## 6.1 Cement

The cement industry is an extremely local industry. The products do not travel far given their high weight and low value. They also have a limited life time, e.g., ready mix concrete needs to be delivered within 90 minutes (Verein Deutscher Zementwerke e.V. 2002, p. 449). Cement is an omnipresent building material word-wide that together with steel is responsible for almost half of all industrial $CO_2$ emissions (Allwood et al. 2012, p. 287). Cement production is a particularly electricity and fuel intensive process with an energy share of larger than 52% of the gross value creation (EEFA – Energy Environment Forecast Analysis GmbH & Co. KG 2013, p. 5). Therefore, energy reduction in the cement industry is a highly relevant technical and socio-political objective (Verein Deutscher Zementwerke e.V. 2002, p. 46). Allwood et al found that „best practice in cement production is only 50 % over the theoretical limit, the global average is around 4.7–5.5 GJ/ton, almost double best practice" (Allwood et al. 2012, p. 293).

The focus of this case is the clinker production process described by Verein Deutscher Zementwerke e.V. 2002, p. 47: Clinker is formed by taking limestone rock, after it has been excavated and crushed, and mixing it with sand and clay to be burned in a kiln. The heat of the kiln causes the material to react, consequently forming a mixture of calcium silicates, also called clinker. According to the EEFA, the kilns consume approximately 22% of all electrical energy, a significant share excluding raw material pre-processing, i.e. crushing and milling that account for around 73%. The primary thermal energy for the kiln comes from conventional

25 Throughout the industrial cases confidential data has been removed, i.e., scale labels, tag names, values


M. Hammer, *Management Approach for Resource-Productive Operations*,
Industrial Management, https://doi.org/10.1007/978-3-658-22939-9_6

fuels such as coal, oil or gas – or alternative fuels including rubber, waste, solvents or renewables (EEFA – Energy Environment Forecast Analysis GmbH & Co. KG 2013, p. 10). The temperature in the kiln reaches 1,450° C and material takes 20 to 40 minutes to pass through (Verein Deutscher Zementwerke e.V. 2002, p. 57).

### 6.1.1 Context

This work has been conducted as part of a proof of concept for the application of advanced analytics to identify profit related process improvement opportunities and was carried out in spring 2016. The focus was to reduce energy consumption in the kiln. Kiln torque has been used as a proxy. A value driver tree for cement, Figure 58, shows how kiln torque is connected to kiln motor energy consumption, overall energy consumption, variable cost and operating margin (Heldmann et al. 2017, p. 84). Overall, there are more than 100 parameters that come into play and determine the operational performance of the kiln. Controllable variables by the operators included for example the fuel ratio and kiln motor speed. Disturbance variables or non-controllable parameters would be the molecular composition of coal or the heating value of rubber. The main output variables considered were the clinker volume and the kiln torque as proxy for energy consumption.

### 6.1.2 Application

The starting situation included the review of existing systems and previous improvement efforts. The investigated site had already implemented an optimizer model in the past, however, it has only been used 62% of time. Even in situations considered as "steady state" operations with >75 t/h clinker production for which the optimizer was originally designed for, the plant ran under operator control at times. The optimizer uses a static set of pre-defined rules to optimize the process. As it is not dynamic the operators regularly update the target values manually. In order to understand the process variability and the two operating regimes better, the stability of the process during the last 158 hours of each of the regimes was analyzed. While the expert optimizer increased the stability, that is the kiln torque in this regime showed a lower standard deviation of 24.5 vs. 32.2 Nm (-24%) when under operator control, the difference has been considered insufficient. Reviewing specific energy consumption for a time period of 18 months, Figure 59, showed considerable variability.

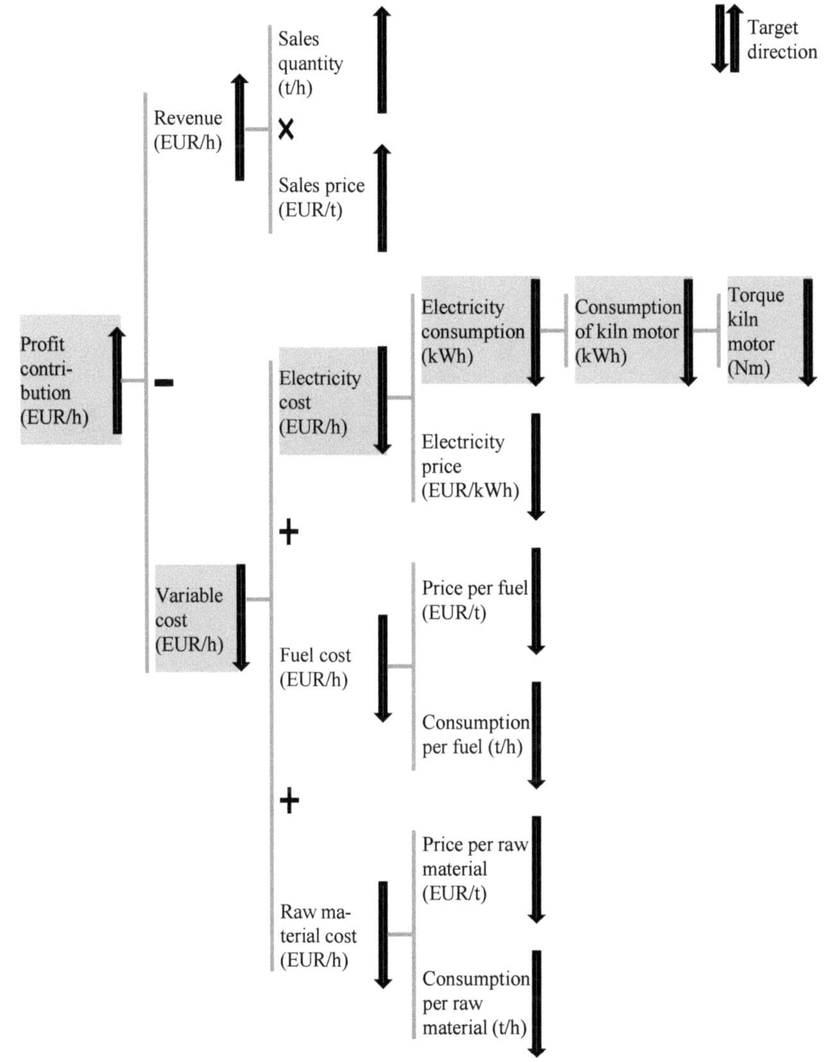


Figure 58: Value driver tree for cement (Heldmann et al. 2017, p. 84)

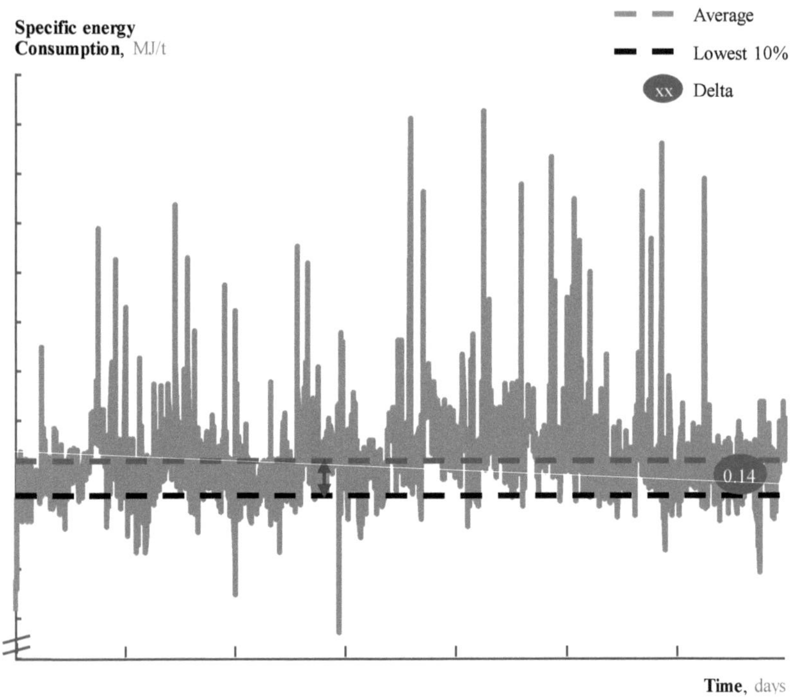


Figure 59: Specific energy consumption

The potential for optimization was to reduce process variability and operate at the specific energy consumption level of the best 10% days. This represented an opportunity of 0.14 MJ/t and a reduction of total energy consumption by 6-8%.

As a next step data on all variables was collected and inconsistent, redundant or extraneous data was removed. The time behavior of the process was assessed to structure the data with consistent time stamps. Thereafter a neural network based model was used to simulate process behavior and determine the key parameters affecting the kiln torque. As per chapter 3.5 (Advanced analytics), "Neural networks can model very complex patterns and decision boundaries in the data" (Baesens 2014, p. 51), are inspired "by the cognitive processes and organizational structure of neurobiological systems" (Corsten, May 1996, p. 67), and belong to the group of non-traditional optimization algorithms.

### 6.1.3 Results

The model, Figure 60, shows that torque is primarily affected by coal feed, total energy and meal temperature. The sensitivity represents the percentage change in torque based on a 1% increase in the parameters. Deviation between the actual and predicted values of torque is calculated as a percentage of the value range. The average deviation of the model is 4.4. Based on industry standards, <5% average deviation is ideal, thus the model is considered highly accurate.

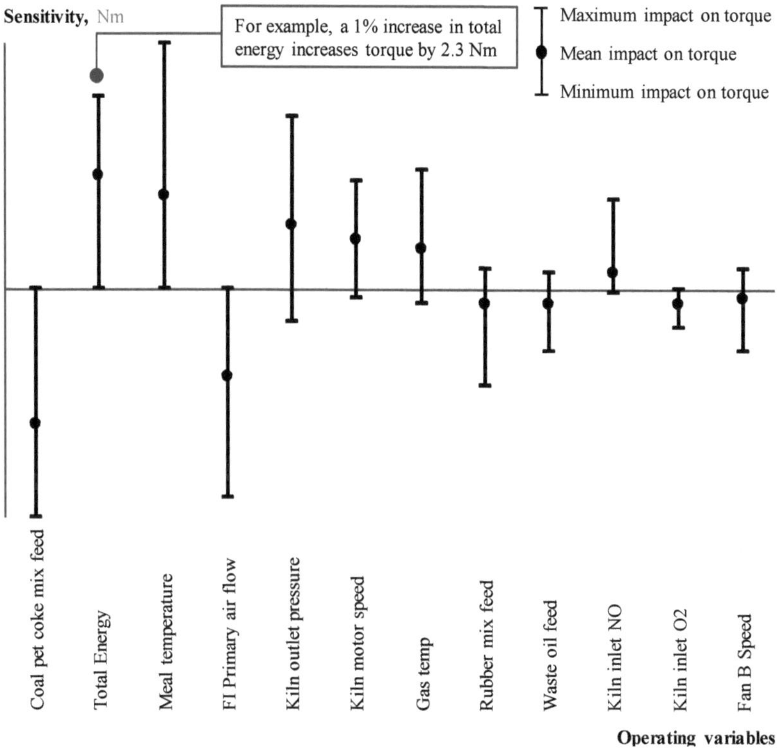


Figure 60: Key parameters and their impact on torque

Expert interviews were conducted to validate the findings and the proof of concept concluded that analytics based models can accurately predict process behavior and can be used for process optimization. Once implemented, an advanced analytics driven optimizer can recommend optimized set points either to operators or the distributed control system (DCS) directly to reduce energy consumption in real-time. In order to derive even more value from the analysis, further implementation recommendations were presented. They include the review of optimization targets potentially even beyond energy consumption in the kiln; enhancing the model with additional data and what-if scenarios; building an ongoing optimizer that includes process constraints and limits for optimization and safety purposes; designing the implementation architecture in line with current IT and security infrastructure; installing the optimizer on-site and handing over the model to process engineers for continuous improvement; training the operators and process engineers in the use of the optimizer; and launching performance management initiatives to ensure ongoing application and tracking of impact.

## 6.2 Ammonia

This chapter gives a brief summary of a pilot application using profit per hour as a target KPI in ammonia production. Part of this research was published in a paper from the 50th CIRP[26] Conference on Manufacturing Systems (Hammer et al. 2017b, p. 715). Ammonia is a large-volume chemical serving as a raw material for the production of nitrogen based fertilizers (Moulijn et al. 2013, p. 171). The most common method of producing Ammonia, although energy intensive and costly, is the Haber-Bosch process, which combines hydrogen from steam reforming of natural gas with nitrogen from air (Moulijn et al. 2013, p. 182).

### 6.2.1 Context

This work was conducted as part of a pilot analytics implementation in the fall of 2016. The method used contained 8 steps (Hammer et al. 2017b, p. 717) to trial profit per hour as a target metric based on analytics. The first step, as per Hammer et al., was the creation of a profit per hour value tree and the identification of key parameters. These were classified, as in the cement case, into three categories: (1) Controllable variables, parameters that can be influenced by the operator, e.g., ratios of steam to gas and air to gas; (2) Disturbance variables, parameters that can´t be influenced, e.g., external temperature, relative humidity, air pressure; and (3) Output variables which are the result of the what happens in the process, e.g., Ammonia and steam volumes, and profit per hour (Hammer et al. 2017b, p. 718).

26 The International Academy for Production Engineering

### 6.2.2 Application

Graphical analysis of profit per hour over output led to three insights: (1) there is a strong correlation between profit per hour and output, (2) clear seasonal impact, and (3) additional variation of approx. 3-5 % at each production rate level (Hammer et al. 2017b, p. 718). A predictive model, based on artificial neural networks, helped to estimate the impact of the external weather conditions, including parameters such as temperature and humidity, and to quantify the remaining non-weather related losses. These residual profit losses were then depicted in a cumulative profit per hour chart, Figure 61, and served to detect controllable elements for process optimization. Nine operating windows could be differentiated. Assignable process disturbances due to internal issues such as equipment reliability, or external shortages were found to make up half of all losses and are marked with letters a, b, c, and d. Stable operating conditions were assigned with numbers 1 to 5 and showed a varying degree of profit losses according to their slope. A further predictive model focusing on the residual losses surfaced five additional controllable optimization parameters. These are being visualized as part of a decision cockpit for operators and are considered for future automated process control (Hammer et al. 2017b, p. 719).

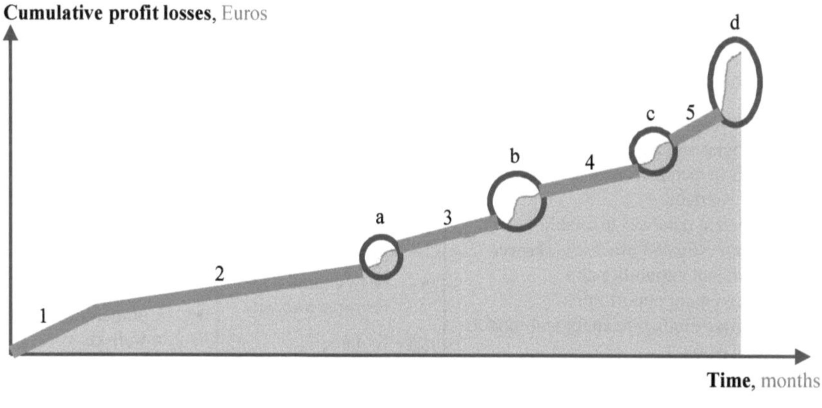


Figure 61: Cumulative profit losses (Hammer et al. 2017b, p. 719)

### 6.2.3 Results

The pilot implementation of profit per hour as a target process control parameter was considered successful under the condition that external, non-controllable variables are isolated. The benefits of advanced process control of influenceable parameters have been estimated at 0.5-2% additional profit per hour (Hammer et al. 2017b, p. 719).

## 6.3 Summary: Challenges and Opportunities in Practice

The two case examples from the process industries indicate that there is a financial opportunity to use advanced analytics and that in general there is sufficient data available, given that the processes are operated on continuous basis. With respect to the optimization target, both cases were grounded in a financial value driver tree. However, while the ammonia case considered all trade-offs by using profit per hour as a target KPI, the cement case focused on energy only. In cement, an improvement in yield, can be achieved by increasing the energy used in the process by burning more fuel leading to higher costs. On the other hand, reducing energy consumption could increase the time the clinker is treated in the kiln and lead to a loss in throughput and profitability. Therefore, to consider all trade-offs and to avoid sub-optima an overarching financial metric, such as profit per hour, seems meaningful. When it comes to the process methodology the two cases used different steps, resulted in different outcomes, but nevertheless are considered successful as part of this research. A need for a structured implementation methodology based on a well-known approach became evident.

| **Learning** | **Delimitations** | **Requirements** |
|---|---|---|
| • Financial value driver tree based on ROIC helped prioritize the focus for improvement<br>• Sufficient data was available<br>• The investigated processes showed significant variability and improvement opportunity<br>• Accurate predictive analytical models could be built<br>• Profit per hour as a target for modelling helps solve trade-offs<br>• Different processes were used, not previously known to the organization<br>• Companies desire ongoing decision support, e.g., operator cockpit or closed-loop, analytics based process control | INCLUDES<br>• Manufacturing in process industries<br>• Continuous operations<br>• High capital and resource intensity<br><br>EXCLUDES<br>• Discrete industries<br>• Batch operations | • Practicality, i.e., minimum required complexity and effort<br>• Structured implementation methodology<br>• Compatibility with a well-known improvement approach<br>• On-going decision support for process improvement |

Table 32: Summary of conclusions from practice perspective

# 7 Interim Conclusion: Scope of Work

In this chapter the research need is summarized and the scope of work is defined through the delimitation and requirements from the previous chapters dealing with theory, related work and observations from practical cases.

## 7.1 Research Gap

The objective of this thesis is to define a structured methodology to increase time-based profit in manufacturing in process industries through the use of analytics. This need comes, to recapitulate, from both practice and theory. A clear research need in the area of industrial analytics has been seen by Diab asking for a "systematic […] approach that […] meet[s] the operational and business requirements […] and technological advances" (Diab et al. 2017, p. 15). Also Henke et al. point out that companies currently face organizational challenges in their attempt to implement "data-driven insights into day-to-day business processes" (Henke et al. 2016a, vi). Therefore, LaValle et al. recommend that managers "focus on achievable steps" (LaValle et al. 2011, p. 26) for implementation. In the VUCA context, laid out in chapter 2, companies need to become agile, i.e., react quickly, based on a common profitability goal for operations aligned across organizational boundaries. Process controls will need to enable "an integration between the business environment, with current cost of material, energy, and maybe even emissions, and the production information in the plant allows to solve optimization problems that optimize the bottom line directly" (Terwiesch, Ganz 2009, p. 141). Rao affirms that, "the selection of optimum process parameters plays a significant role […] to increase productivity" in manufacturing (Rao 2011, p. 3). Such operational aspects require additional research in the area of performance management systems (Sager et al. 2016, p. 66), especially for dynamic performance management systems that lack a structured framework (Bititci et al. 2000, p. 694) and need to be capable of providing short-term, data-driven recommendations (Becker 2016, p. 143). Horvath et al. see a need for profit-focused value driver models based on operative KPIs (Horvath et al. 2015, p. 105). Automated data capture and analyses are required to cope with changing conditions and dynamic bottlenecks in near real time (Neugebauer et al. 2016, p. 3). Gausemeier and Klocke recommend "to develop appropriate


M. Hammer, *Management Approach for Resource-Productive Operations*,
Industrial Management, https://doi.org/10.1007/978-3-658-22939-9_7

ontologies and apply them [...] for optimizing manufacturing systems" (Gausemeier, Klocke 2016, p. 75). Brecher points out that socio-technical production systems are highly complex, even more so when exposed to significant external volatility, requiring advanced, cybernetic, and self-optimizing control approaches (Brecher, Özdemir 2014, p. 2).

## 7.2 Delimitation of Research Focus and Summary of Requirements

In this section the scope of work is outlined based on the delimitations of research focus and summary of requirements, Table 33, from the previous chapter covering the industry, digitization, management, operations and practice perspectives.

The resulting scope of work can be synthesized into the following three requirements:

1. Help manufacturers cope with the VUCA context through an **operations improvement approach** that is generically applicable in process industries, independent from sector, location or plant size. The approach should be **built upon a structured implementation methodology**; compatible with a well-known improvement approach; practical, requiring minimum complexity and effort; and deliver sustainable results through the integration of technical, managerial, and people aspects.

2. Focus on **time-based profit as a leading operational KPI**, linking the operations and management level using a ROIC-based value driver tree; and maximizing cumulative profits as the overarching goal.

3. Leverage **digital technologies**, consolidating data from various data sources with consistent time stamps, using predictive and prescriptive analytics, linking analytics and advanced process control **for on-going, closed-loop decision support** and process improvement.

| Chapters | Delimitation | Requirements |
|---|---|---|
| 2. Industry perspective<br>• Megatrends affecting industry<br>• Manufacturing<br>• Process industries | INCLUDES<br>• Manufacturing at a process industry plant, regardless of geography and sector<br>EXCLUDES<br>• Discrete manufacturing, the larger supply chain, and service industries | • Leverage digital technologies<br>• Help manufacturers cope with VUCA context<br>• Maximize profits<br>• Focus on time utilization<br>• Develop a generic improvement approach for process industries, independent from sector, location or plant size |
| 3. Digitization perspective<br>• Industry 4.0<br>• Internet of Things<br>• Big Data<br>• Advanced analytics | INCLUDES<br>• Big Data capabilities, e.g., streaming of data, data lakes and advanced (predictive and prescriptive) analytics<br>EXCLUDES<br>• Hardware, equipment upgrades with new technologies, e.g. sensors, communication, etc. | • Consolidate data from various data sources with consistent time stamps<br>• Use of predictive and prescriptive analytics<br>• Link analytics and advanced process control<br>• Develop an implementation approach consistent with existing operations improvement methodologies |
| 4. Management perspective<br>• Decision making<br>• Performance measures<br>• Performance measurement and management systems<br>• Decision support systems | INCLUDES<br>• Time-based profit optimization<br>• Dynamic, closed-loop performance management<br>• Operations orientation (internal focus) considering external factors and overall strategic objectives<br>• Target group are decision makers in a manufacturing site, e.g., plant managers, process engineers and operators<br>EXCLUDES<br>• Capital and financing aspects, e.g., debt/equity optimization | • Profit orientation with the goal of maximizing ROIC<br>• Profit rate as leading operational KPI<br>• Linking operations level with management level through value driver tree<br>• Decision support, e.g., cockpit or closed loop automatic decision making |

| | | |
|---|---|---|
| 5. Operations perspective<br>• Resource-productive operations<br>• Lean<br>• Six Sigma<br>• Theory of constraints<br>• Agility<br>• Advanced process control | INCLUDES<br>• Maximizing industrial productivity of assets and resources in process industries<br>• Focus on bottleneck<br>• Loss thinking with reference to the theoretical limited<br>• Structured approach for operations improvement<br>• Closed loop, advanced process control enhanced by advanced analytics<br>EXCLUDES<br>• Agility monitoring of the external environment and handling of external influences, such as price and demand volatilities | • Structured implementation methodology<br>• Compatibility with a well-known improvement approach<br>• On-going process improvement through closed-loop process control<br>• Sustainability of results through the integration of technical, managerial, people aspects |
| 6. Observations of practice<br>• Cement<br>• Ammonia | INCLUDES<br>• Manufacturing in process industries<br>• Continuous operations<br>• High capital and resource intensity<br>EXCLUDES<br>• Discrete industries<br>• Batch operations | • Practicality, i.e., minimum required complexity and effort<br>• Structured implementation methodology<br>• Compatibility with a well-known improvement approach<br>• On-going decision support for process improvement |

Table 33: Delimitation of research focus based on related work and theory

# 8 Methodology Conception: Framing a Time-Based and Analytics Supported Operations Management Approach

In this chapter the methodology to answer the research questions from chapter 1 will be outlined. The overall objective is to provide industrial companies with a step-by-step process methodology to implement a time-based and analytics-supported operations management approach. In section 8.1 the basic concept and characteristics of the approach are introduced. Section 8.2 covers the theoretical classification of the methodology. Section 8.3 deals with criteria when the approach is meaningful. Section 8.4 looks at pre-conditions to enable the approach.

## 8.1 Concept

In manufacturing process parameters have to be chosen in the best possible way taking process safety, quality, cost and delivery times into account (Rao 2011, pp. 2–3). In order to make trade-off decisions an overarching criteria has to be stated. Stakeholders of for-profit manufacturing companies ultimately aim for profit maximization (Hitomi 1996, p. 320). Effective performance management analytics require a combination of IT, management accounting, and the analytical methods (Schläfke et al. 2012, p. 114). The same need for an inter-disciplinary approach exists for dynamic process control (Roffel, Betlem 2006, xiii-xiv). In 1978 Skinner investigated the relationships between technology, constraints, economics and management (Skinner 1978, p. 96). Figure 62, gives an overview of these aspects adapted to the concept of this work. The operations management approach for profit per hour is made possible by advances in technology in the context of Industry 4.0 and includes Big Data analytics, as discussed in chapter 3. In a set of five defined digital operating models, the approach is classified as “data powered” and builds in intelligence from analytics and focuses on ROIC as a KPI (World Economic Forum 2016, p. 17). Also constraints apply, namely, the delimitations of this work to manufacturing in process industries (chapter 2), and time (chapter 4).


M. Hammer, *Management Approach for Resource-Productive Operations*,
Industrial Management, https://doi.org/10.1007/978-3-658-22939-9_8

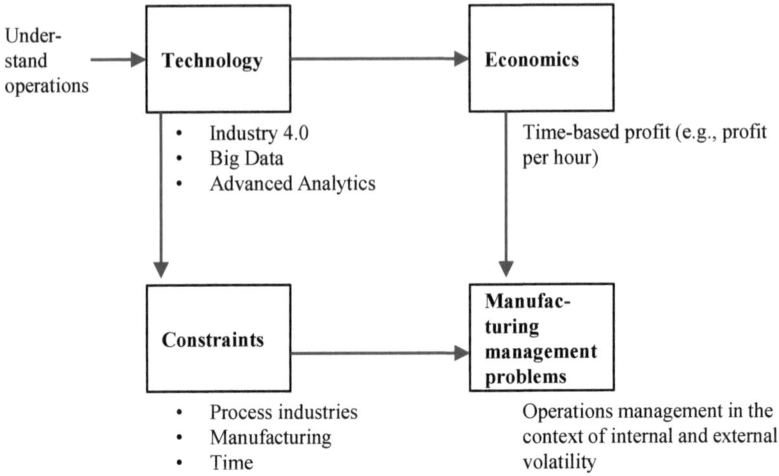


Figure 62: Technology, economics and manufacturing management (adapted from Skinner 1978, p. 96)

### 8.1.1 Technology

Advances in analytics algorithms and techniques, including machine learning, are used to analyze large amounts of data gathered from industrial control systems [...] to drive intelligent operational and business processes, [and enable] the convergence of analytics in the OT and IT worlds (Diab et al. 2017, pp. 2–3). From a technology point of view, Figure 63 illustrates the components of a system that takes in data from a plant (and also its environment), uses analytical models as basis for decisions and can prescribe actions back to the MES. There are two possible end-states, depending whether the decision maker is actually a human operator/manager, or whether the entire system operates autonomously. In the first case, information as a basis for decision making and suggested actions need to be displayed in a dashboard to the operators. In the second case, the algorithm works in a closed-loop mode and controls the process within predefined boundaries.

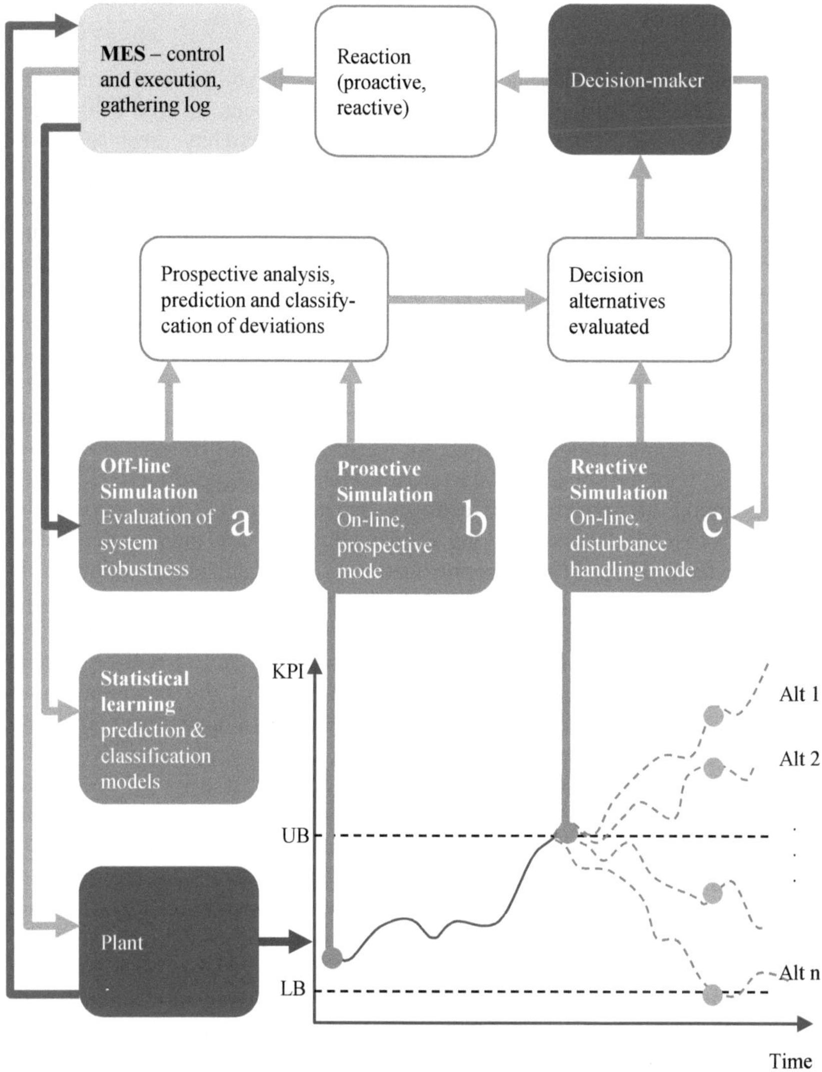


Figure 63: Plant-level active disturbance handling by using reactive/proactive operation modes of simulation (Monostori et al. 2016, p. 626)

### 8.1.2 Economics

KPIs will gain further significance with the rise in data volume and complexity (Losbichler, Gänßlen 2015, p. 312). Although KPIs have been covered in literature for specific functions, Epstein and Lee point out that, “there have been relatively few attempts to integrate the relationships among variables across disciplines, and relate the management actions pertaining to them to overall firm profitability” (Epstein, Lee 2000, pp. 44–45). In line with the overall goal to accumulate profits, profit per time period becomes both a leading and a lagging financial parameter. What the author would like to add is a point of reference into the concept, the theoretical limit (chapter 5) for profit per hour. This allows the quantification of profit losses which shall be minimized. It has to be noted that profit losses are additive. As profit is highly volatile, and incurred profit losses can never be recuperated, the time dimension is an important element. Furthermore, the theoretical limit might change over time, for reasons of simplification it is assumed constant in the period of observation as part of this work. According to Horngren et al, the timing of performance feedback depends on “(1) how critical the information is for the success of the organization, (2) the management level receiving the feedback, and (3) the sophistication of the organization’s information technology” (Horngren et al. 2015, p. 910). In the case of profit per hour the information is critical to the operations management team and also operators and with the latest technology actual values can be computed and visualized in near real-time. Figure 64, integrates the economic aspects of the profit per hour management approach. The approach integrates both management control and operations control (Anthony 1965, p. 93) into one overall approach. Time dependent metrics for profit do exist but are not commonly used for operations control. Profit per hour serves as a leading target process control parameter at the operations level, and the resulting cumulative profit, e.g., ROIC, is the corresponding lagging indicator at the management level. In the light of implementation, Gray and Wilkinson highlight that “financial considerations are powerful motivational factors for both the implementation of any change itself, and for how the change is implemented” (Gray, Wilkinson 2016, p. 337). Breaking down profitability into underlying value drivers as discussed in chapter 4 with respect to ROIC, enables organizations to implement driver-based decision making processes. For Clark and Dostal this will lead to increased business insights based on driver-based dashboards linking outcome metrics to drivers mathematically and the ability to conduct “what-if” analyses (Clark, Dostal 2013, p. 2).

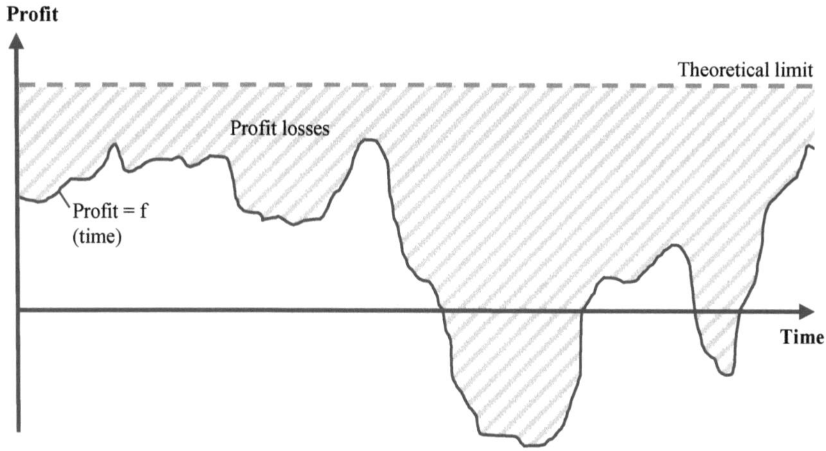


Figure 64: Economic aspect of time-based profit management approach

## 8.2 Classification

In this section the work considers application oriented theory, systems theory and model theory.

### 8.2.1 Application Oriented Theory

The practice focus of application oriented research, according to Ulrich is constitutive, i.e., the direct purpose is to support practical actions grounded in science. The link to practice is of central importance (Ulrich 1981, p. 10). Economic science should not only support decision makers in developing and evaluating possible courses of actions, but also determining how to proceed given their objectives (Heinen 1991, p. 11). Human actions, and economic actions in particular, can be described as rational processes, as per Domschke, following the general phases of planning (decision preparation), decision, execution and control. In this respect, the main task of operations research is to apply or develop an optimization model for solving a real decision problem (Domschke et al. 2015, p. 1).

### 8.2.2 System Theory Classification

A system is defined as "a set of things working together as parts of [...] a complex whole".[27] Systems thinking is a generic approach helping to structure and interpret complex situations by thinking holistically and considering different perspectives (Züst 1997, p. 34). Figure 65 illustrates the basic terms in systems thinking.

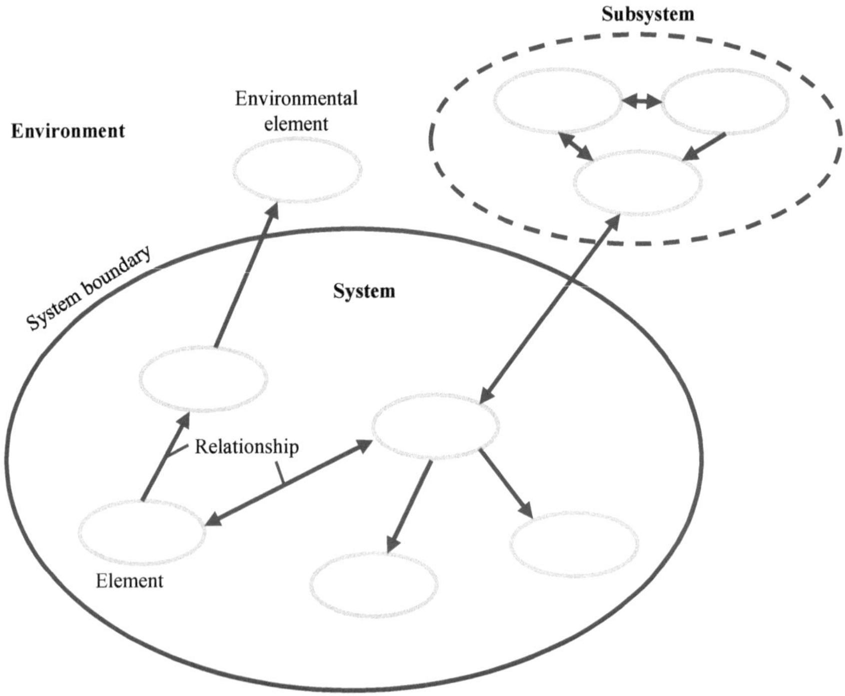


Figure 65: Basic terms in systems thinking (Haberfellner et al. 2012, p. 34)

In line with this definition there are three systems perspectives: (1) environment oriented, (2) causal oriented, and (3) structure oriented (Haberfellner et al. 2012, pp. 42–43). Systems can be considered blackbox, greybox, or whitebox depending on the degree of knowledge of the internal structure and relationships between systems inputs and outputs (Haberfellner et al. 2012, pp. 38–39). Law and Kelton point out that when experiments with the actual system cannot be performed,

27 https://en.oxforddictionaries.com/definition/system, last accessed 11.08.2017

experiments with a model of the system have to be conducted. This can be done through physical or mathematical models using analytical solutions or simulation (Law, Kelton 1991, p. 4). For Bishop, modeling systems using dynamic scenarios and sensitivity analysis "creates the best quantitative representation of continuous variables that describe the future state" (Bishop et al. 2007, p. 20). Systems engineering provides a universally applicable procedural model consisting of four components that can be combined in a modular way: (1) top down, (2) principle of building variants, (3) phased procedure, and (4) the problem solving cycle (Haberfellner et al. 2012, p. 124). Hitomi distinguishes six aspects of systems engineering in manufacturing: (1) the basic function, structure and design of the manufacturing system (systems engineering approach), (2) the optimization of manufacturing system (management science/operations research approach), (3) process control and automation (control engineering approach), (4) production information management (information technology approach), (5) economics of manufacturing (economics approach), and (6) social aspects of manufacturing excellence (social science approach) (Hitomi 1996, p. 57). In a socio-technical context "human beings are random, nondeterministic systems" (Scaife 2016, pp. 93–94). A classification of systems including adjacent theory such as cybernetics is shown in Figure 66. Cybernetics goes back to Norbert Wiener in 1948 (Wiener 1994).

This research looks at socio-technical systems and aims to develop a methodology, which is defined as "a system of methods used in a particular area of study".[28] Where a method is a "systematic process of achieving certain ends with accuracy and efficiency".[29]

28 https://en.oxforddictionaries.com/definition/methodology, last accessed 09.08.2017
29 http://www.businessdictionary.com/definition/method.html, last accessed 09.08.2017

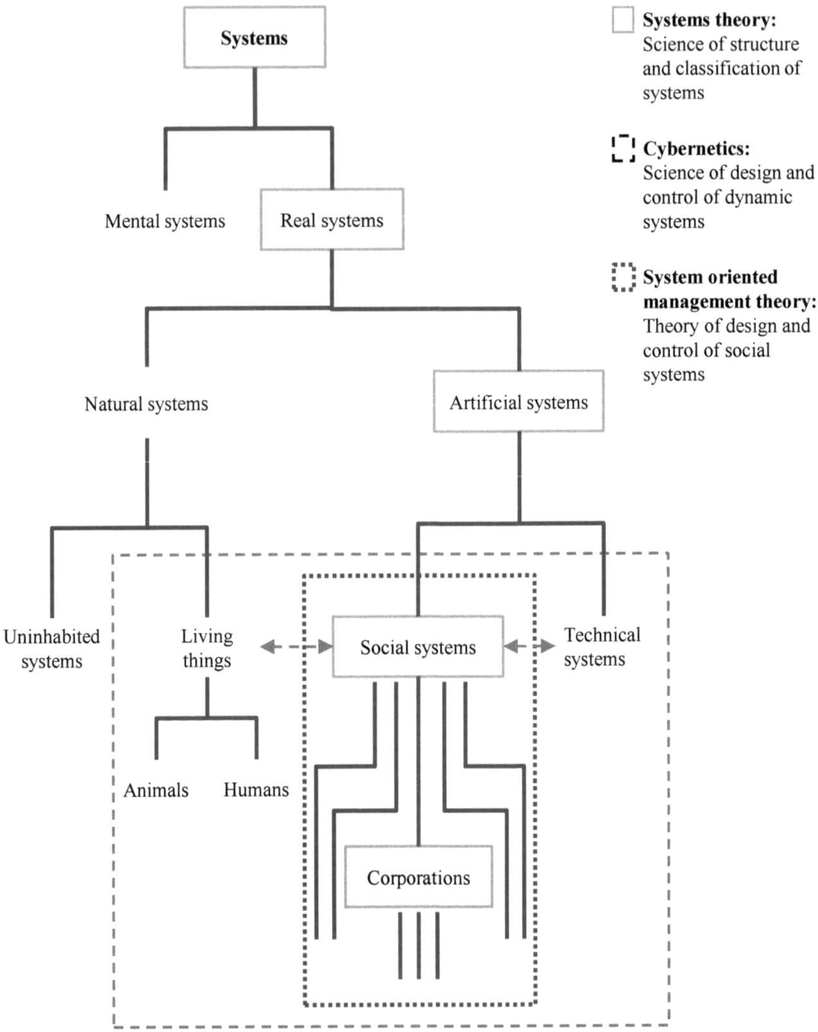


Figure 66: Systems theory, cybernetics, and management theory (Ulrich 2001, p. 44)

### 8.2.3 Model Theory Classification

Models can be distinguished in several ways, e.g., they can be deterministic if all information and relationships are known, or stochastic when the model is based on uncertain, probabilistic variables (Law, Kelton 1991, p. 6). Schweitzer, Krause 1997, p. 9 provide an overview according to structural properties of economic models, Figure 67.

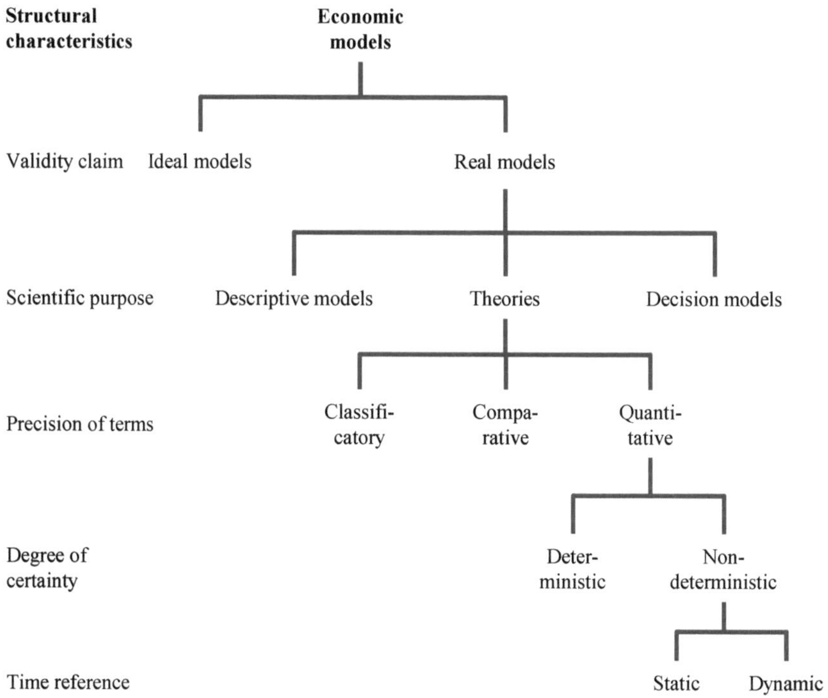


Figure 67: Classification of economic models (Schweitzer, Krause 1997, p. 9)

Depending on the scope of the model it can be a total or a partial model (Domschke, Scholl 2005, pp. 32–33) and also of predictive nature (Domschke, Scholl 2005, p. 31). A realistic representation of corporate and economic behavior, according to Forrester, requires dynamic, non-linear, stable models (Forrester 1961, p. 49).

Forrester states:

> "The nonlinearities of maximum factory capacity, labor and credit shortage, and the dependence of decisions on complex relationships between variables, all compellingly insist on being included in a usefully realistic model of the industrial enterprise. Since time and changes with time are the essence of the manager´s task, a useful model must be dynamic and capable of adequately generating its own evolution through time" (Forrester 1961, p. 52).

### 8.2.4 Summary of Relevance

In the scope of this work, the methodology deals with a dynamic, non-linear/stochastic model of an industrial system. The methodology will be a procedural model with defined system boundaries, i.e. a partial model with clear scope on one site excluding aspects of supply chain and the exhaustive coverage of externalities. Related to this work, Hutchinson 2007, p. 140 specifically proposed further research using a system dynamics approach considering the moderating role of management accounting systems between a time-based manufacturing strategy and manufacturing performance, Figure 68.

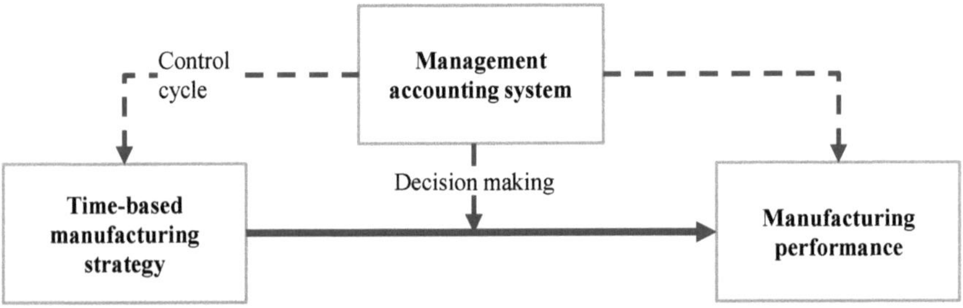


Figure 68: System-dynamics based conceptual framework for time-based manufacturing strategy (Hutchinson 2007, p. 140)

## 8.3 Applicability

In order to answer RQ1 (under what conditions does a profit per hour management approach help to take the best available decisions), the author formulates the following proposition: profit per hour is a suitable operational target KPI for industrial operations management in manufacturing, when (1) trade-off decisions between conflicting targets (e.g., throughput, energy, yield, ...) are required, (2) time is the constraint (e.g. high OEE, continuous vs. batch), (3) "real time" decision making is required, e.g. due to high volatility, (4) cumulative profit maximization is the desired long term goal, (5) invested capital (fixed cost) and/or resource intensity (variable cost) is high (e.g. process industries).

### 8.3.1 Trade-Off Decisions Are Required

Industrial companies gain strategic, competitive advantage through the performance of their production system measured by factors such as process costs, timing, quality or flexibility (Ramsauer 2009, 50). As a consequence a variety of trade-offs arise in production, e.g., between resource utilization and quality (Brignall et al. 1991, p. 34). Epstein and Lee point out that the "prevalent tendency to focus on individual target variables results in a significant impediment to cross-functional integration in organizations" (Epstein, Lee 2000, p. 44). Figure 69 provides examples of interdependencies among throughput, yield, energy and environment.

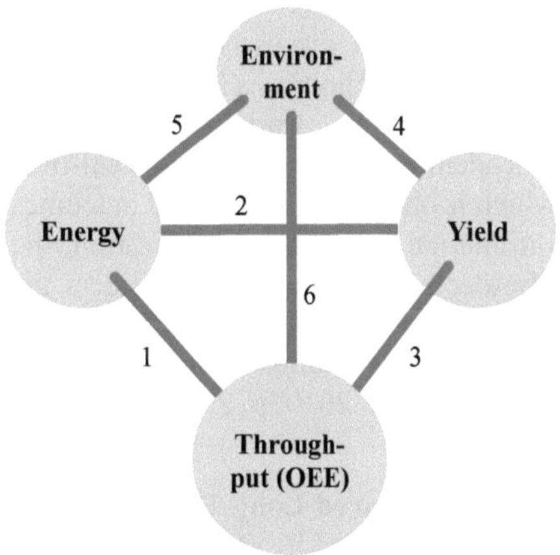


**Examples of Interdependencies**

1. Lower energy consumption can be achieved with lower throughput
2. Increasing yield can increase energy consumption
3. Increasing yield can reduce throughput
4. Yield increase also reduces waste to be disposed
5. Improving energy consumption can reduce CO2 emissions
6. Increasing throughput can increase waste

Figure 69: Trade-offs for resource-productive operations (Hammer, Somers 2016, p. 89)

In order to reach the highest overall productivity, managers need to handle uncertain conditions while balancing several criteria which are in contrast to each other (Rao 2013, p. 1). Technology is already in use to help, as discussed in chapter 4.4 (decision support systems) and chapter 5.6 (advanced process control systems). For example, real-time energy management systems communicate with process control systems as well as cost accounting/finance systems such as SAP to make decisions (Feldmann 2013, p. 10).

### 8.3.2 Time is the Constraint

For the purpose of this discussion, time is considered as linear, continuous, economic (Voss, Blackmon 1998, p. 150) and absolute, as per the belief of Aristoteles and Newton (Hawking 1988, p. 33). Other concepts, such as space-time, elaborated in Einstein´s general theory of relativity (Einstein 1916, p. 769) or the cyclical perception of time in some cultures (Voss, Blackmon 1998, p. 149) will not be included. Time is a crucial factor across industries as lost time cannot be recovered. Time is of particular relevance in process industries as it often presents a constraint. The importance of time is evidenced by continuous 24/7 operations, and already high levels of OEE in markets with sufficient demand.

### 8.3.3 "Real Time" (Short Interval) Decision Making is Required

Given the increased volatility of the environment, as discussed in chapter 2, decisions need to be made in shorter intervals. Profit per hour as a leading decision metric presents a clear criteria for short-interval decisions. Darby sees a need for more exchange between industry and academia with respect to real-time optimization (Darby et al. 2011, p. 883), which is one of the anticipated outcomes of this thesis. While this thesis focuses on internal operations optimization, the best case in the author´s opinion, would be decision-making that considers the commercial conditions from markets and customers in real-time. A sector where this is already done is the electricity market where generation and consumption are balanced directly via the market price (Conejo et al. 2010, p. 2).

### 8.3.4 Cumulative Profit Maximization is the Desired Long Term Goal

The profit maximization hypothesis is the most common objective in economic literature (Adam 1970, p. 59). The economic principle and maxim that companies must earn the highest possible profits on invested capital is a structural element of market economy systems (Gutenberg 1963, p. 8). It also demands that corporate decisions are made both for the short and long term (Gutenberg 1963, p. 10). According to a recent study, managing for the long term leads to higher growth in average revenue by 47% and earnings by 36%, and in addition, to faster growth in market capitalization (Barton et al. 2017).

### 8.3.5 High Invested Capital, High Resource Intensity and/or Resource Scarcity

In situations with "high capital and manufacturing costs, there is an economic need to operate these machines as efficiently as possible in order to obtain the required pay back" (Rao 2011, p. 3). Process operating situations that are relevant to maximizing operating profits, according to Edgar et al. 2001, pp. 7–8 and Seborg et al. 2004, p. 513 include:

> **(1) Sales limited by production**: If additional products can be sold beyond current capacity, sales can be increased by increasing production. This can be achieved by optimizing operating conditions and production schedules. This situation implies a higher profit margin on the incremental sales.
> **(2) Sales limited by market:** This situation is susceptible to optimization only if improvements in efficiency at current production rates can be obtained, hence, the economic incentive for implementation in this case may be less than in the first example because no additional products are made. An increase in thermal efficiency, for example, usually leads to a reduction in manufacturing costs (e.g., utilities or feedstocks).
> **(3) Large throughput:** Units with large production rates (or throughputs) offer great potential to increase profits. Small savings in production costs per unit throughput or incremental improvements in yield, plus large production rates, can result in major increases in profits. Most large chemical and petroleum processes fall into this classification.
> **(4) High raw material or energy consumption:** They are major cost factors in a typical plant and thus offer potential savings. For example, the optimal allocation of fuel supplies and steam in a plant can reduce costs by minimizing fuel consumption.

## 8.4 Pre-Conditions

The approach is enabled by a combination of technology, human factors and management. In this section, with focus on answering RQ2 (In practice, what keeps companies from implementing a profit per hour approach), the pre-conditions are investigated and required elements are elaborated. The author´s reasons why companies are currently not following a profit per hour management approach are: (1)They are **not aware** or it is **not meaningful to them**, i.e. they do not meet criteria discussed in the previous section; (2) they **lack infrastructure** (e.g. sensors/meters), **data** (e.g., volume, frequency, quality) to compute the metric, or **do not have access to (advanced) algorithms** required to calculate profit per hour as a target function; (3) they **lack the required skills** (e.g., IT, analytics, functional expertise); (4) they **lack an implementation process** (e.g., methodology) or fail in the change management process, and (5) they **struggle to adapt the accounting procedures**. A recent study of complex operations by Gundersen based on 7 companies found seven success criteria, Table 34, ranging from mindset, leadership, training to data capture and data basis.

| No. | Success criteria | Capabilities for best practice | Typical issues |
|---|---|---|---|
| 1 | Data capture and data basis | Use of advanced sensors and automated data capture, rich data sources, capacity to handle and store large datasets | • Data is not updated<br>• Data is not sufficiently structured<br>• No data sources exist to support work process and decision point |
| 2 | Communication infrastructure and data transmission | Capacity for large data quantities without latency and with sufficient uptime and security, handle multiple technologies | • Communication infrastructure does not exist with sufficient capacity |
| 3 | Information access, integration layer | Users must have access to appropriate applications and information must be available across applications | • Manual interfaces or lack of information sharing across applications<br>• Lack of access to applications at information point of origin<br>• Application catering for the right information does not exist |
| 4 | Information visualization and workspaces | Enable cross-disciplinary and proactive use of relevant information, where work-spaces that are adapted, presented and visualized with the work process context in mind, information can come from various sources and must be aggregated to fit the decisions relevant for the specific work processes | • Workspaces/information visualization does not support work processes and decision points (or not defined) |
| 5 | Collaboration functionalities and work arenas | Technology and physical space for access to information and connection between team members independent of location | • Collaboration infrastructure does not support work processes and decision points (or not defined)<br>• Collaboration technology not used to its potential<br>• Collaboration technology not compatible or is not available |

| | | | |
|---|---|---|---|
| 6 | Organization, roles and responsibilities (Governance) | Harmonized and documented work processes, clear competence requirements, mandates and decision authority, clear and standar-dized roles, responsibilities and relational links, clearly stated requirements for information needs, best practices etc. for describing tasks within work processes, collaborative work processes (between disciplines/skills and locations) | • Gap between actual operations and formal procedures and work instructions<br>• Unclear roles, responsibilities, work processes and decision points<br>• Unclear communication lines and division of authority in interfaces between organization units and between disciplines |
| 7 | Mindset, leadership and training | Transparent leadership, utilize new ways of working, integration competence, sustainable change, continuous improvement, learning organization (active training) | • Lack of policy and culture for coordination, information sharing, common understanding of goals between organizational units, both internally, between organizations and at external organizations<br>• New strategies, structures and processes not implemented, lack of plans for transitions except the occasional new organization chart<br>• No attention to organizational learning processes and training of basic collaboration practices |

Table 34: Success criteria and issues in management of complex operations (Gundersen 2017, pp. 87–88, 93)

Success criteria 1-5 confirm the author's hypothesis of a lack of infrastructure or other data related issues. Number 6 relates to the hypothesis of a lack of methodology and number 7 links to gaps in skills and training. When it comes to data, it is important to point out that issues associated with cost allocation, as pointed out in chapter 4.2, are the final reason which keeps companies from implementing a profit per hour approach. The author´s operations management approach aims to optimize the profit per hour and requires that the revenues of the production of a customer order are compared to the cost at the time of production. This leads to differences in external cost accounting and internal management accounting in terms of value and timing.

### 8.4.1 Technology

Technology is an essential enabler. Next to continued reductions in cost for computing or storage, developments in the area of analytics and visualization software and interoperability between systems is required (Manyika et al. 2015, pp. 11–12). Monostori et al confirm: "The existence of legacy systems hinders the stepwise introduction of CPPS solutions into existing manufacturing systems or, the transformation of a whole traditional system to become Industry 4.0-ready" (Monostori et al. 2016, p. 627). Technical issues such as these are not new and were stated earlier in the context of planning and control systems: "Connectivity between applications was difficult or expensive to implement and maintain" (Shobrys, White 2002, p. 150); and in the area of performance management: "[there is an] absence of a flexible platform to allow organizations to effectively and efficiently manage the dynamics of their performance measurement systems" (Bititci et al. 2000, p. 694). While there has been some progress in the area of PMS, still in 2016, similar technical infrastructure challenges remain, e.g., the capability "to read information not only from databases available in the manufacturing system, but also from other functional models applied by decision makers during their planning activities" (Almeida, Azevedo 2016, p. 138). The rise of data lakes capable of storing data from a variety of sources including structured and unstructured data will ease analytics (Martin 2016, p. 35). Figure 70 illustrates the target state with a data lake as an analytics enabler.

Beyond the data processing infrastructure, analytics depends on information sources that "go beyond sensor data and tend to include environmental and context data, including usage information (e.g. high load) of the machinery" (Becker 2016, p. 145). However, while "businesses today are constantly generating enormous amounts of data [...,] that doesn't always translate to actionable information" (Veeramachaneni 2016). This has to do with the fact that some organizations start with collecting data rather than identifying the business problem first (Franks 2014, p. 36). Furthermore, "companies need to ensure that the right data are available and that the data quality is good" (Schläfke et al. 2012, p. 115). Seufert found that while data quality is essential, more than 50% of companies either do not explicitly manage this subject or handle it decentrally (Seufert et al. 2014, p. 21). Mining data is of multidisciplinary nature including data science, knowledge discovery, statistics, pattern recognition, computational neuroscience, machine learning, and AI (Dean 2014, p. 56).

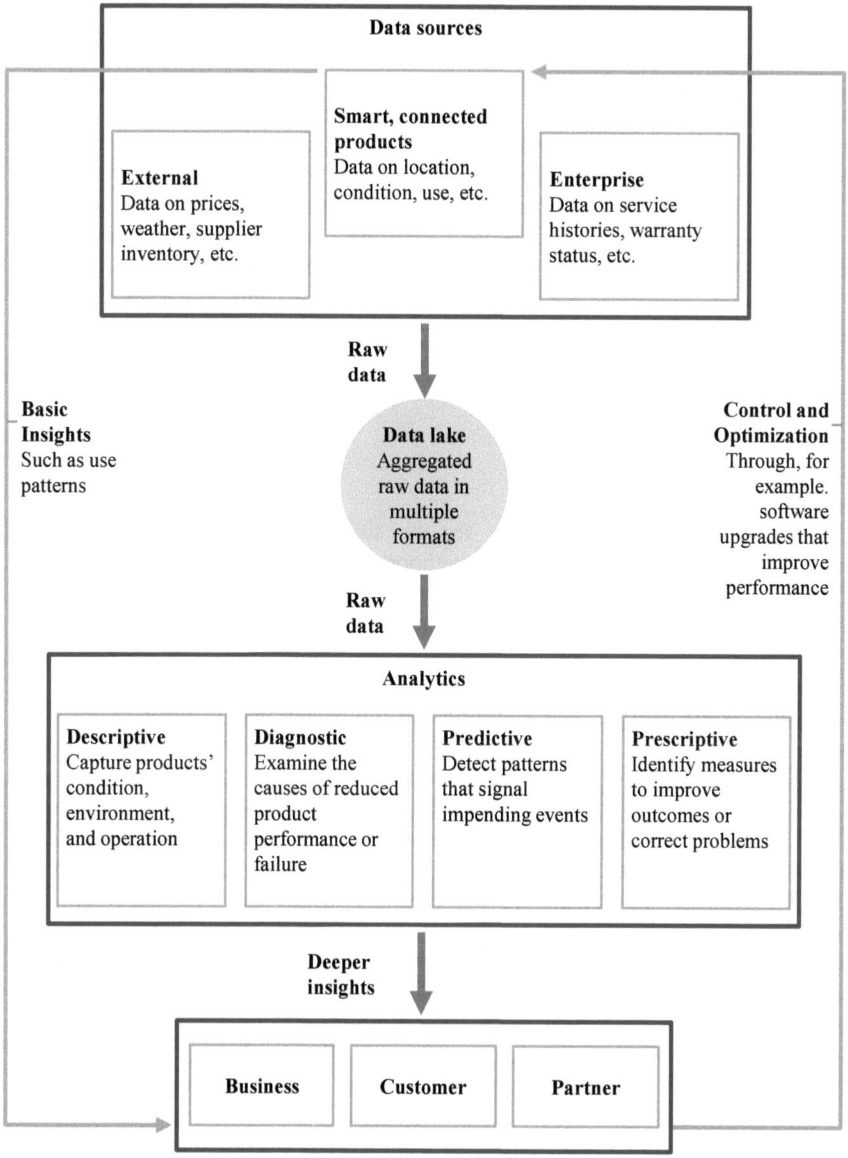


Figure 70: Data lake (Porter, Heppelmann 2015)

The BDVA Big Data Value Association 2016, pp. 27–28 sees the following five challenges: (1) Semantic and knowledge-based analysis: Improvement to the analysis of data to provide a near real-time interpretation of the data (i.e. sentiment, semantics, etc.). Furthermore, ontology engineering for Big Data sources, interactive visualization & exploration, real-time interlinking and annotation of data sources, scalable and incremental reasoning, linked data mining, cognitive computing, (2) Content validation: Implementation of veracity (source reliability / information credibility) models for validating content and exploiting content recommendations from unknown users, (3) Analytics frameworks & processing, (4) Advanced business analytics and intelligence, and (5) Predictive and prescriptive analytics: Machine learning, clustering, pattern mining, network analysis and hypothesis testing techniques applied on extremely large graphs containing sparse, uncertain and incomplete data.

### 8.4.2 People

"Skills of talented human beings are the single most important resource in successfully exploiting Big Data" (Davenport 2014a, p. 110). However according to Bill Joy, the cofounder of Sun Microsystems "No matter who you are, most of the smartest people work for someone else" (Lakhani, Panetta 2007). Even though the benefits of business analytics are clear, the required skills might be lacking (Schläfke et al. 2012, p. 119), as mentioned in chapter 3.5. A recent survey of 545 companies confirmed this as for around half of the companies missing know-how is the biggest hurdle for benefiting from Big Data (Bange et al. 2015, p. 35). Companies therefore struggle to move from the early stages of analytics adoption, Table 35, towards using prescriptive analytics. Four areas of expertise are required for the optimization of manufacturing processes using advanced analytics, as per Rao 2011, p. 3; Chen et al. 2012, p. 1183; and Feldmann et al. 2016, pp. 4–5: (1) Domain expertise to understand the business issues and translate them into analytics opportunities based on the knowledge of the manufacturing process including constraints, specifications machine capacities, etc.; (2) IT expertise to capture data from sensors and store information using local or cloud-based software platforms; (3) Advanced analytics knowledge of mathematics, statistics, numerical optimization techniques; and (4) Change management skills to communicate findings, interact with the frontline and implement improvements. Next to skills, the successful implementation of improvement projects requires will and capacity (Monroe 2015, p. 61). Recent operations research found exceptionally few companies "able to develop the right mind set to support real sustainable value creation and continuous improvement" (Benzi 2017, p. 117). Also considerable capacity is required to deal with change management issues, working with the frontline in adapting operational processes and roles (Davenport 2014a, p. 184). Iafrate emphasizes that in the digital world, "the main goal is to move from a data organization (struggling with the data management) to a learning organization (leveraging all the value behind the data, with the right processes and organization)" (Iafrate 2014, p. 27).

| | Aspirational | Experienced | Transformed |
|---|---|---|---|
| **Motive** | Use analytics to justify actions | Use analytics to guide actions | Use analytics to prescribe actions |
| **Key obstacles** | • Lack of understanding how to leverage analytics for business value<br>• Executive sponsorship<br>• Culture does not encourage sharing of information | • Lack of understanding how to leverage analytics for business value<br>• Skills within line of business<br>• Ownership of data is unclear or governance is ineffective | • Lack of understanding how to leverage analytics for business value<br>• Management bandwidth due to competing priorities<br>• Accessibility of the data |

Table 35: Three stages of analytics adoption (LaValle et al. 2011, p. 24)

### 8.4.3 Process Methodology

The author postulates the thesis that in order for companies to implement a profit per hour operations management approach they would need to apply a standardized, repeatable, step-by-step process methodology considering one of the two design end-states, i.e., a live decision cockpit for managers/operators or fully automated advanced process controls. As per the requirements in chapter 7, a standardized, generic, well known step-by-step methodology for operations improvement shall be used. Table 36 shows a selection of 14 common methodologies in the area of operations and also Big Data, data mining, and knowledge discovery. The number of steps varies between 4 and 10 steps. At the lower end there is Demming´s Plan-Do-Study-Act (PDSA) loop while on the higher end there are, for example, TQM and KDD. The comparison also illustrates the compatibility and emphasis of the approaches. While there is not only one approach that can work for the profit per hour management approach, the following two criteria help to make a selection. First, the approach should be an operations approach and secondly it should be one that is already well known and using data. DMAIC is a "structured methodology and industry accepted universal language of improvement" (Burton 2011, p. 53) and is thus chosen by the author.

<table>
<tr><th colspan="7">OPERATIONS IMPROVEMENT PROCESS METHODOLOGIES</th></tr>
<tr><th>PDSA (Deming 2000, p. 132)</th><th>TOC (Goldratt 1990, p. 8)</th><th>DMAIC (Lunau 2009, p. 10)</th><th>8D (disciplines) (Riesenberger, Sousa 2010, p. 2225)</th><th>USAF 8-steps (Plenert 2011, p. 115)</th><th>TQM (Plenert 2011, p. 104)</th><th>Process Reengineering (Plenert 2011, p. 110)</th></tr>
<tr><td rowspan="6">Plan</td><td rowspan="3">Identify the constraint</td><td>Define</td><td>Team formation</td><td>Clarify the problem</td><td>Identify problems/ opportunities</td><td>Mobilization (Develop and communicate a vision, identify champions and process owners, assemble the teams)</td></tr>
<tr><td>Measure</td><td>Problem analysis</td><td>Break down the problem/identify performance gaps</td><td>Prioritize these problems</td><td rowspan="4">Diagnosis (train and educate, current process analysis, select and scope the process, understand the current customer, model the process, identify problems, set targets for new designs)</td></tr>
<tr><td rowspan="4">Analyze</td><td>Containment actions</td><td rowspan="2">Set improvement targets</td><td>Select the biggest bang-for-the-buck project</td></tr>
<tr><td rowspan="3">Exploit the constraint</td><td rowspan="3">Root cause analysis</td><td>Develop an implementation plan</td></tr>
<tr><td>Determine root causes</td><td>Use operations research and MIS tools where appropriate</td></tr>
<tr><td>Develop countermeasures</td><td>Develop guide posts and an appropriate measurement system</td><td rowspan="2">Redesign (create breakthrough design concepts, redesign the entire system, build prototype, information technology)</td></tr>
<tr><td rowspan="2">Do</td><td>Subordinate the processes</td><td rowspan="2">Improve</td><td rowspan="2">Corrective actions</td><td rowspan="2">See countermeasures through</td><td>Training</td></tr>
<tr><td>Elevate the constraint</td><td>Implementation</td><td rowspan="4">Transition (finalize transition design, implementation phase, measure benefits, communicate to avoid resistance)</td></tr>
<tr><td rowspan="2">Study</td><td rowspan="3">Repeat the process – find another constraint</td><td rowspan="3">Control</td><td>Verification of the effectiveness of the corrective actions</td><td rowspan="2">Confirm results & process</td><td rowspan="2">Feedback—monitoring—control—change</td></tr>
<tr><td>Preventive actions</td></tr>
<tr><td>Act</td><td>Congratulate the team.</td><td>Standardize successful processes</td><td>After successful project implementation and on-going status, repeat cycle</td></tr>
</table>

| BIG DATA, DATA MINING AND KNOWLEDGE DISCOVERY PROCESS METHODOLOGIES | | | | | | |
|---|---|---|---|---|---|---|
| **Analytics-based decision making** (Davenport 2013, p. 4) | **SMART** (Marr 2015, p. 21) | **Stepwise approach to Big Data Analysis** (Berman 2013, p. 157) | **Generic analytics process flow** (Franks 2014, p. 179) | **SEMMA** (Dean 2014, p. 61) | **CRISP-DM** (Shearer 2000, p. 14) | **KDD** (Fayyad et al. 1996, p. 42) |
| Recognize the problem or question<br>Review previous findings | Start with strategy | A question is formulated<br>Resource Evaluation<br>A question is reformulated | Identify business problem | Sample | Business understanding | Developing an understanding of the application domain and the relevant prior knowledge and identifying the goal of the KDD process from the customer's viewpoint |
| Collect the data | Measure metrics and data | Query output adequacy<br>Data description<br>Data reduction | Acquire data<br>Prepare data | Explore | Data understanding<br>Data preparation | Creating a target data set<br>Data cleaning and preprocessing<br>Data reduction and projection |
| Analyze the data | Analyze your data | Algorithms are selected | Performa analysis | Modify<br>Model | Modelling | Matching the goals of the KDD process (step 1) to a particular data-mining method<br>Exploratory analysis and model and hypothesis selection<br>Data mining |
| Present and act on the results | Report your results<br>Transform your business and decision-making | Results are reviewed and conclusions asserted<br>Conclusions are examined and subjected to validation | Evaluate results<br>Deploy and drive value | Assess | Evaluation<br>Deployment | Interpreting mined patterns<br>Acting on the dis covered knowledge |

Table 36: Comparison of process methodologies

Next to the DMAIC methodology, Six Sigma bundles a wide range of specific tools. While Six Sigma traditionally tends to be project focused solving specific problems, in this work it is used for ongoing optimization based on continuous variables, e.g., mass flows, temperatures, pressures. Beyond implementation, an ongoing process of alignment and improvement is required, Figure 71.

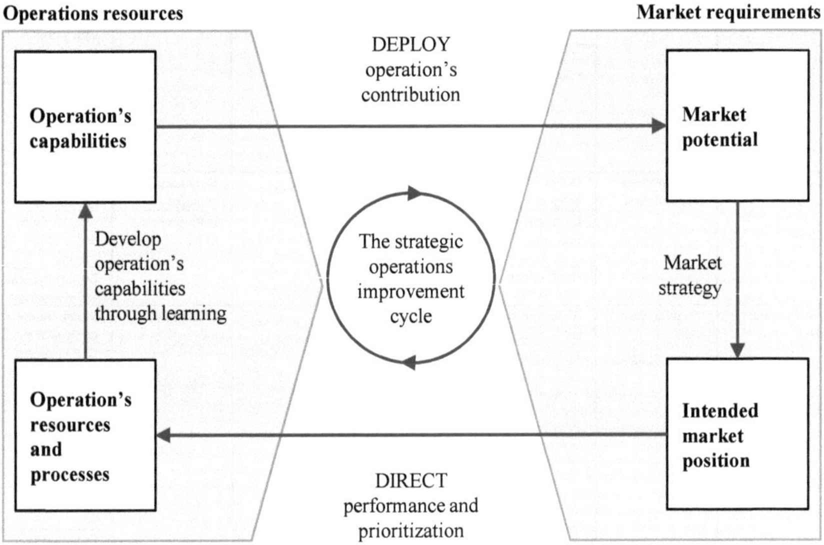


Figure 71: Direct, develop, deploy strategic improvement cycle (Slack, Lewis 2011, p. 220)

## 8.5 Summary: Constituents of a Time-Based and Analytics-Supported Operations Management Methodology

The approach is made possible through a combination of technology and economics taking constraints into account as illustrated in section 8.1. The methodology has been classified according to application-oriented theory, model theory and systems theory in section 8.2. The applicability against five criteria (section 8.3) and the preconditions (section 8.4) have been discussed in detail. The standardized method for implementation will be detailed in chapter 9 and is structured around the DMAIC framework; well-known in industry; generically applicable across sectors; practical; proven to deliver sustainable results through the integration of technical, managerial, and people aspects.

# 9 Methodology: Implementing an Analytics, Time and Six Sigma Based Operations Management Approach

In this chapter the previously conceived methodology will be explained in detail. The framework, Figure 72, follows the five phases of the Six-Sigma approach with 17 specific activities and tools for each phase stated by the author. This chapter gives the answer to RQ3 on how to implement a profit per hour management approach. As with all approaches, a customization, i.e. an extension of activities or adaptation of tools, to specific circumstances is required as part of a broader rollout – this need for adaptation and continuous improvement is also pointed out by Schwaninger 2013, p. 56.

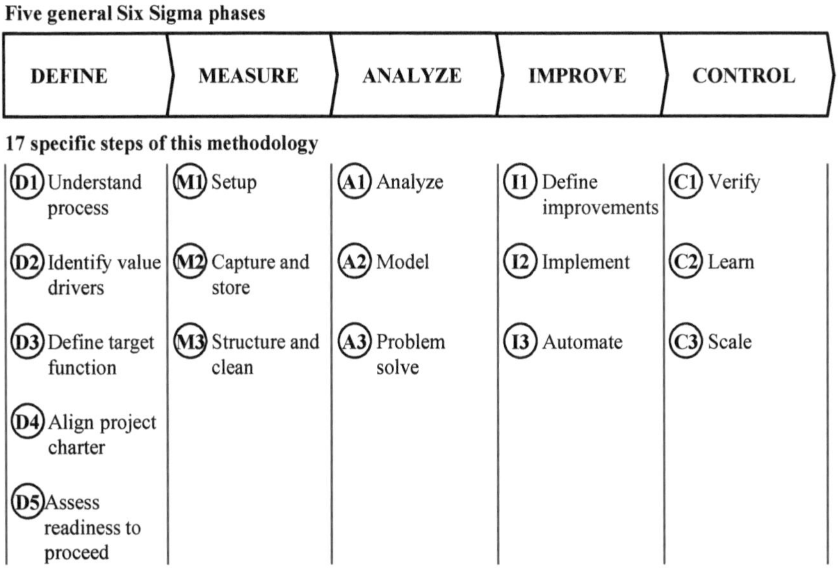


Figure 72: Methodology overview


M. Hammer, *Management Approach for Resource-Productive Operations*, Industrial Management, https://doi.org/10.1007/978-3-658-22939-9_9

## 9.1 Phase 1 – Define

The first phase, Define, is an important fundament and enabler for the subsequent phases. It deals with assessing the starting point and readiness of an organization. It also reviews the business itself and its value drivers to derive the most relevant field of actions.

**D1 Understand Process**

Before starting any optimization effort, as in Lean (chapter 5), it is necessary to understand the process through the involvement of site personnel, walking the shop floor and reviewing available information. A solid understanding will help not only with aspects of optimization, feasibility, but also with change management and organizational alignment. In addition to go & see, helpful Lean Six Sigma tools in this step include value stream mapping, as detailed in the book Learning to See (Rother, Shook 1999), and SIPOC (supplier-input-process-output-customer) (Lunau 2009, p. 34).

Expected results include:
- Process description
- Process flow diagram
- Typical problems and opportunity areas

**D2 Identify Value Drivers**

The concept of value drivers and the underlying theory in management accounting has been reviewed in chapter 4. As concluded as part of RQ1 "applicability" we take a financial optimization focus as given. Therefore the identification of value drivers starts with analyzing the ROIC tree, Figure 73, and for operational management we will exclude the invested capital branch, as this is not an influenceable area in the short term. Looking at profit in further detail, all information leading up to this, i.e. revenue and cost drivers, need to be collected. Understanding the sensitivities and "the Power of 1%" gives insights on value at stake and helps to prioritize. According to Gilchrist, "in most industries, a modest improvement of 1% would contribute significantly to the return on investment of the capital and operational expenses incurred by deploying the Industrial Internet" (Gilchrist 2016, p. 4).

Expected results include:
- Value driver tree for ROIC created
- Value drivers identified and their sensitivities analyzed

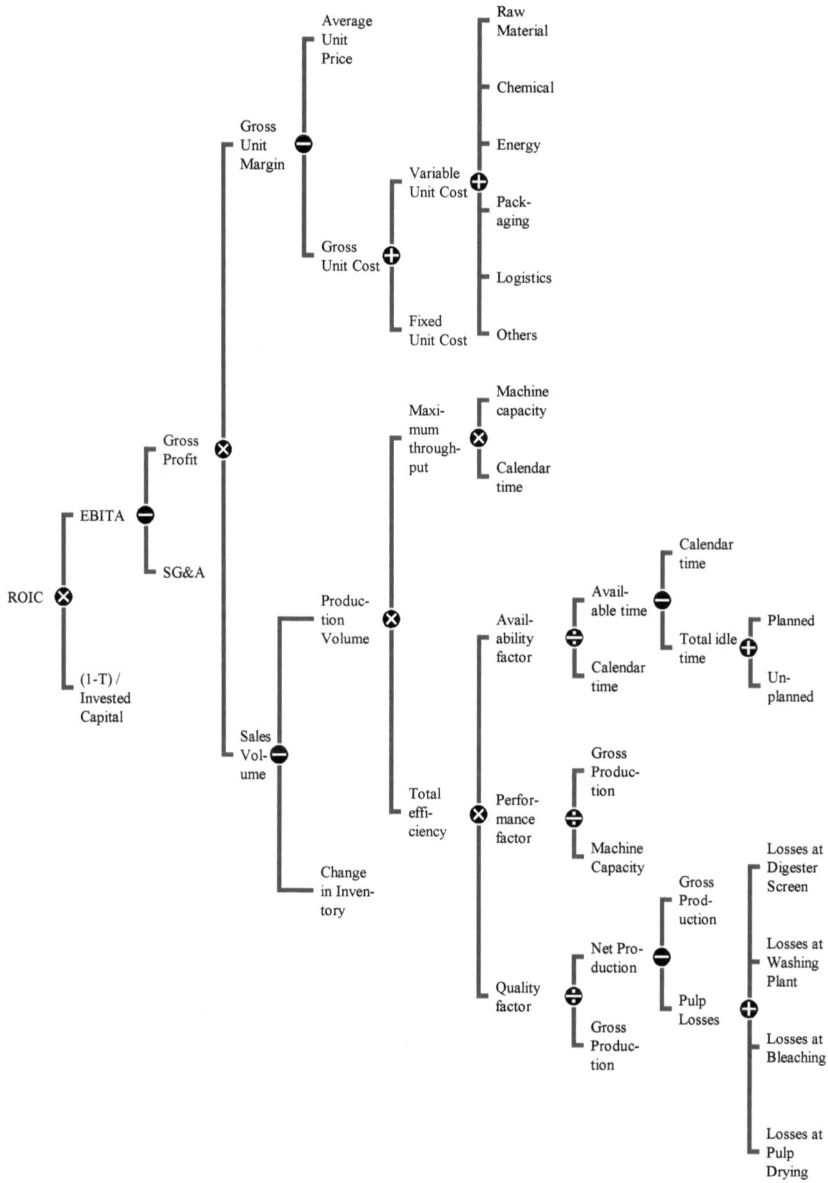


Figure 73: Example ROIC tree for pulp and paper

**D3 Define Target Function**

For optimization purposes a target has to be defined. Classically this would be increasing throughput, maximizing yield, reducing scrap or other cost items. As per the previous discussion in chapter 8, using an overarching profit target, such as profit per hour is the default target and recommended for continuous process manufacturers. However, there might be exceptions and reasons to consider only a sub-set of profit per hour as target. In the cement case of chapter 6, energy consumption at the kiln has been selected as target based on its high sensitivity on profit.

Expected results include:

- Profit per hour function
- Influencing parameters and constraints

**D4 Align Project Charter**

A critical element of preparation is the alignment of stakeholders to a project charter prior to proceeding with further observations, measurements and data analyses.

| | |
|---|---|
| **1. Business Case**<br>Describe the starting situation and emphasize what the project means and its importance. | **2. Problems and Goals**<br>Describe problems and goals the SMART way (Specific, Measurable, Agreed to, Realistic, Time bound). Do not guess causes or propose solutions, but depict the current and target state. Besides the baseline (the basis for savings achieved by the project and the additional turn - over), estimate the monetary benefits of the project (net benefit). |
| **3. Focus and Scope**<br>Which issues are within and which are outside the project scope? What is to be the focus? For the DMAIC approach, which process forms the basis? | **4. Roles and Milestones**<br>Fix the starting date of the project and its duration […], name the involved persons, and determine the resources needed. A separate project schedule for the whole project is required. Further possible components of the project charter are:<br>– Key quality indicators […]<br>– Improvements or project benefits which cannot be calculated in metrics.<br>– Risks that may impede carrying out the project or realizing the full benefit. |

Table 37: Project charter (Lunau 2009, pp. 30–31)

The project charter, Table 37, clarifies the scope, expected impact, roles and discussing it also helps to address concerns upfront, e.g., will automation and advanced process control replace work places.

Expected results include:

- Project charter created and aligned within the organization

**D5 Assess Readiness to Proceed**

A structured maturity questionnaire can be used to identify strengths, weaknesses and potential risks. Walker uses a framework called SIGMA assessing the strategic readiness according to 5 levels, from novice to expert. SIGMA refers to: source of data, innovation, growth mindset, market opportunities, analytics (Walker 2015, p. 264). Similarly, Loshin, also uses a 5 point scale for quantifying organizational readiness. His assessment is based on 5 dimensions: feasibility, reasonability, value, integrability, and sustainability (Loshin 2013, p. 12). Davenport´s Big Data Readiness Assessment Survey, on the other hand, is structured around 6 categories with the abbreviation DELTTA: data, enterprise, leadership, targets, technology and, analytics and data scientists. For each category he defined 5 questions, i.e. a total of 30 questions. Answers should be given in numeric form using a 5 step scale ranging from disagree strongly to agree strongly (Davenport 2014a, pp. 205–209). As part of the proposed methodology, a combination of the aforementioned questionnaires seems most efficient; not only striking a balance between 5 (few) and 30 (many) questions, but also tying the readiness to the DMAIC framework. The result is a set of 18 questions, Table 38, for the 3 phases of measure (data related), analyze (analytics/modelling related), and implement (related to organizational aspects). The proposed dimensions help to assess the readiness of an organization to proceed. Further questions for define and control are not required, as everything that can be measured, analyzed, and implemented naturally can be defined and controlled.

Expected results include:

- Readiness assessment conducted

| # | DMAIC phase | Dimension |
|---|---|---|
| 1 | M | **Sensors for data capture:** Are readings from operations available? What kind of sensors are used? |
| 2 | M | **Coverage of data capture:** To what extent are production parameters captured? |
| 3 | M | **Granularity of measuring:** At what granularity level is the process flow measured? |
| 4 | M | **Data collection:** At what frequency is data stored? |
| 5 | M | **Accuracy of data:** How accurate is the stored data? |
| 6 | M | **Streaming and accessibility of data:** Is data being streamed? How accessible is the stream? |
| 7 | A | **Structural data practices:** How is data structured, stored and accessed? |
| 8 | A | **Data cleaning:** How is data cleaned and blended? |
| 9 | A | **Focus of analysis:** What is the objective function and focus for any analysis and modelling? |
| 10 | A | **Depth of analysis:** What level of dependents are used in the modelling and analysis? How is the element of time taken into account? |
| 11 | A | **Type of modelling used:** How advanced are the modelling techniques? |
| 12 | A | **Degree of automated analysis:** To what degree are the analysis and modelling automated? |
| 13 | I | **Presenting results:** How are the results presented and insights derived? |
| 14 | I | **Leveraging insights for operational decisions:** How is the model output used for operational decision-making? |
| 15 | I | **Leveraging insights for long-term decision-making:** How are insights incorporated into longer term operational strategy, e.g., plant optimization through capital investments? |
| 16 | I | **Capabilities and understanding:** Are in-house capabilities to run advanced analytics and modelling available? |
| 17 | I | **Staff development:** What initiatives are used to increase knowledge and awareness of the possibilities to optimize the production processes? |
| 18 | I | **Objectives and vision:** Are advanced analytics incorporated into the company's strategic vision and culture? |

Table 38: Dimension of readiness assessment

## 9.2 Phase 2 – Measure

### M1 Set Up

In this step the available systems and the data landscape has to be understood. According to Finlay, this includes current decision-making systems, existing meta data, data sources and people working in operational areas (Finlay 2014, pp. 158–159). In addition to knowing what systems exist, e.g., a data lake, and who is using them, insights into available parameters, direct/indirect measurements, and accuracy of sensors are needed.

Expected results include:

- Overview of systems and sources of information
- Parameters recorded

### M2 Capture and Store

This step is about capturing and storing data from the previously identified sources. Typically the first time this is done through collecting a batch of historic data. At a later stage online streaming into a data-lake can be configured. For the first set up a significant period of data needs to be available. A practitioner rule is to collect as much data as possible, but for data in seconds/minutes/hours intervals often 6-24 months of data is sufficient. Be aware that depending on the number of variables, number of systems and time horizon the data download can take several hours. Once the data has been received an immediate backup copy should be made before proceeding to manipulate the data.

Expected results include:

- Raw data from different sources, e.g., process control and ERP systems, collected and stored

### M3 Structure and Clean

Once the data is available it has to be structured and cleaned. At first each data tag has to be classified with source, variable type (e.g., input, output, controllable, disturbance), units, associated process steps and descriptions. Thereafter the matching of time stamps has to be performed to create a consistent data set. A consistency check of the data is conducted to identify missing values, negative values, errors or any other data anomalies. In order to able to structure and clean the data the process, system constraints and major process changes in the period of the investigation need to be well understood.

Expected results include:
- Knowledge of data collection frequency from different sources, missing data, anomalies, and time behavior of the process
- Availability of a structured and clean data set for analyses

## 9.3 Phase 3 – Analyze

**A1 Analyze**

To start with, the variables are analyzed through the means of descriptive analytics tools such as visualization of time-series, identifying trends such as increases, decreases, frequencies, variability and different operating modes. Other visualization tools are for example heat maps and tree maps giving an indication whether parameters are relevant and on or off-target. Descriptive analytics also includes classical statistical analysis such as regressions and also clustering. The aim of all analyses in this step is to develop data-based improvement hypothesis and to quantify the improvement opportunity.

Expected results include:
- Data visualized, analyzed and data sets for modelling prepared
- Key parameters and improvement hypotheses identified

**A2 Model**

For modelling, different data sets are used for training, test and validation. In this step predictive analytics such as decision trees, neural networks or genetic algorithms are applied to mirror the process and predict its behavior, i.e., a digital twin is created, Figure 74. The model serves four purposes: (1) to create a reference based on historic data, (2) to predict the process behavior going forward, (3) to quantify improvements comparing optimized/unoptimized process behavior, and (4) to monitor performance on ongoing basis.

Expected results include:
- Predictive model and optimizer available
- Quantification and explanation of opportunities

**A3 Problem Solve**

After the conclusion of the analyses and modeling steps the site personnel comprised of a cross-functional team of engineers, operators, supervisors and managers start problem solving improvements. Here principles and tools from lean and Six Sigma are applied, such as "go & see" the process, root-cause problem solving using cause-effect diagrams, 5-Why's or FMEA; to understand the current state and designing the future state of the process.

End results include:
- Problem solving workshops conducted
- Understanding of current state and envisioned future state

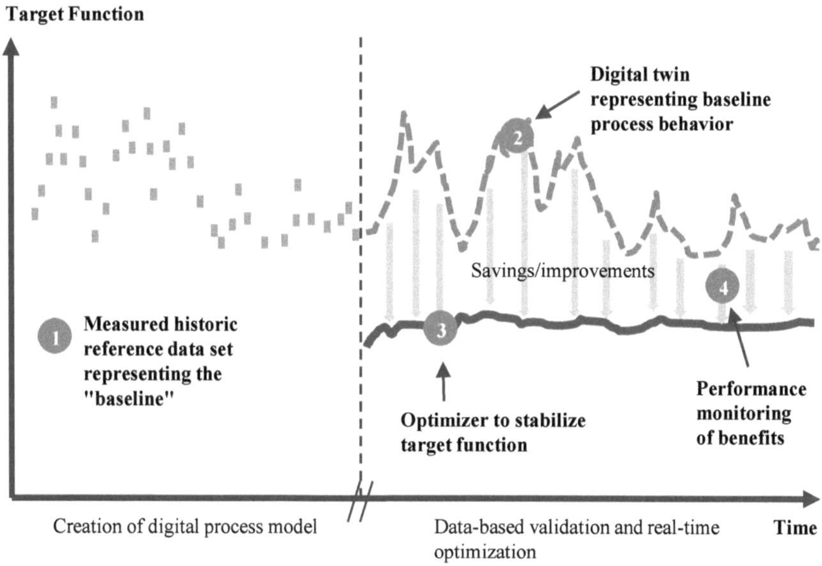


Figure 74: Digital twin as result of modelling and basis for optimization

## 9.4 Phase 4 – Improve

### I1 Define Improvements

The improvements are selected based on problem solving workshops, brainstorming of potential solutions, definition of criteria, prioritization using for example an effort-benefit matrix and evaluation of feasibility.

Expected results include:
- List of improvement measures to bridge the gap between current and future state

**I2 Implement**

It almost goes without saying, that only implemented improvements will deliver benefits. What is important to point out, in line with the lean philosophy discussed in chapter 5.2, is that according to Drew et al, sustainable operational improvements depend on three aspects:

> "(1) Operating system: The way in which assets and resources are configured to deliver value to the customer with minimum losses, (2) Management infrastructure: The management organization, processes and systems required to support and sustain the operating system, and (3) Mindsets and behaviors: The ways of thinking and acting at all levels of the organization that are required to underpin the formal systems and structures" (Drew et al. 2004, p. 17).

One important outcome is the implementation of a profit per hour dashboard, Figure 75, allowing operators and their supervisors to manage the operations through setting leading parameters that minimize profit losses and thus maximize cumulative profits.

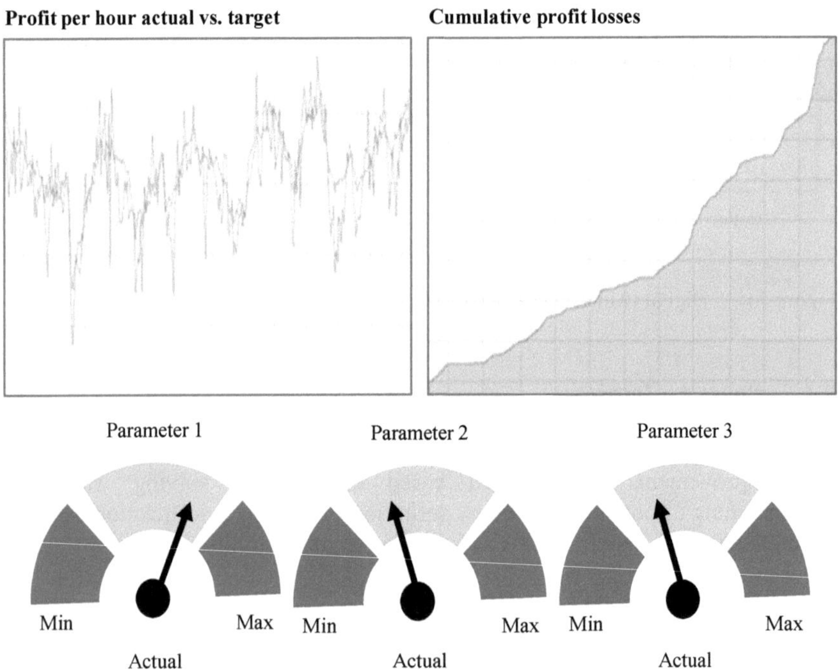


Figure 75: Example of profit per hour dashboard

Expected results include:

- Implementation plan
- Changes of technical, managerial and people related nature
- Dashboard

**I3 Automate**

In this proposed but optional step, decision making is automated, also referred to as closing the loop, based on model predictive control (see chapter 5.3). In certain process industries, for example, power plants or refineries, automatic operations are well-accepted practice. The role of the operators is to supervise the plant and intervene in case of deviations or abnormal conditions. Also, a defined process for updating and continuously improving the controls is required. Next to time-based updates specific triggers such as model accuracy or time in automatic operating mode can be defined.

Expected results include:

- Online optimizer (optional)
- Process for updates and continuous improvement

## 9.5 Phase 5 – Control

The last phase, control, includes the validation of improvement, sustaining measurement systems, process owner transition, the identification of new improvement opportunities, knowledge repository, and celebration (Burton 2011, pp. 293–294). These tasks are grouped into three steps in this section: verify, learn, scale.

**C1 Verify**

The verification step entails both checking the progress of improvement activities (e.g., using a Gantt chart), and the evaluation of realized benefits, (e.g., quantifying the savings based on the dashboard implemented in step I2). Furthermore, the finance and accounting department provides cost savings reports as part of the routine financial reporting cycle.

Expected results include:

- Implementation progress
- Savings

**C2 Learn**

Learning is essential for three reasons: (1) to continuously improve the process in scope of optimization, (2) to roll out optimization efforts to other processes and sites, and (3) to share best-practices in order to become more efficient. Slack & Lewis lay out a double loop learning process, Figure 76.

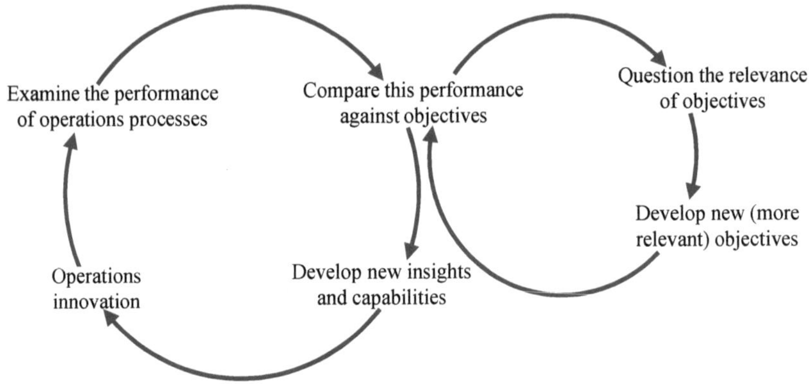


Figure 76: Double-loop learning (Slack, Lewis 2011, p. 331)

In its first loop the framework reviews the optimization results against the predefined objectives, and in its second loop it triggers managers and engineers to step back to review and amend the objectives. Sharing knowledge also requires documenting the process, learning, and results and developing best-practices. These serve to support internal dissemination and as basis for training. Finally, the last step is to fully integrate analytics in the organization and standard business processes. Loshin lays out a series of helpful questions for doing so, covering participants in the process, desired outcomes of the process, available information, knowledge and actionable results delivered by data analytics, additional training needs, and how business processes need to be adjusted (Loshin 2013, pp. 110–111).

Expected results include:

- Documented learning
- Tools and best-practices

**C3 Scale**

The purpose of this last step is to plan and execute the role-out of the improvements and approach at scale. Figure 77 gives a typical example including all sites, grouped by regions and technologies. Sites that have been covered previously are marked with a tick. The rollout logic can be either by region or technology based on the availability of skills, work capacity and value at stake.

Expected results include:

- Roll out plan / opportunities

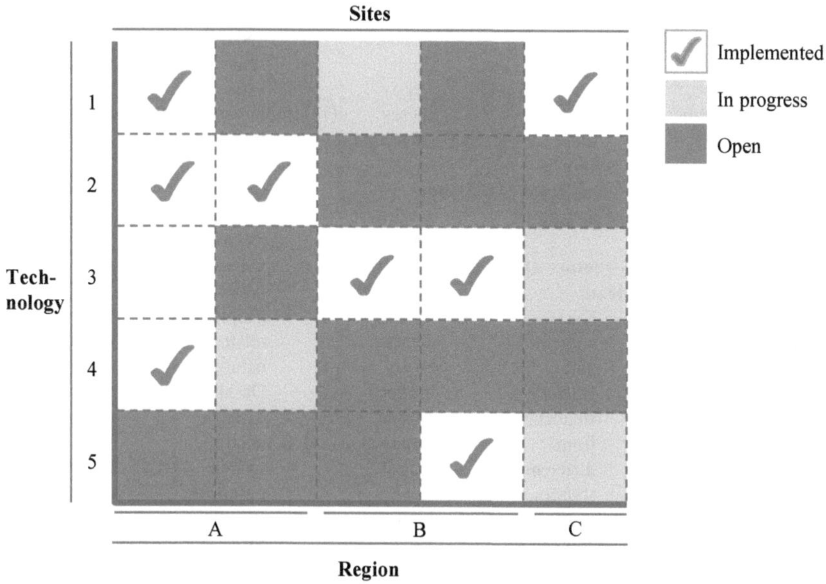


Figure 77: Scale-up matrix with sites, regions and technologies

## 9.6 Summary of Methodology

At the end of chapter 9, Figure 78, summarizes the expected end results of the 17 steps and five phases.

| DEFINE | MEASURE | ANALYZE | IMPROVE | CONTROL |
|---|---|---|---|---|
| **D1 Understand process**<br>▪ Process description<br>▪ Process flow diagram<br>▪ Typical problem and opportunity areas<br><br>**D2 Identify value drivers**<br>▪ Value driver tree for ROIC<br>▪ Sensitivity analysis<br><br>**D3 Define target Function**<br>▪ Profit per hour function<br>▪ Influencing parameters and constraints<br><br>**D4 Align project charter**<br>▪ Project charter<br><br>**D5 Assess readiness to proceed**<br>▪ Readiness assessment checklist | **M1 Setup**<br>▪ Overview of systems and sources of information<br>▪ Parameters recorded<br><br>**M2 Capture and store**<br>▪ Raw data from different sources collected and stored<br><br>**M3 Structure and clean**<br>▪ Knowledge of data collection frequency from different sources, missing data, anomalies, and time behavior of the process<br>▪ Availability of a structured and clean data set for analyses | **A1 Analyze**<br>▪ Data visualized, analyzed and data sets for modelling prepared<br>▪ Key parameters and improvement hypotheses identified<br><br>**A2 Model**<br>▪ Predictive model and optimizer available<br>▪ Quantification and explanation of opportunities<br><br>**A3 Problem solve**<br>▪ Problem solving workshops conducted<br>▪ Understanding of current state and envisioned future state | **I1 Define improvements**<br>▪ List of improvement measures to bridge the gap between current and future state<br><br>**I2 Implement**<br>▪ Implementation plan<br>▪ Changes of technical, managerial and people related nature<br>▪ Dashboard<br><br>**I3 Automate**<br>▪ Online optimizer<br>▪ Process for updates and continuous improvement | **C1 Verify**<br>▪ Implementation progress<br>▪ Savings<br><br>**C2 Learn**<br>▪ Documented learnings<br>▪ Tools and best-practices<br><br>**C3 Scale**<br>▪ Roll out plan / opportunities |

Figure 78: Summary of methodology

# 10 Methodology Validation: Prototypical Application in the Pulp Manufacturing Industry

In this chapter the conceived methodology is validated by taking a case study approach. The research is based again on process industries and deals with pulp manufacturing. It includes insights on the process, examples, and sanitized results.

## 10.1 Context

The aim of this case study is to apply the time-based and analytics-supported operations management approach for profit per hour maximization in the context of pulp manufacturing. The specific aims are to: (1) use profit per hour as operational target metric, (2) confirm that the 17-step methodology outlined along the DMAIC phases works, and (3) summarize the benefits of this approach. This case study has been conducted by the researcher in a sounding board/partner role to an industrial solutions provider serving process industries including the pulp & paper, metals, chemicals, among others. The company operates in more than 40 countries and employs over 25,000 people. One of their offerings is a process optimization platform[30], which has been used for process improvement and automation at a customer site, the scope of this case study. The site is an integrated mill with an annual production of approx. 220,000 tons of pulp and 1 million tons of high quality multi-coated papers used for premium quality publications worldwide. The mill pays a lot of attention to manufacturing excellence and has a long record of continuous improvement. Technical upgrades, such as a recent general rebuild of critical parts of the liquor boiler and recovery plant, contribute positively to the environment as they decrease noise pollution and $NO_X/SO_2$ emissions. Next to very high recycling rates resulting in low raw material losses and less water consumption, all effluents are fully treated before discharge to the river. The mill generates its own electricity from a combined heat and power plant, using a high proportion of renewable fuels. The integrated pulp plant processes

30 The specific process optimization platform is not a pre-requisite for the methodology described in chapter 9.


M. Hammer, *Management Approach for Resource-Productive Operations*,
Industrial Management, https://doi.org/10.1007/978-3-658-22939-9_10

locally harvested wood from sustainable forest (70% sawmill waste, 30% thinnings) and uses total chlorine free (TCF) bleaching technology.

## 10.2 Application

The application of the methodology follows the steps outlined in chapter 9, Figure 78. The results were obtained through a series of working sessions and interviews with the responsible lead engineer from the industrial services company in which the researcher had the role of being the sounding board and partner. Specific interview results, such as the readiness assessments and questions and answers are documented in Appendix A and B respectively.

**D1 Understand Process**

Cellulose pulp is obtained from fibrous materials, taken from wood and non-wood species through a chemical, sulfite based process. Early patents of the process go back to Julius Roth in 1857 and Benjamin Tilghman in 1867 and the operation of the first mill using this process started in Sweden in 1874. It subsequently became the dominant pulp making process in industry, but nowadays accounts for less than 10% due to the rise of the alternative "kraft" process. While the kraft process can handle all species of wood producing stronger pulp, key advantages of sulfite pulping remain easily bleached, bright pulps with high yield (Biermann 1996, pp. 91–92). Pulp making needs to meet multiple objectives, from outstanding product quality, to lowest possible impact on the environment (Sixta 1998, p. 25). The mill in this case study uses a bisulfite process, i.e., a full chemical pulping process with magnesium as base, therefore also referred to as magnefite process (Biermann 1996, p. 95). This modification has comparatively low sensitivity to wood species while keeping yield and brightness high (Sixta 1998, p. 25).

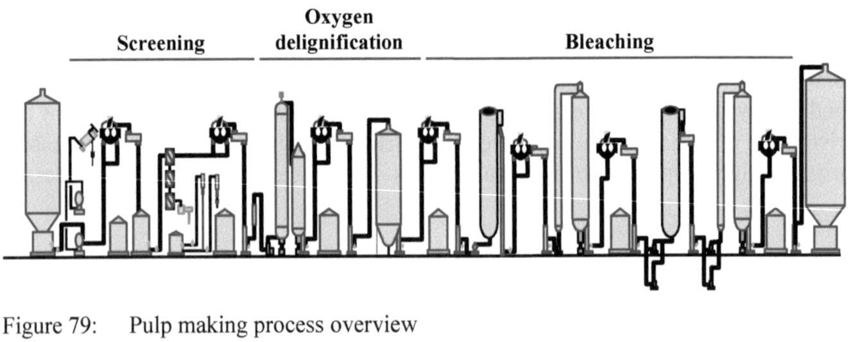


Figure 79: Pulp making process overview

The overall pulp making process is illustrated in Figure 79 and spans from feeding wood chips into the process up until the end of the bleaching plant. This process consists of the pre-treatment of wood chips, cooking, washing, oxygen delignification, screening and bleaching. During the cooking process cellulose fibers from the wood are released and lignin is dissolved. In the subsequent washing step inorganic and organic compounds are sent to the recovery plant, where the chemicals are regenerated for further use as cooking agent. The objective of oxygen delignification is to dissolve the remaining lignin still present maintaining pulp properties such as viscosity. Screening separates uncooked fiber and any contaminants. Finally, bleaching increases the brightness of the pulp to a typical range of 85-90 ISO brightness.

Results:
☑ Process description and process flow diagram available
☑ Process understood
☑ Typical problems and opportunity areas identified

Observations:
Multiple discussions with the engineers required to understand the complex process. Functional expertise is critical at this stage and in line with the focus of process engineers: "There are fewer and fewer process engineers and they focus on domain know-how" (Appendix B).

**D2 Identifying Value Drivers**
As a starting point, the strategic value drivers for the pulp manufacturing site were reviewed and mapped against the hierarchical levels and functionalities of the industrial service providers´ process optimization platform, Figure 80. Based on a qualitative assessment the optimization of production offered a high impact opportunity across levels. A profit per hour value driver tree, Figure 81, for the pulp manufacturing process was developed next and main revenue and cost items were highlighted as per the defined methodology.

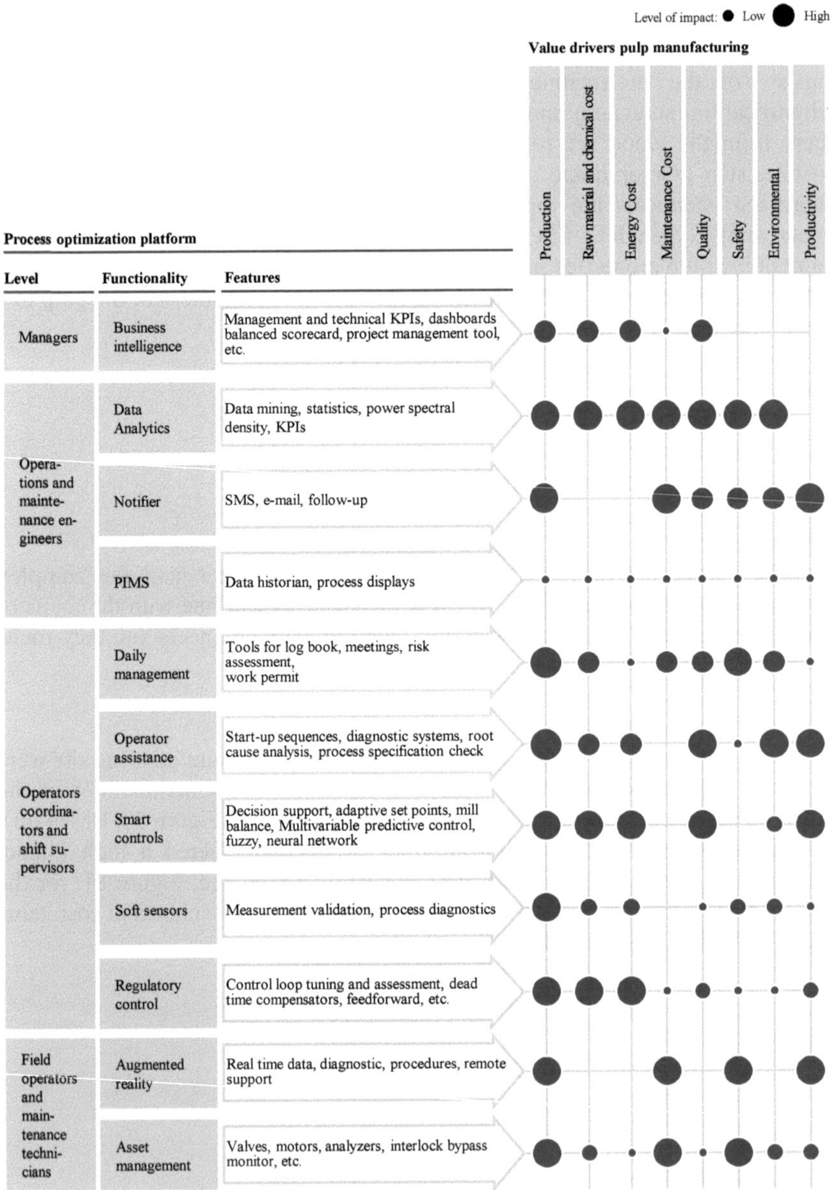


Figure 80: Overview of process optimization functionality and value drivers

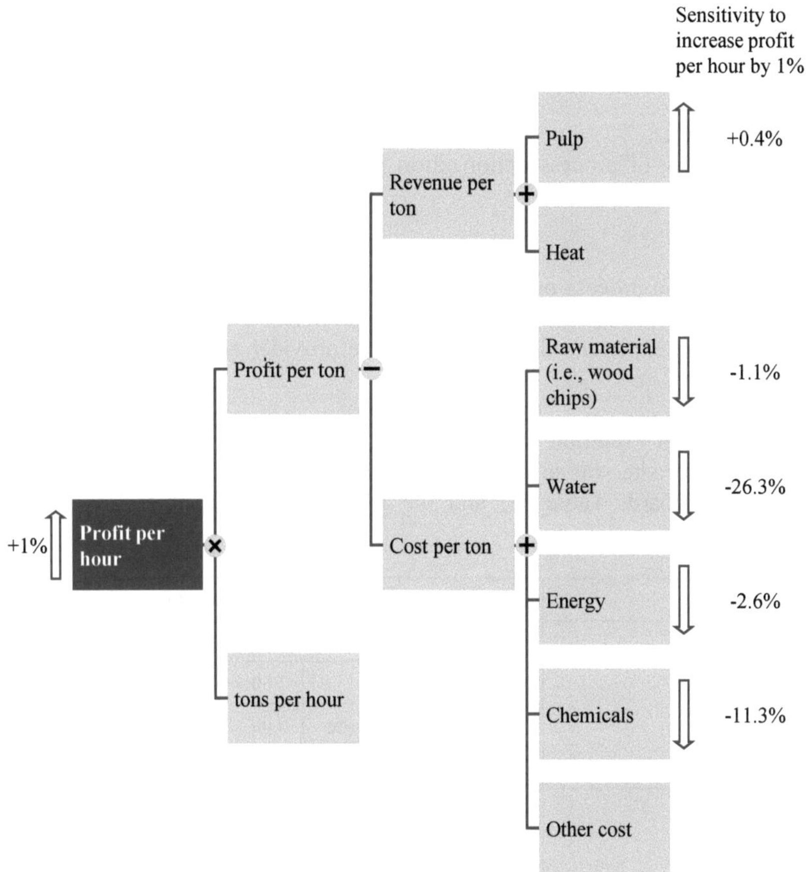


Figure 81: Value driver tree[31]

The elaboration of a profit per hour value driver tree required data on cost, production output, specific consumption per resource, and the market price for cellulose. An analysis of the sensitivities of key parameters to increase profit per hour by 1% was conducted and showed that profit is highly sensitive to changes in pulp revenues, raw materials and energy cost.

31 Excludes cost elements where data was not available, e.g., SO2.

Results:

☑ Value driver tree for ROIC created

☑ Value drivers identified and their sensitivities analyzed

Additional result:

☑ Functionality of process optimization platform understood and mapped to value drivers

Observations:

While the specific process optimization platform used in this case is not a prerequisite, and alternatives exist, it is advantageous in terms of project time and cost to work with an experienced industrial service provider and a proven analytics platform.

**D3 Define Target Function**

The target at the site was to optimize for specific cost per output using a cost optimizer dashboard, Table 39, and the Maximum Sustainable Rate (MSR) concept.

| Area | Raw material | Cost [Euro/ton] |
|---|---|---|
| $O_2$ | $H_2O_2$ | 3.98 |
| | NaOH | 7.60 |
| | Steam medium pressure | 0.00* |
| | $O_2$ | 0.56 |
| EP | $H_2O_2$ | 5.51 |
| | NaOH | 3.26 |
| | Steam low pressure | 0.00* |
| HC | $H_2O_2$ | 4.26 |
| | NaOH | 2.86 |
| | Steam low pressure | 0.00* |
| | $H_2SO_4$ | 0.23 |

* The steam related values show zero as the steam was turned off at the time

Table 39: Cost optimizer

MSR, Figure 82, is a common concept for output optimization and is defined by the top decile production rate in a given time period, e.g., one year. An average rate at 90-91% of MSR, also referred to as efficiency, is considered acceptable, >92 excellent.

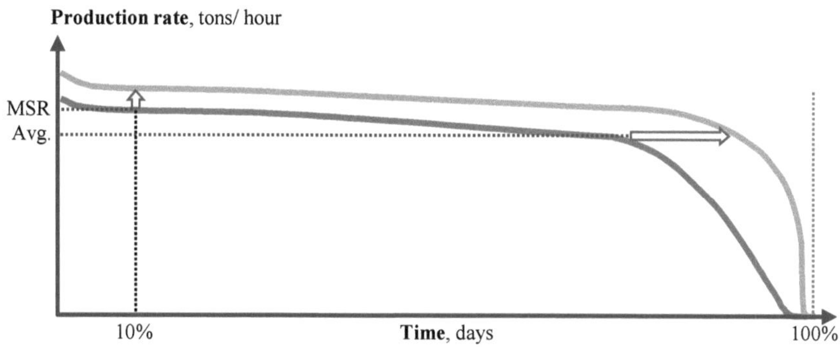


Figure 82: Maximum Sustainable Rate (MSR)

To transition from an output optimization to profit per hour maximization, output in tons/hour and profit/ton was converted to profit contribution per hour, which is shown in Figure 83. The graph contains 4135 hourly profit values from the first calendar half of 2017[32]. A variability with a relative standard deviation of 13% can be observed. Taking the gap between the actual profit per hour values and the top decile as a point of orientation, profit losses in the order of 10.3% became visible and presented an opportunity for improvement. Specific losses from varying operating modes became apparent through steeper slopes in the cumulative profit loss chart, Figure 84. For example, the circle highlights a technical problem in evaporation leading to less chemicals and less acid in the recovery and the digester, and resulting ultimately in reduced throughput and increased profit losses.

Results:
☑ Profit per hour calculated
☑ Influencing parameters and constraints known

32 The remaining 245 values were excluded, either as they represented outliers, referred to non-production periods or as no readings were available.

Observations:
"The approach is suitable for continuous operations for integrated optimization of cost and production", and "the key strength is the clear link to the end goal of generating profits"(Appendix B).

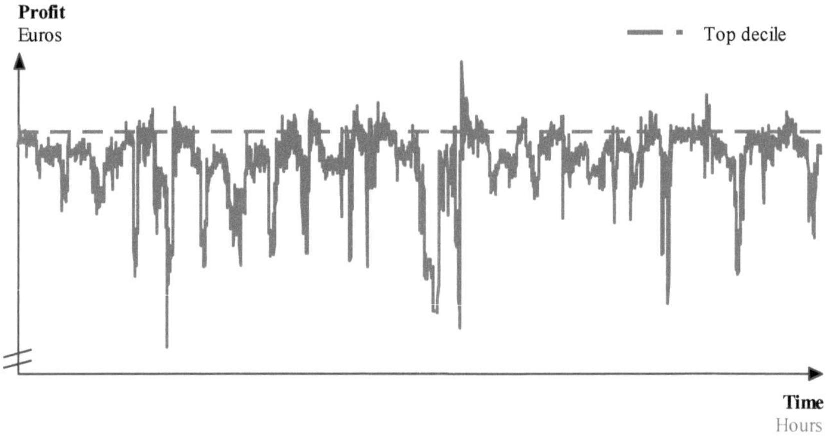


Figure 83: Profit per hour

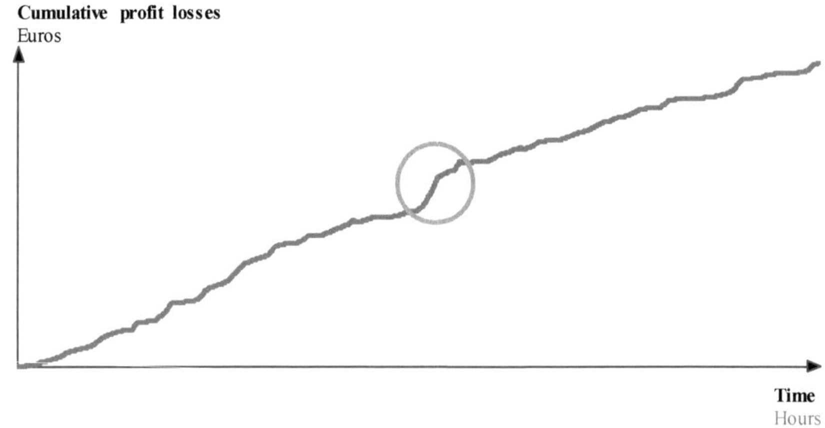


Figure 84: Cumulative profit losses compared to the top-decile

**D4 Project Charter**

A structured project charter was made available electronically to the team and its stakeholders. It includes the definition of the project, customer expectations, economic analysis, risks, stakeholders, assumptions, constraints, goals in the initiation phase. Furthermore, the project charter helps with planning, executing, measuring & controlling, and closing, Figure 85.

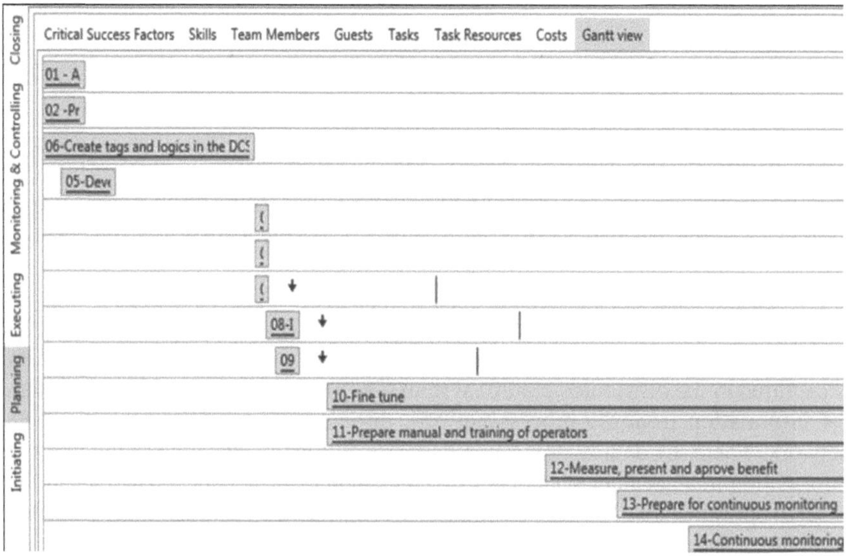


Figure 85: Project charter

Results:

☑ Project charter available and aligned within the organization

Observations:

The project charter needs to be iterated and partially adapted over time. The team comprised personnel from the industrial services provider (process optimization specialist supported by data scientists) and from the manufacturer (project manager, process engineers, automation specialist, financial controller, and department/mill manager).

**D5 Readiness**

Before executing the project the assessment of pre-conditions was done. First, the economic evaluation was performed, e.g. payback of implementing a process optimization platform. Secondly, technical requirements were discussed, e.g., the topology of network, interface and server configuration, hardware, software licenses, remote and local access rights, tag list, etc. Furthermore, the developed readiness assessment was applied, the results of which are summarized in Appendix A.

Results:

☑ Readiness assessment performed

Observations:

The questions cover a good mix of technical and organizational elements. "New tools, such as the gap analysis and the readiness assessment are useful" (Appendix B).

**M1 Setup**

Figure 86 provides an overview of the systems and network topology. Process data is captured in the distributed control system (DCS) and an OPC A server transfers the information from the process network through a firewall to the mill office network. There the data is stored in a database and made available to the process information management system (PIMS), decision making expert (DME) and the process optimization platform. The platform can be accessed on site through office computers and mobile or augmented reality devices. Furthermore, there is an option for remote support through the internet secured by firewalls and virtual private networks (VPN). At the mill in scope the process optimization systems do not currently interact with other systems such as ERP systems. At other sites interfaces exist to enable risk-based maintenance and servicing contracts to be performed.

Results:

☑ Overview of systems available

☑ Sources of information and recorded parameters understood

Observations:

Not all interfaces are in place at the start and creating them takes effort, e.g., link to ERP systems. High concern about cyber-security and provision of remote access to data systems.

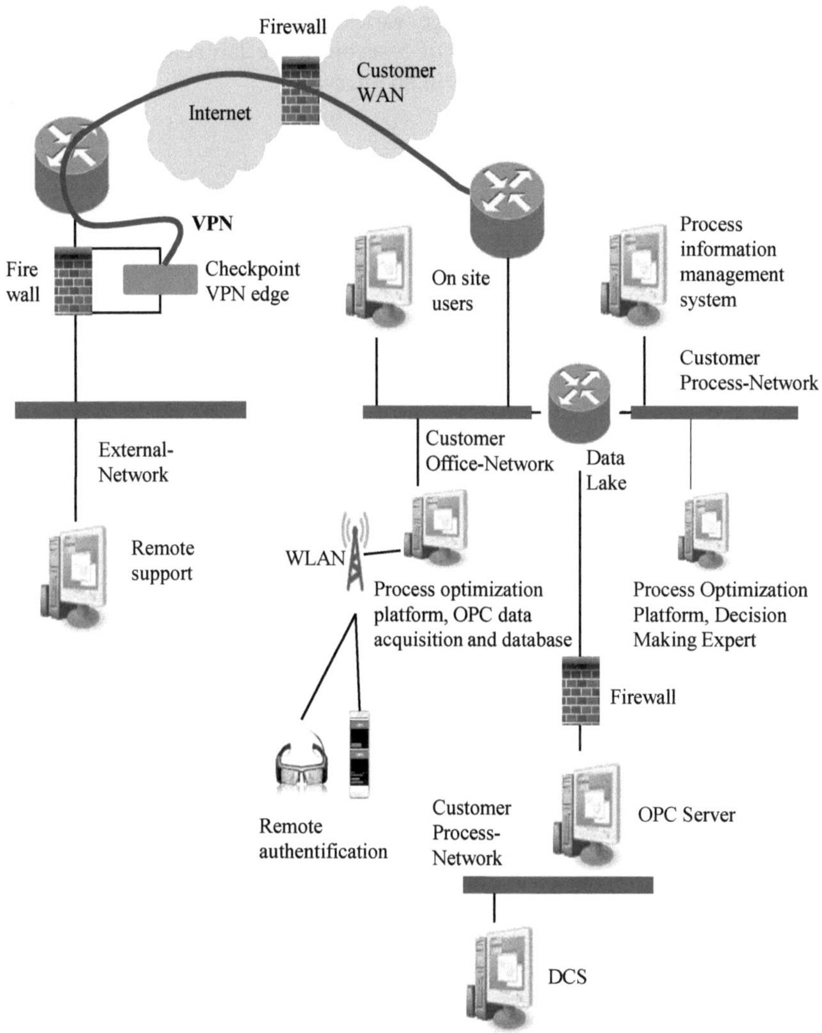


Figure 86: Systems overview

**M2 Capture and Store**
In this phase all available tags, i.e. approx. 3,000 parameters, from the distributed control system (DCS) were captured. Further data, such as laboratory information regarding quality, alarms or operator inputs were also included in the data lake.

The frequency of capture and storage varies by source. While DCS data is collected typically in short intervals of 5 seconds, the lab results available are available only at the end of shifts, i.e. in 8h intervals.

Results:

☑ Raw data from different sources collected and stored

Observations:

Seamless data capture available in this process. A data lake capable to handling real-time data streams from various OT/IT systems is useful.

**M3 Structure and Clean**

There is a defined process for the identification and removal of duplicates and outliers, and for interpolation, aggregation and shifting of data to match time stamps. This is required to correct for varying frequencies of data capture and retention times in the process.

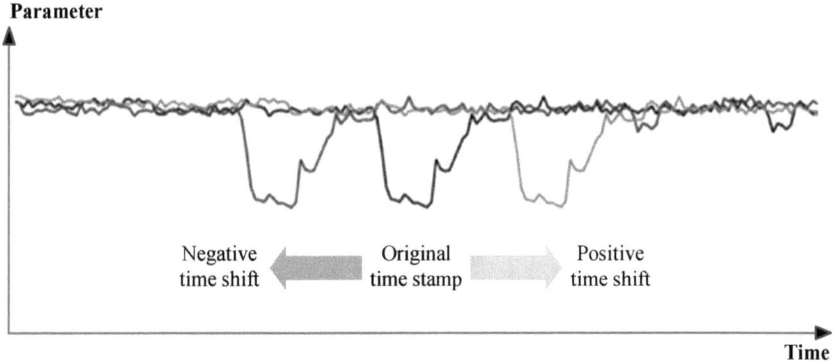


Figure 87: Shifting of data to match time stamps

The time shifting of parameters, Figure 87, is typically done manually and the shift remains fixed. There is an opportunity to make it variable, as a function of production output, going forward.

Results:

☑ Knowledge of data collection frequency from difference sources, missing data, anomalies, and time behavior of the process acquired

☑ A structured and clean data set for analysis is available

Observations:
The automation of data cleaning procedures including time stamping and dead time correction is a critical feature.

**A1 Analyze**
Common process measures in pulp making are the kappa number, a measure of the lignin content of pulp important in the delignification process (Biermann 1996, p. 72), and brightness, a measure of the whiteness on a percentage scale (Biermann 1996, p. 123). Kappa can be tied to the raw materials yield/cost and brightness effects mainly the chemicals cost. Further parameters are the pH-level, temperature and consistency that should remain constant within the limits.

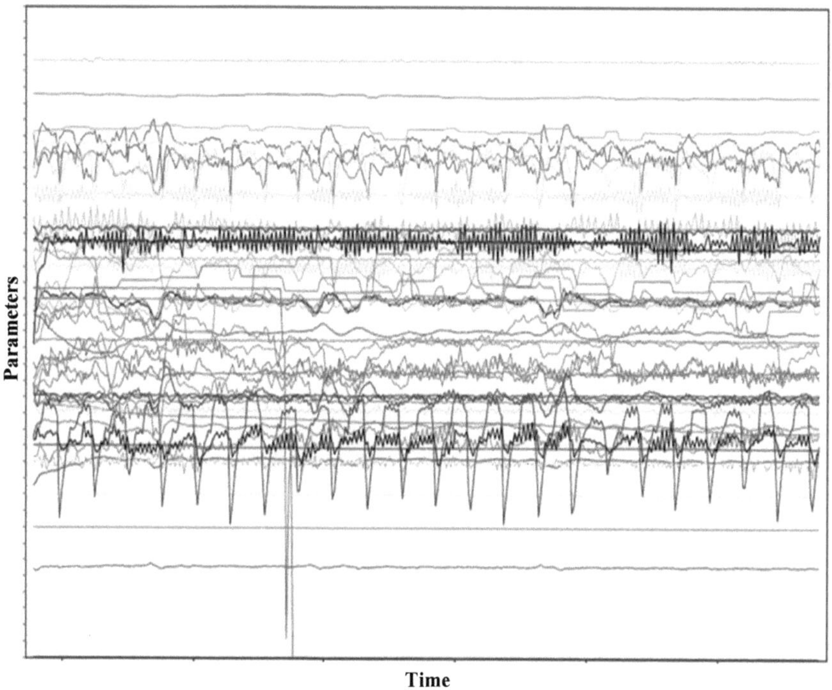


Figure 88: Visualization of trends in the bleaching process

Basic analysis included visualizing trends and checking if parameters stay within the defined upper and lower control limits. Figure 88 includes, among others, parameters on brightness, steam, oxygen, and throughput. Analyses can show increasing trends, decreasing trends, stability, variability, frequencies and different operating modes. Through the use of heat maps correlations were found and investigated. Figure 89 shows a high correlation between quantities of NaOH, a base with pH >7, and $H_2O_2$, an acid with pH <7. A good correlation between the two parameters helps to achieve a stable pH-level in the overall process.

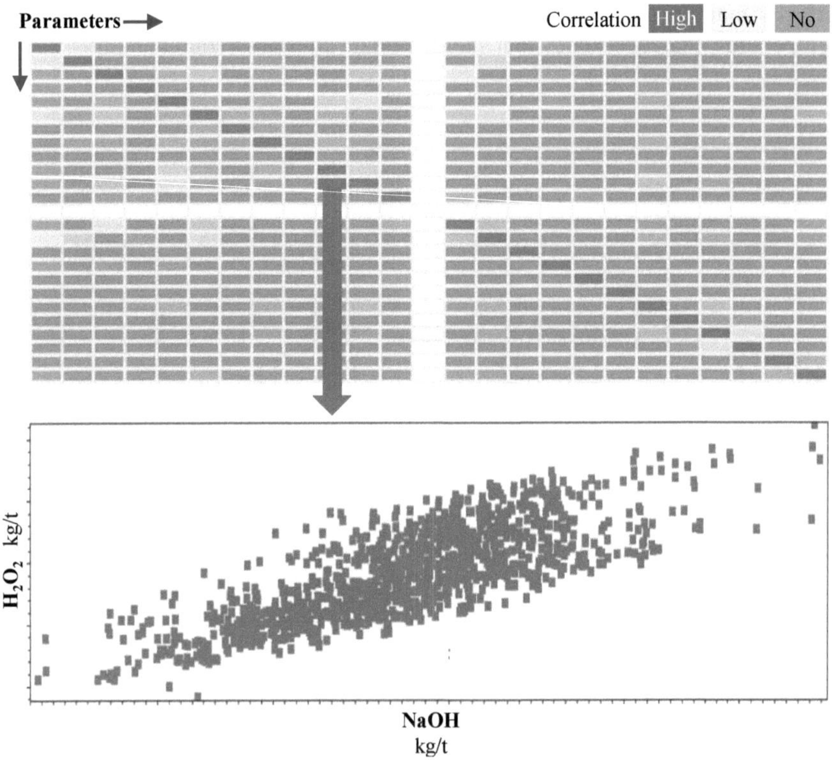


Figure 89: Heat map Fiberline

Next to heat maps there are tree maps, Figure 90, visualizing parameters with respect to their specification. For each one of the 5 departments shown, i.e., washing, $O_2$ bleaching, bleaching, cooking and screening, the parameters are represented by size of importance and by color with respect to their target range.

The tools covered so far help with data visualization and feature selection, i.e., the reduction of parameters to focus on in subsequent steps.

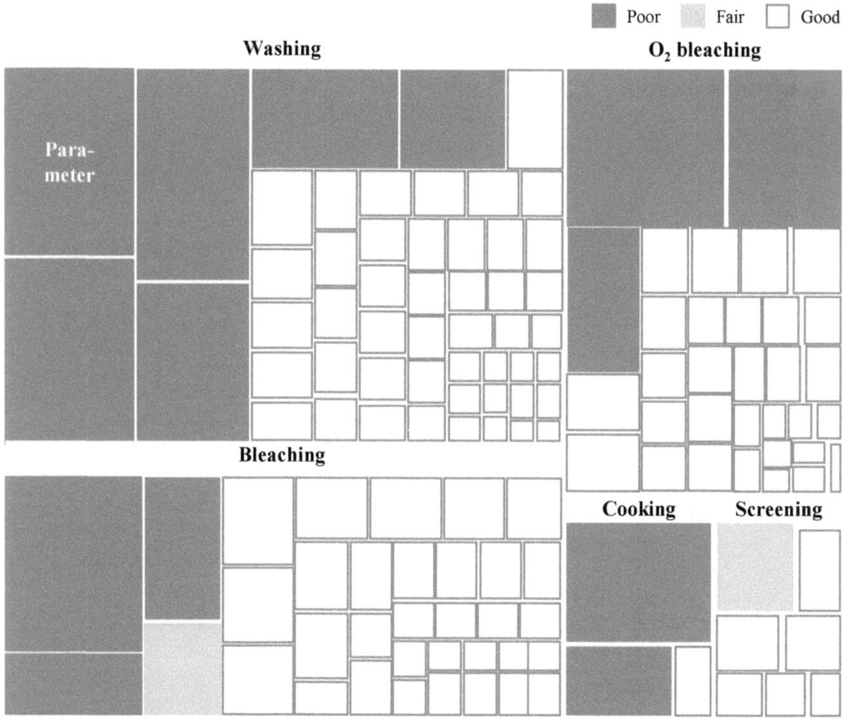


Figure 90: Tree map

Performing a cluster analysis, Figure 91, resulted in the identification of the best and worst parameters based on the average and spread of the middle two quartiles in the boxplots. By comparing the top 5 good/bad parameters improvement ideas for delignification efficiency were derived. For example, increasing the level of consistency and narrowing its variation from 2.9-3.2% to 3.2-3.3% through better discharge control.

Results:
☑ Data visualized, analyzed and data sets for modelling prepared
☑ Key parameters and improvement hypotheses identified

Observations:
The process optimization platform covers a wide range of analysis capability, not all functions were used as part of this project. "Most of our clients do not have or use machine/deep learning algorithms yet" (Appendix B).

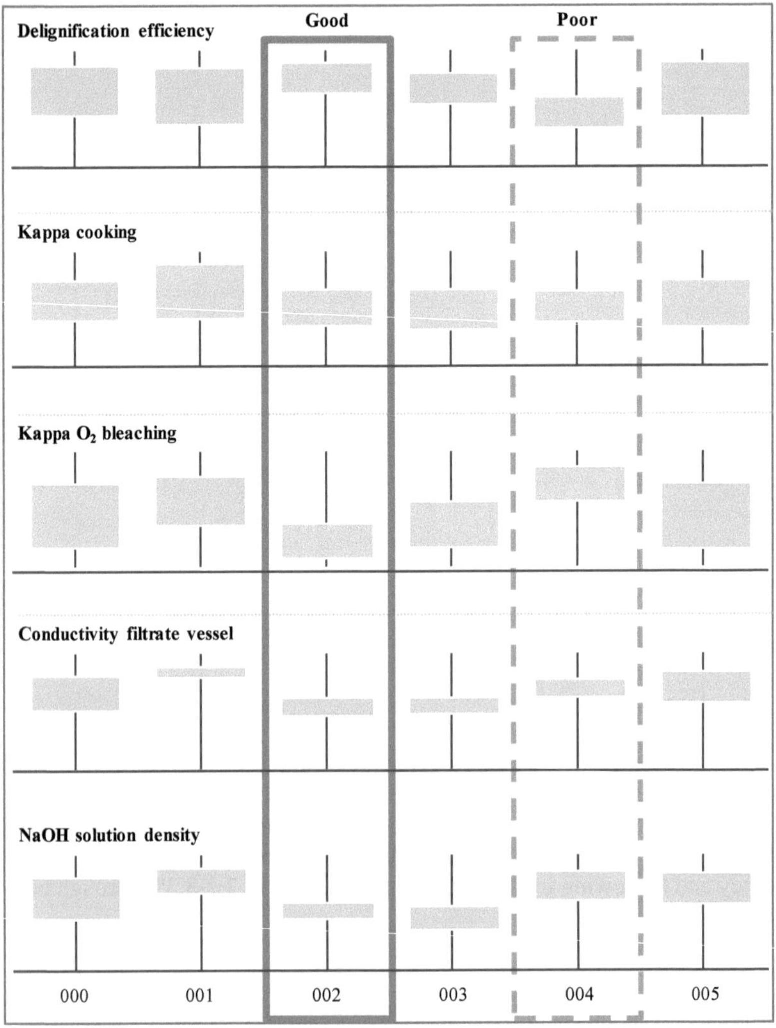


Figure 91: Cluster analysis

**A2 Model**

The focus for modelling were the 15 parameters influencing brightness. Data for 2 months in 5 second intervals represented an initial dataset comprised of around 15 million data points. In the model phase a predictive decision tree based model was built for acid pH in the delignification process with an accuracy of an $R^2$ of 0.89. Figure 92 shows the good fit of the model illustrating the actual values and the model values.

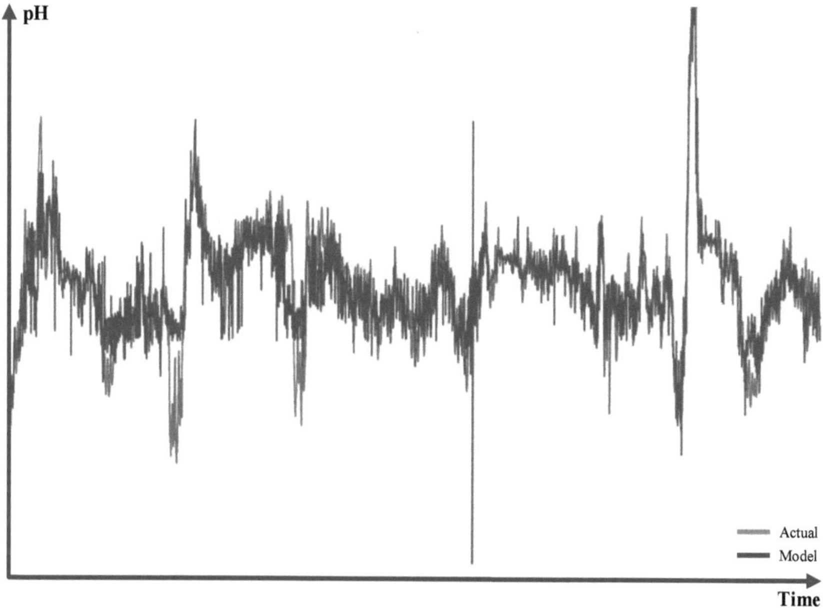


Figure 92: Predictive model for acid pH

Results:

☑ Predictive model and optimizer available
☑ Quantification and explanation of opportunities available

Observations:

In this case the analytics skills were not available internally in the pulp plant. "Often external providers are brought in to provide help with data analytics (Appendix B). The predictive models developed by the industrial service provider reached a high accuracy and good fit.

**A3 Problem Solve**

Daily interactions with operators and weekly working sessions with the process specialists were conducted by the industrial service provider to review specific process steps, such as delignification, cooking or the bleaching process. For the delignification process optimization of the 3 main controls were reviewed: (1) pH control of the pulp to the reactor changing the $H_2O_2$ dosage, (2) kappa control through adjusting the oxygen dosage, and (3) brightness control in alignment with kappa control also adapting $H_2O_2$. For the cooking process, where digester gas passes through chemical recovery, the discussions centered on discharge control. There are 7 digesters and around 20 discharges per day in total. Approx. every 70 minutes a digester is discharged and pressure drops from 7 to 2.5 bars. This also leads to variation in pH and $SO_2$ concentration. The aim was to predict the flow of strong gas to the chemical recovery process. Increasing strong gas correlates with lower pH and raising $SO_2$ levels. A control for the pH was developed using the predictive model from the strong gas flow.

Results:

☑ Problem solving workshops conducted

☑ Understanding of current state and envisioned future state

Observations:

"People need to be convinced and trained" (Appendix B). Aspects like this one underline that change management is crucial. Practices from lean and Six Sigma can be leveraged.

**I1 Define Improvements**

In this step a list of improvements was created. For delignification, as a first example, an improvement opportunity was identified through the application of clustering: a reduction of chemicals through improved process control while maintaining kappa and brightness specifications. A second improvement example, an opportunity to improve consistency by reducing the consumption of cold liquor, was recognized through the use of a decision tree based model of the cooking process. The solution was the design of a new discharge model.

Results:

☑ List of improvement measures to bridge the gap between current and future state available

Observations:
Interdependencies are considered through the common profit target KPI. "The approach helps as it is holistic and avoids shifting costs within the process, i.e., the savings in one don´t lead to higher costs in another" (Appendix B).

**I2 Implement**
Three improvements were implemented: a) advanced process control in delignification, b) new discharge control and c) target value prediction for $SO_2$.

a) The process control improvements for kappa in delignification are illustrated in Figure 93. The advanced process controls can be set to auto or manual modes. Furthermore, target values can be set by operators locally, automatically calculated internally or received from an external system, e.g. upper level control.

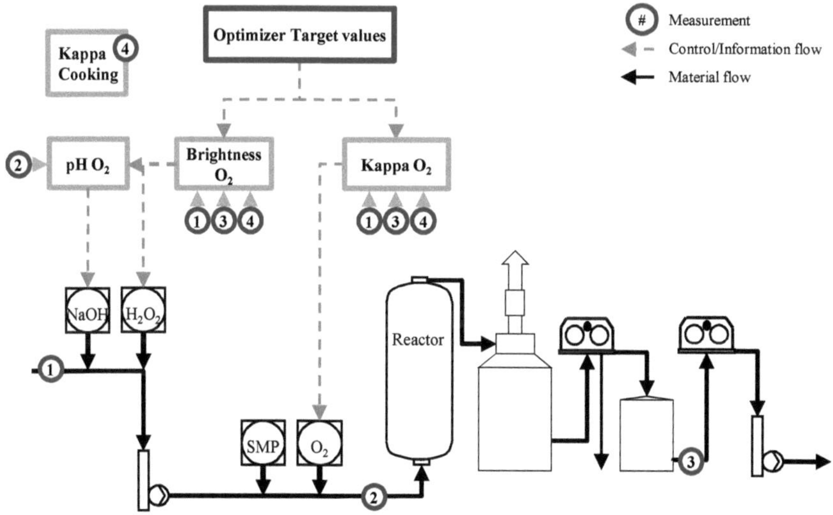


Figure 93: Advanced process control diagram for delignification

b) New discharge control, Figure 94: The improved flow control of the discharge flow leads to reduced production losses, i.e. remaining pulp in digester after discharge; and less disturbance in consistency in the fiberline with positive effects on pulp quality.

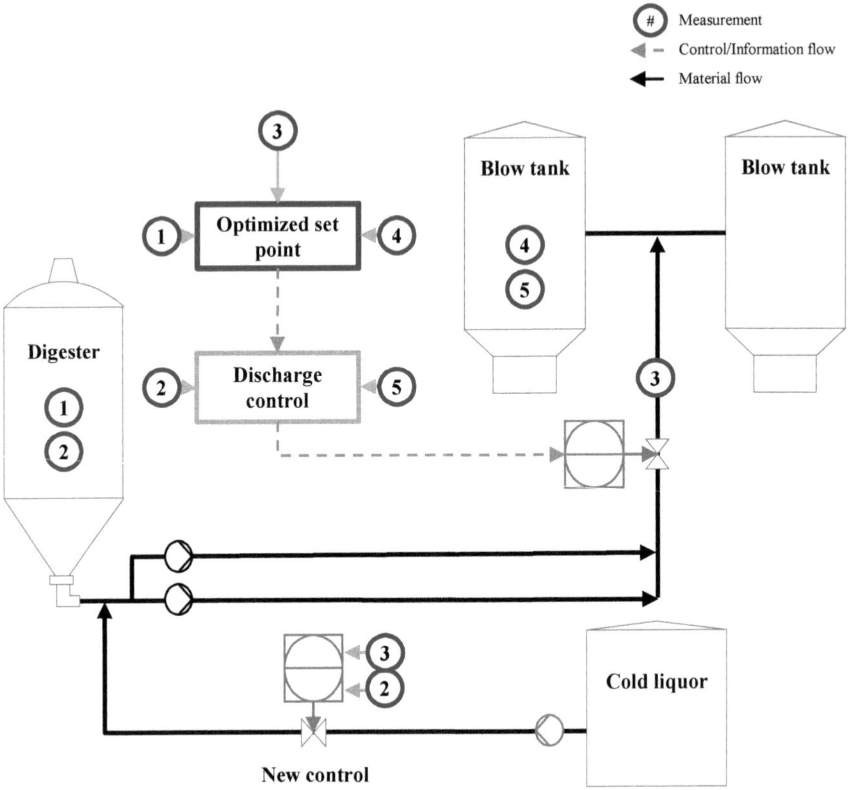


Figure 94: Discharge control diagram

c) Target value prediction for $SO_2$: The predictive model, as shown in Figure 92, helps to reduce the variability in pH and variability of kappa in cooking.

For all three improvements the deliverables are an operator manual and documentation explaining how the process controls work including risks and benefits, training, and onsite support during the initial phases. From a performance management point of view, all input/output measures are displayed in a dashboard, see Figure 95. The deviations shown in Kappa $O_2$ and conductivity in vessel 3 were due to a technical problem in the washing press. In addition to that, a further indicator measuring the time in auto-control mode was implemented.

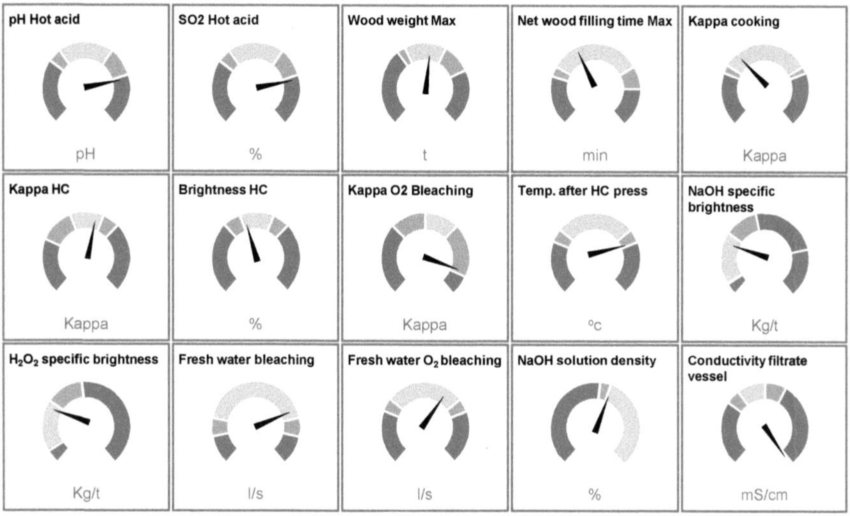


Figure 95: Dashboard

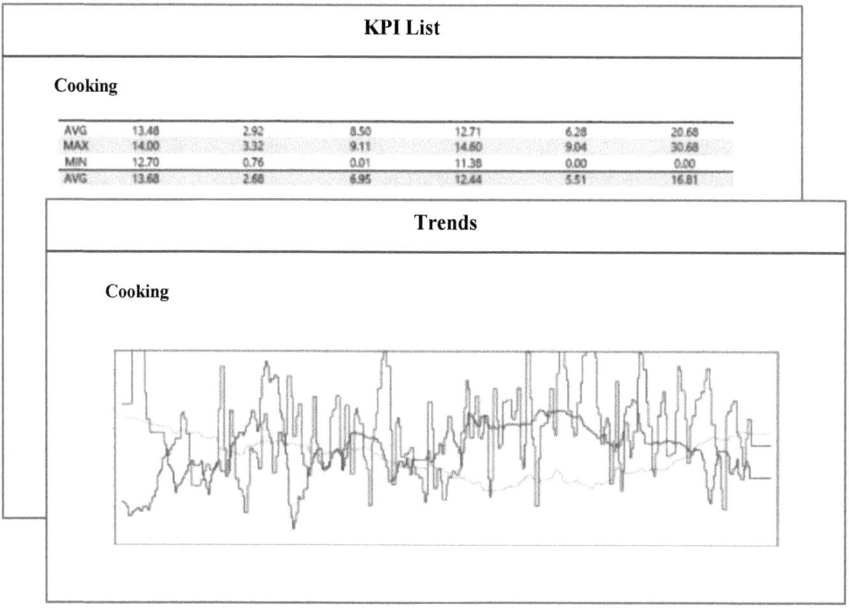


Figure 96: Extract of shift report

The shift reports summarizing the performance are made available electronically and an extract for cooking is shown in Figure 96.

Results:

☑ Implementation plan
☑ Changes of technical, managerial and people related nature
☑ Dashboard

Observations:
The previous steps resulted in a deep understanding of the process and the sensitivity of parameters with respect to profit and facilitated the design of the dashboard.

**I3 Automate**
An online optimized, model predictive control was configured, Figure 97. The target is to optimize the delignification process through optimal brightness in $O_2$ bleaching. The model is regularly checked, e.g., once per quarter, and when necessary tuned, for example, when the model usage drops below 70%. In the case of deviation the system automatically generates a report email which is sent to the process or maintenance engineers.

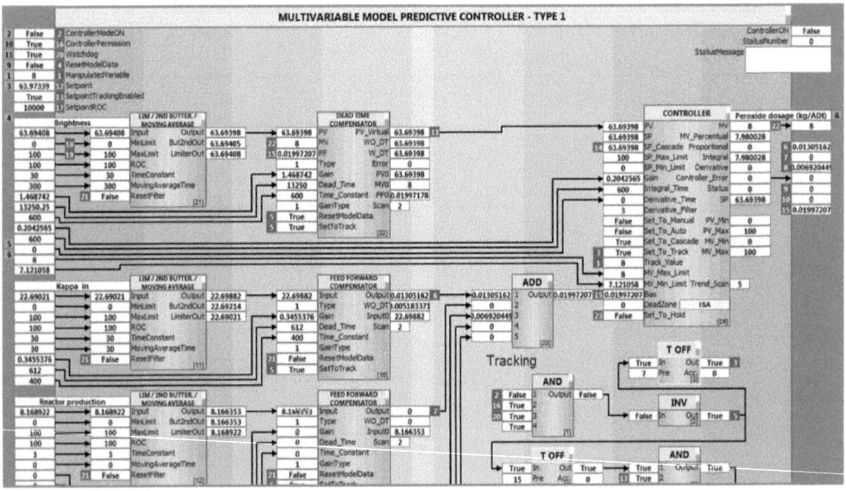


Figure 97: Model Predictive Control for $O_2$ bleaching

Results:

☑ Online optimizer installed

☑ Process for updates and continuous improvement implemented

Observations:

While the full automation of control based on MPC is optional, it delivers better results. Trust from operators and managers into the model has to be gained first.

**C1 Verify**

The benefits of the three specific improvement initiatives are reviewed in Table 40 and resulted in a profit per hour increase of approx. 1-2%. Further process improvements will be initiated to tackle the additional profit losses identified.

| Initiative | Status | Savings |
|---|---|---|
| Chemicals reduction | Implemented | 3.7 % NaOH, 1.6% $H_2O_2$ |
| Discharge control | Implemented | 6.7 % energy savings at a specific equipment in the digester |
| $SO_2$ concentration | Ongoing | To be quantified after implementation |

Table 40: Status of initiatives

Results:

☑ Implementation progress assessed

☑ Savings quantified

Observations:

The help of the accounting department is essential to establish the baseline, quantify the benefits, and verify the sustainability of improvement results.

**C2 Learn**

Learning from implementation is captured in the logbook and a project summary is shared in the format of a 1-page minute. Details such as the operator manual, project documentation and analysis are distributed on demand within the global team. The industrial service provider also uses a global knowledge sharing and skills management tool. Additional insights from the structured interviews about the application of the methodology and time-based profit KPI are included in Appendix B.

Results:
☑ Learning documented
☑ Tools and best-practices available

Observations:
"Large sites have processes for topics such as improvement, innovation, idea generation and problem solving [...]. What is lacking is demonstrating the importance of change top-down by management" (Appendix B).

**C3 Scale**
For scaling the process optimization opportunities across sites, regions and business areas a matrix is used, Figure 98, that indicates which operations have been already covered and which ones are to be tackled next.

Results:
☑ Roll out plan / opportunities

Observations:
The roll-out speed and sequence is not only determined by the expected value at stake and time to capture, but is also heavily influenced by available resources and local knowledge.

## 10.3 Conclusion

What has been found is that the methodology works and that profit per hour is a useful target control metric. Significant improvement opportunities surfaced through the data and analytics based profit investigation. The process optimization platform providing the capability for data analytics and process control supported three specific improvement initiatives, of which two have been concluded with measured benefits. Both the structured methodology and the profit per hour concept are planned to be used by the industrial services provider in the future and be part of the rollout.

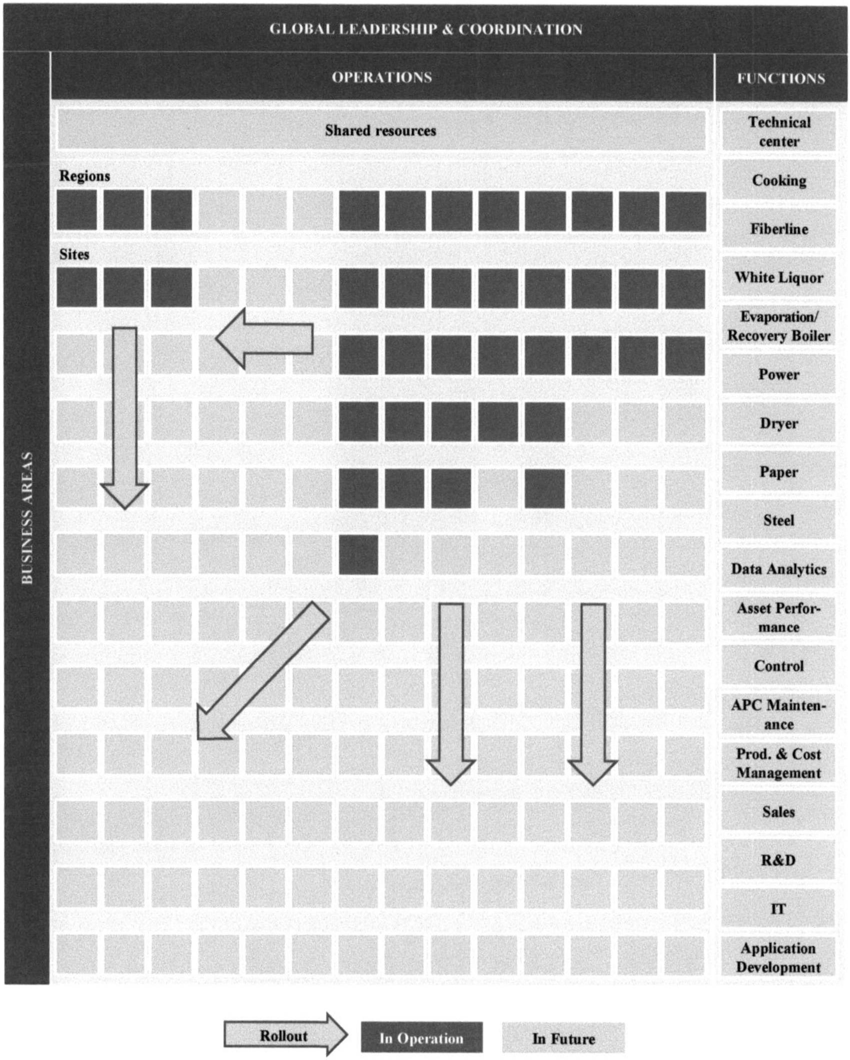


Figure 98: Roll-out opportunities

# 11 Conclusion

In this closing chapter, section 11.1 summarizes the results, section 11.2 discusses the findings, in the light of the research objectives and questions in chapter 1, and section 11.3 provides an outlook on future research needs.

## 11.1 Summary

Chapter 1 introduced the context and challenges industrial companies are currently facing. This includes high external volatility, competitive pressures and technological disruption. The last of these, under the theme of digitization, however also presents opportunities such as the use of Big Data and analytics for improved decision making in operations management, and increasing profits through a time-based profit metric. The chapter defined the research objectives, questions and laid out an application oriented research design. It concluded with the heuristic used for the theory and related work in the subsequent chapters. Chapter 2 looked at the megatrends and current challenges in industry, in particular manufacturing in process industries. Increasing volatility, uncertainty, complexity and ambiguity present significant challenges and opportunities to adopt agility and leverage digital technologies. Chapter 3 summarized the relevant aspects of digitization, the broader trends of Industry 4.0 and the Industrial Internet of Things, and Big Data and advanced analytics specifically. Chapter 4 considered the management perspective and discussed fact based decision making using performance measures, performance management and decision support systems. The key outcome is a profit orientation which links profit rate as a leading indicator with ROIC as a lagging indicator using value driver tree logic. Chapter 5 defined resource-productive operations and the contribution of operational improvement methods, in particular, lean, six sigma, the theory of constraints, agility, and advanced process control systems. Elements of all approaches fed into the resulting methodology of this work. Chapter 6 contributed learning from practice through case studies in cement and ammonia, both process industries. Chapter 7 provided an interim conclusion based on theory and practice. It framed the scope of work, specific requirements and its delimitation. Chapter 8 conceived the theoretical framework for an analytics and time based profit management approach, defined criteria for when it is meaningful, and derived pre-conditions to


M. Hammer, *Management Approach for Resource-Productive Operations*,
Industrial Management, https://doi.org/10.1007/978-3-658-22939-9_11

be in place prior to implementation. Important concepts in the areas of systems thinking, e.g. value drivers, limits and boundaries; and in the area of operational improvement were reviewed. The chapter closed with the choice of DMAIC phases for the methodology. Chapter 9 laid out the details of the implementation methodology along 17 steps including the expected end results for each one. Chapter 10 presented a third and final industrial application case study as a validation of the methodology. The criteria and pre-conditions defined in chapter 7 were met in the case of pulp manufacturing. Chapter 11 concludes this work with this summary, discussion and outlook.

## 11.2 Discussion

This thesis, "Achieving resource-productive operations through a time-based and analytics-supported operations management approach – Design of a structured implementation methodology based on Six Sigma to maximize profits", set itself four objectives at the outset: (1) the identification of criteria for this approach; (2) the identification of pre-conditions; (3) the conception of a methodology for implementation; and (4) its validation. Based on these objectives, three research questions were formulated and elaborated on in this work: RQ1 (Under what conditions does a profit per hour management approach help to take the best available decisions? When does it fail?) was answered in the course of chapter 8 (Methodology conception) and Appendix B. RQ2 (In practice, what keeps companies from implementing a profit per hour approach? What are the pre-conditions and why?) was discussed as part of the empiric research in chapters 6 and 10 (Learning from practice, Methodology validation), chapter 8 (Methodology conception) and Appendix B (Pulp manufacturing case study – interview questions and answers). RQ3 (How would companies implement a profit per hour operations management approach?) was dealt with in chapter 9 (Methodology) and chapter 10 (Methodology validation). In conclusion it can be said that the research objectives have been met and the research questions were able to be answered.

As the three different case studies in the process industries revealed, the structured methodology conceived for analytics-supported optimization with a profit rate focus is both feasible and highly relevant. It meets the current requirements found during the theoretical and practical investigation of this work, as summarized in chapter 7: (1) Helping manufacturers cope with the VUCA context through an operations improvement approach, that is generically applicable in process industries, independent from sector, location or plant size; that is built upon a structured implementation methodology; compatible with a well-known improvement approach; practical, requiring minimum complexity and effort; and delivers sustainable results through the integration of technical, managerial, people aspects; (2) focusing on time-based profit as a leading operational KPI, linking the operations and management level using a ROIC-based value driver tree; and maximizing cumulative profits as an overarching goal; and (3) leveraging digital technologies, consolidating data from various data sources with consistent time stamps, using predictive and prescriptive analytics, linking analytics and advanced process control for on-going, closed-loop decision support and process improvement.

**Applicability**

As long as the defined preconditions are in place, the applicability extends beyond process industries, e.g., discrete manufacturing or services; and operating modes, e.g., also factories in batch production regime. Next to the process methodology, these preconditions are technology, i.e., infrastructure that generates, captures and processes data for advanced analytics and process controls; and skilled people with cross-functional expertise including functional, IT, analytics and change management knowledge.

**Contributions**

This research work contributes novel findings to both academia and practice: (1) a new and unique methodology for implementation of a time-based and analytics-supported operational management approach along the five phases of Six Sigma including 17 detailed steps; (2) the definition of applicability and preconditions for adopting this approach in industry and proof that it works; and (3) the documentation of three unique current practical case examples and extensive review of present literature.

**Limitations**

Because the system boundaries were clearly defined and the focus of this work is internal optimization of manufacturing operations in process industries, external effects such as the direct impact of market price volatility were not investigated.

**Validity**

According to Meredith, "case and field studies exhibit the same level of rigor and adhere to the same requirements of good research as rationalist studies, but achieve these goals by different means" (Meredith 1998, pp. 452–453). As outlined in the research design, chapter 1.4, relevant criteria for exploratory and descriptive case study research are the justification of the research approach, construct validity, external validity, and reliability (Yin 2003, p. 28; Voss et al. 2016, p. 192). The research approach includes theoretical sampling with the goal, as per Eisenhardt, to replicate or extend the emergent theory (Eisenhardt 1989, p. 537). The three cases in this work build upon each other. The Cement case demonstrated the successful application of advanced analytics techniques to optimize energy consumption, a highly relevant sub-parameter of ROIC in this industry. The Ammonia case piloted the use of profit per hour as a target optimization parameter. The final case study in the pulp manufacturing industry completes the research with the prototypical application of the conceived implementation methodology. As per Yin, the validation using a single case is "worth conducting because the descriptive information alone [that] will be revelatory" (Yin 2003, p. 43). As far as the construct validity is concerned, and in line with Yin 2003, p. 34, the researcher had key informants review the draft case study reports and included multiple sources of evidence. For example, the pulp manufacturing case study was reviewed and iterated with the engineer of the industrial solutions provider in a series of eight workshops. With respect to external validity and to overcome the paradox of sampling (Kaplan 1998, p. 239), "researchers must consider the possible effects of industry, organization size, manufacturing processes, and inter-organizational effects" (Stuart et al. 2002, p. 426). The author took these effects into account by selecting cases from manufacturing in process industry only, thus reducing the influence of industry. While not investigated in this work, the approach developed should work beyond the defined industry focus, as mentioned under applicability. Finally, the author aimed to clearly describe the investigated literature and case study to enhance research reliability. He discussed the findings with other researchers, presented the intermediate results to the scientific community at conferences and through the publication of articles.

## 11.3 Outlook

The author sees the definition of specific rules and ongoing procedures for profit rate maximization, linking the internal and external context, e.g., as part of the sales & operations planning (S&OP) process, as the most relevant future research need. Especially how to handle and include external influences, such as price and demand volatilities. According to Chopra and Meindl, S&OP helps to maximize profitability when faced with predictable variability in a supply chain by managing both supply and demand (Chopra, Meindl 2016, p. 242). A short definition is provided by Dougherty: "S&OP is a business process that gives managers control based on a current knowledge of the market and the company's internal capabilities, while fostering effective and timely cross-functional communication and decision making." (Dougherty 2012, p. 16). Thomé et al. studied the impact of sales and operations planning practices on manufacturing operational performance and found positive effects across countries and industries (Thomé et al. 2014, p. 2117). A balanced supply chain involves functional trade-offs between purchasing (low purchase price), production (economies of scale), finance (low working capital), distribution (low transportation cost) and the market (wide product range) (Stevens 1989, p. 4). The goal of the S&OP process is to find the optimal trade-offs for maximizing profits (Thomé et al. 2012, p. 10). Big Data presents an opportunity to make more, and previously invisible data, accessible; resulting in lower uncertainty and better decisions (APICS Suppy Chain Council 2015, p. 9). For Dogan et al. "supply chain predictive analytics [...] could be the key differentiator in rapidly building and sustaining a high-performing supply chain in the decade ahead" (Dogan et al. 2015, p. 37). According to Wallace, S&OP is "a medium-to-long term planning tool that provides visibility into the future, thereby avoiding surprises when demand shifts" (Wallace 2012, p. 9). A research opportunity is to introduce real time advanced analytics of internal and external Big Data into the S&OP process.

A final question has been raised by (Mayer-Schönberger, Cukier 2013, p. 195): "as Big Data transforms our lives—optimizing, improving, making more efficient, and capturing benefits— what role is left for intuition, faith, uncertainty, and originality?"

# Bibliography

Abel, Dirk; Epple, Ulrich; Spohr, Gerd-Ulrich (Eds.) (2008): Integration von advanced control in der Prozessindustrie. Rapid control prototyping. Weinheim: Wiley-VCH.

Abele, Eberhard; Reinhart, Gunther (2011): Zukunft der Produktion. Herausforderungen, Forschungsfelder, Chancen. München: Hanser.

Ackoff, Russell Lincoln (1978): The art of problem solving, accompanied by Ackoff's fables. New York, Chichester: Wiley.

Adam, D.; Backhaus, K.; Bauer, M.; Dinge, A.; Johannwille, U.; Voeth, M.; Welker, M. (1998): Koordination betrieblicher Entscheidungen. Die Fallstudie Peter Pollmann. 2., neu bearb. und erw. Aufl. Berlin, Heidelberg, New York: Springer (Springer-Lehrbuch).

Adam, Dietrich (1970): Entscheidungsorientierte Kostenbewertung. Wiesbaden: Gabler.

Adam, Dietrich (1997): Produktions-Management. 8., vollst. überarbeitete und wesentlich erw. Aufl. Wiesbaden: Gabler.

Agachi, Paul Şerban (2006): Model based control. Case studies in process engineering. Weinheim: Wiley-VCH.

Aggarwal, Shilpa; Manuel, Nimal (2016): Big data analytics should be driven by business needs, not technology. McKinsey & Company. Available online at http://www.mckinsey.com/business-functions/mckinsey-analytics/our-insights/big-data-analytics-should-be-driven-by-business-needs-not-technology, checked on 8/16/2017.

agiplan; Fraunhofer IML; Zenit (2015): Studie "Erschließen der Potenziale der Anwendung von 'Industrie 4.0' im Mittelstand". agiplan GmbH. Mühlheim an der Ruhr.

Åhlström, Pär (2016): The research process. In Christer Karlsson (Ed.): Research methods for operations management. Second edition. New York: Routledge, pp. 46–78.

Akkermans, Henk A.; van Wassenhove, Luk N. (2013): Searching for the grey swans. The next 50 years of production research. In International Journal of Production Research 51 (23-24), pp. 6746–6755. DOI: 10.1080/00207543.2013.849827.


M. Hammer, *Management Approach for Resource-Productive Operations*,
Industrial Management, https://doi.org/10.1007/978-3-658-22939-9

Albrecht, Florian; Faatz, Laura; Abele, Eberhard (2013): Multidimensional Evaluation of the Changeability of Interlinked Production Processes with Material Flow Simulation. In Procedia CIRP 7, pp. 139–144. DOI: 10.1016/j.procir.2013.05.024.

Aldinger, Lars Alexander (2009): Methode zur strategischen Leistungsplanung in wandlungsfähigen Produktionsstrukturen des Mittelstandes. Dissertation. Universität Stuttgart. Institut für Industrielle Fertigung und Fabrikbetrieb.

Allwood, Julian M.; Cullen, Jonathan M.; Carruth, Mark A. (2012): Sustainable materials. With both eyes open. Cambridge: UIT Cambridge.

Almeida, António; Azevedo, Américo (2016): A Multi-Perspective Performance Approach for Complex Manufacturing Environments. In Journal of Innovation Management 4 (2), pp. 125–155.

Anderson, Jim (1996): Control for profit. In Trans Inst MC 18 (1), pp. 3–8.

Anderson, Jim; Backx, Ton; van Loon, Joost; King, Myke (1994): Getting the most from Advanced Process Control. In Chemical Engineering (March), pp. 78–89.

Anthony, Robert N. (1965): Planning and Control Systems. A framework for analysis. Boston: Division of Research Graduate School of Business Administration Harvard University.

APICS Suppy Chain Council (2015): Exploring the Big Data Revolution. APICS Suppy Chain Council. Available online at http://www.apics.org/docs/default-source/shopapics/big-data-folio-final.pdf, checked on 8/16/2017.

Arrow, Kenneth J. (1964): Control in Large Organizations. In Management Science 10 (3), pp. 397–408.

Aschenbrücker, Andreas; Horváth, Péter; Michel, Uwe (2014): Controlling im volatilen Umfeld. In Controller Magazin January/February, pp. 4–10.

Ashayeri, J.; Teelen, A.; Selen, W. (1996): A Production and Maintenance Planning Model for the Process Industry. In International Journal of Production Research 34 (12), pp. 3311–3326.

Auschitzky, Eric; Hammer, Markus; Rajagopaul, Agesan (2014): How big data can improve manufacturing. McKinsey & Company. Available online at http://www.mckinsey.com/business-functions/operations/our-insights/how-big-data-can-improve-manufacturing, checked on 8/16/2017.

Azzone, Giovanni; Masella, Cristina; Bertelè, Umberto (1991): Design of Performance Measures for Time-based Companies. In Int Jrnl of Op & Prod Mnagemnt 11 (3), pp. 77–85. DOI: 10.1108/01443579110143412.

Baesens, Bart (2014): Analytics in a big data world. The essential guide to data science and its applications. Hoboken, New Jersey: Wiley (Wiley & SAS business series).

Bange, Carsten; Grosser, Timm; Janoschek, Nikolai (2015): Big Data Use Cases. Getting real on data monetization. BARC - Business Application Research Center. Würzburg.

Bange, Carsten; Marr, Bernard; Bange, Axel (2009): Performance Management: Aktuelle Herausforderungen und Perspektiven. BARC. Würzburg.

Bartezzaghi, Emilio (1999): The evolution of production models. Is a new paradigm emerging? In Int Jrnl of Op & Prod Mnagemnt 19 (2), pp. 229–250. DOI: 10.1108/01443579910247446.

Barton, Dominic; Court, David (2012): Making advanced analytics work for you. A practical guide to capitalizing on big data. In Havard Business Review (October), pp. 1–7.

Barton, Dominic; Manyika, James; Williamson, Sarah Keohane (2017): Finally, Proof That Managing for the Long Term Pays Off. In Havard Business Review (February). Available online at https://hbr.org/2017/02/finally-proof-that-managing-for-the-long-term-pays-off, checked on 8/16/2017.

Bauer, Margret; Craig, Ian K. (2008): Economic assessment of advanced process control – A survey and framework. In Journal of Process Control 18 (1), pp. 2–18. DOI: 10.1016/j.jprocont.2007.05.007.

Bauer, Ulrich (2013): Mehrwert Techno-Ökonomie - Eine Standortbestimmung. In Christian Ramsauer (Ed.): Industrial Engineering und Innovation. Techno-Ökonomie an der TU Graz ; Festschrift anlässlich des 70. Geburtstages von Em.Univ.-Prof. Josef W. Wohinz. Graz: Verl. der Techn. Univ (Festschriften TU Graz), pp. 9–26.

Bauernhansl, Thomas (2014): Die Vierte Industrielle Revoluation - Der Weg in ein wertschaffendes Produktionsparadigma. In Thomas Bauernhansl, Michael ten Hompel, Birgit Vogel-Heuser (Eds.): Industrie 4.0 in Produktion, Automatisierung und Logistik. Anwendung, Technologien, Migration. Wiesbaden: Springer Vieweg, pp. 5-36.

Bauernhansl, Thomas (2016): Weckruf für Unternehmen. Warum wir ein einheitliches Verständnis für Industrie 4.0 brauchen. In ZWF 111 (7-8), pp. 453–457.

Baur, Cornelius; Wee, Dominik (2015): Manufacturing's next act. McKinsey & Company. Available online at http://www.mckinsey.com/businessfunctions/operations/our-insights/manufacturings-next-act, checked on 8/16/2017.

BDV PPP & BDVA (2016): BDV Big Data Value. Default presentation. Available online at http://www.bdva.eu/sites/default/files/BDVA%20Default%20Slide%20Pack.pdf, checked on 8/16/2017.

BDVA Big Data Value Association (2016): Big Data Value Strategic Research and Innovation Agenda. Version 2.0 January 2016. Available online at http://www.bdva.eu/sites/default/files/EuropeanBigDataValuePartnership_SRIA__v2.pdf, checked on 8/16/2017.

Becker, Tilman (2016): Big Data Usage. In José María Cavanillas, Edward Curry, Wolfgang Wahlster (Eds.): New Horizons for a Data-Driven Economy: A Roadmap for Usage and Exploitation of Big Data in Europe. s.l.: Springer Open, pp. 143-165.

Becker, Tilman; Curry, Edward; Jentzsch, Anja; Palmetshofer, Walter (2016): Cross-sectorial Requirements Analysis for Big Data Research. In José María Cavanillas, Edward Curry, Wolfgang Wahlster (Eds.): New Horizons for a Data-Driven Economy: A Roadmap for Usage and Exploitation of Big Data in Europe. s.l.: Springer Open, pp. 263-276.

Bellman, Richard (1964): Control Theory. In Scientific American 211, pp. 186–200.

Benjamin Franklin; William Temple Franklin (1818): Memoirs of the Life and Writings of Benjamin Franklin. Vol. III. London: H. Colburn.

Bennett, Nathan; Lemoine, G. James (2014): What VUCA Really Means for You Harvard Business Review.pdf. In Havard Business Review (January-February), p. 27. Available online at https://hbr.org/2014/01/what-vuca-really-means-for-you.

Benzi, Antonio (2017): ICT and International Manufacturing Strategy. In Louis Brennan, Alessandra Vecchi (Eds.): International Manufacturing Strategy in a Time of Great Flux. 1st ed. 2017: Springer International Publishing (Measuring Operations Performance), pp. 105-121.

Berman, Jules J. (2013): Principles of big data. Preparing, sharing, and analyzing complex information. Amsterdam: Elsevier Morgan Kaufmann.

Biermann, Christopher J. (1996): Handbook of pulping and papermaking. 2nd ed. San Diego, London: Academic Press.

Biron, Joe; Follett, Jonathan (2016): Foundational Elements of an IoT Solution. The Edge, The Cloud, and Application Development. O'Reilly. Sebastopol, CA.

Bishop, Peter; Hines, Andy; Collins, Terry (2007): The current state of scenario development. An overview of techniques. In Foresight 9 (1), pp. 5–25. DOI: 10.1108/14636680710727516.

Bititci, Umit S.; Turner, T. J.; Begemann, Carsten (2000): Dynamics of performance measurement systems. In International Journal of Operations & Production Management 20 (6), pp. 692–704.

Blessing, Lucienne T.M; Chakrabarti, Amaresh (Eds.) (2009): DRM, a Design Research Methodology. London: Springer.

Bourne, Mike (2008): Performance measurement: learning from the past and projecting the future. In Measuring Business Excellence 12 (4), pp. 67–72. DOI: 10.1108/13683040810919971.

Braunscheidel, Michael J.; Hamister, James W.; Suresh, Nallan C.; Star, Harold (2011): An institutional theory perspective on Six Sigma adoption. In Int Jrnl of Op & Prod Mnagemnt 31 (4), pp. 423–451. DOI: 10.1108/01443571111 119542.

Brecher, Christian; Özdemir, Denis (2014): Introduction. In Christian Brecher (Ed.): Advances in production technology. New York: Springer, pp. 1-10.

Brignall, T. J.; Fitzgerald, L.; Johnston, R.; Silvestro, R. (1991): Performance Measurement in Service Businesses. In Management Accounting 69 (10), pp. 34–36.

Brisk, M. L. (2004): Process Control: Potential Benefits and Wasted Opportunities. In Proceedings of 5th Asian Control Conference, 20–23 July 2004,, pp. 10–16.

Brisk, Michael (2005): Process control, advancing or retreating? In The Chemical Engineer (769), pp. 38–39.

Bughin, Jacques (2016): Big data, Big bang? In Journal of Big Data 3 (1), p. 1452. DOI: 10.1186/s40537-015-0014-3.

Bughin, Jacques; Hazan, Eric; Labaye, Eric; Manyika, James; Dahlströhm, Peter; Ramaswamy, Sree; Cochin de Billy, Caroline (2016): Digital Europe: Pushing the frontier, capturing the benefits. McKinsey Global Institute. Available online at http://www.mckinsey.com/business-functions/digital-mckinsey/our-insights/digital-europe-realizing-the-continents-potential, checked on 8/16/2017.

Burton, Terence T. (2011): Accelerating lean six sigma results. How to achieve improvement excellence in the new economy. Ft. Lauderdale, FL: J. Ross Pub.

Buschbacher, Florian (2016): Wertschöpfung mit Big Data Analytics. In Utz Schäffer, Jürgen Weber (Eds.): Controlling & Management Review Sonderheft 1-2016. Wiesbaden: Springer Fachmedien, pp. 40–45.

Busi, Marco; Bititci, Umit S. (2006): Collaborative performance management. Present gaps and future research. In Int J Productivity & Perf Mgmt 55 (1), pp. 7–25. DOI: 10.1108/17410400610635471.

Canney, William M. (2003): The future of advanced process control promises more benefits and sustained value. In Oil & Gas Journal 101 (April 21), pp. 48–54.

Canney, William M. (2005): Are you getting the full benefits from your advanced process control systems? In Hydrocarbon Processing 84 (June), pp. 55–58.

Carvalho, Helena; Duarte, Susana; Cruz Machado, V. (2011): Lean, agile, resilient and green. Divergencies and synergies. In Lean Six Sigma Journal 2 (2), pp. 151–179. DOI: 10.1108/20401461111135037.

Cavanillas, José María; Curry, Edward; Wahlster, Wolfgang (2016): The Big Data Value Opportunity. In José María Cavanillas, Edward Curry, Wolfgang Wahlster (Eds.): New Horizons for a Data-Driven Economy: A Roadmap for Usage and Exploitation of Big Data in Europe. s.l.: Springer Open, pp. 3-12.

Chandler, Alfred D. (1977): The visible hand. The managerial revolution in American business. Cambridge, MA, London: Harvard University Press.

Chatterjee, Bikash (2016): Applying lean six sigma in the pharmaceutical industry. Farnham: Gower.

Chen, Hsinchun; Chiang, Roger H. L.; Storey, Veda C. (2012): Business Intelligence and Analytics: From Big Data to Big Impact. In MIS Quarterly 36 (4), pp. 1165–1188.

Choi, Bong; Kim, Jongweon; Leem, Byung-hak; Lee, Chang-Yeol; Hong, Han-kuk (2012): Empirical analysis of the relationship between Six Sigma management activities and corporate competitiveness. In Int Jrnl of Op & Prod Mnagemnt 32 (5), pp. 528–550. DOI: 10.1108/01443571211226489.

Chopra, Sunil; Meindl, Peter (2016): Supply chain management. Strategy, planning, and operation. Sixth Edition. Boston: Pearson.

Christensen, John; Hemmer, Thomas (2006): Analytical Modeling of Cost in Management Accounting Research. In Christopher S. Chapman, Anthony G. Hopwood, Michael D. Shields (Eds.): Handbook of management accounting research, vol. 2. 1st ed. 2 volumes. Amsterdam, London: Elsevier (Handbooks of Management Accounting Research), pp. 557–571.

Christopher, Martin; Holweg, Matthias (2011): "Supply Chain 2.0". Managing supply chains in the era of turbulence. In Int Jnl Phys Dist & Log Manage 41 (1), pp. 63–82. DOI: 10.1108/09600031111101439.

Christopher, Martin; Holweg, Matthias (2017): Supply chain 2.0 revisited. A framework for managing volatility-induced risk in the supply chain. In Int Jnl Phys Dist & Log Manage 47 (1), pp. 2–17. DOI: 10.1108/IJPDLM-09-2016-0245.

Chu, Li Ping (2016): Data Science for Modern Manufacturing. 1. ed. Sebastopol, CA: O'Reilly Media, Inc.

Cisco (2016): Cisco Global Cloud Index: Forecast and Methodology, 2015–2020. White Paper. Available online at http://www.cisco.com/c/dam/en/us/solutions/collateral/service-provider/global-cloud-index-gci/white-paper-c11-738085.pdf, checked on 8/16/2017.

Clark, Gregg; Dostal, Pilar (2013): The future of decision-making. Using driver analytics to improve insights and decisions. EY (5 Insights for executives). Available online at http://www.ey.com/Publication/vwLUAssets/The_future_of_decision_making/$FILE/The_future_of_decision_making.pdf, checked on 8/16/2017.

Codreanu, Aura (2016): A VUCA Action Framework for a VUCA Environment. Leadership Challenges and Solutions. In Journal of Defense Resources Management 7 (2 (13)), pp. 31-38.

Conejo, Antonio J.; Carrión, Miguel; Morales, Juan M. (2010): Decision making under uncertainty in electricity markets. New York: Springer (International series in operations research & management science, 0884-8289, 153).

Cooper, Robin; Kaplan, Robert S. (1988): Measure Costs Right: Make the Right Decisions. In Havard Business Review (September-October), pp. 96–103.

Corsten, Hans; May, Constantin (1996): Artificial neural networks for supporting production planning and control. In Technovation 16 (2), pp. 67–76.

Curry, Edward; Becker, Tilman; Munné, Ricard; Lama, Nuria de; Zillner, Sonja (2016): The BIG Project. In José María Cavanillas, Edward Curry, Wolfgang Wahlster (Eds.): New Horizons for a Data-Driven Economy: A Roadmap for Usage and Exploitation of Big Data in Europe. Springer Open, pp. 13-26.

Curtis, Graham; Cobham, David P. (2005): Business information systems. Analysis, design, and practice. 5th ed. Harlow: FT Prentice Hall.

Cutler, C. R.; Perry, R. T. (1983): Real time optimization with multivariable control is required to maximize profits. In Computers & Chemical Engineering 7 (5), pp. 663–667. DOI: 10.1016/0098-1354(83)80010-6.

Darby, Mark L.; Nikolaou, Michael; Jones, James; Nicholson, Doug (2011): RTO. An overview and assessment of current practice. In Journal of Process Control 21 (6), pp. 874–884. DOI: 10.1016/j.jprocont.2011.03.009.

Davenport, Thomas H. (1993): Need radical innovation and continuous improvement? Integrate process reengineering and TQM. In Planning Review 21 (3), pp. 6–12. DOI: 10.1108/eb054413.

Davenport, Thomas H. (2013): Keep up with your quants. An innumerate´s guide to navigating big data. In Havard Business Review (July-August), pp. 1–5.

Davenport, Thomas H. (2014a): Big data @ work. Dispelling the myths, uncovering the opportunities. Boston, MA: Harvard Business Review Press.

Davenport, Thomas H. (2014b): How strategists use "big data" to support internal business decisions, discovery and production. In Strategy & Leadership 42 (4), pp. 45–50. DOI: 10.1108/SL-05-2014-0034.

Davenport, Thomas H.; Prusak, Lawrence (2000): Working knowledge. In Ubiquity (August). DOI: 10.1145/347634.348775. Available online at http://ubiquity.acm.org/article.cfm?id=348775, checked on 8/16/2017.

Davies, T. C. (1950): How the DuPont Organization Appraises its Performance. In American Management Association (Ed.): Financial Management Series (94), pp. 3–7.

Dean, Jared (2014): Big data, data mining, and machine learning. Value creation for business leaders and practitioners. Hoboken, New Jersey: John Wiley & Sons (Wiley and SAS business series).

Deming, W. Edwards (2000): The new economics. For industry, government, education. 2nd ed. Cambridge, Mass., London: MIT Press.

Dennis, Daina; Meredith, Jack (2000a): An Empirical Analysis of Process Industry Transformation Systems. In Management Science 46 (8), pp. 1085–1099. DOI: 10.1287/mnsc.46.8.1085.12031.

Dennis, Daina R.; Meredith, Jack R. (2000b): An analysis of process industry production and inventory management systems. In Journal of Operations Management 18 (6), pp. 683–699. DOI: 10.1016/S0272-6963(00)00039-5.

Deubel, Thomas (2017): Profitabel - Der Effekt von Agilität auf das Unternehmensergebnis. In Christian Ramsauer, Detlef Kayser, Christoph Schmitz (Eds.): Erfolgsfaktor Agilität. Chancen für Unternehmen in einem volatilen Marktumfeld. 1. Auflage. Weinheim: Wiley-VCH, pp. 101-125.

Dhawan, Rajat; Singh, Kunwar; Tuteja, Ashish (2014): When big data goes lean. In McKinsey Quarterly (2), pp. 97–102.

Diab, Wael William; Harper, K. Eric; Lin, Shi-Wan; Sobel, William (2017): Industrial Analytics: The Engine Driving the Industrial Revolution. industrial internet Consortium. Available online at http://www.iiconsortium.org/pdf/Industrial_Analytics-the_engine_driving_IIoT_revolution_20170321_FINAL.pdf, checked on 8/16/2017.

DIN 8580:2003-09 Manufacturing processes - Terms and definitions, division.

Dobbs, Richard; Manyika, J.; Woetzel, Jonathan R. (2015): No ordinary disruption. The four global forces breaking all the trends. First edition. New York: PublicAffairs.

Dogan, Can A.; Gjendem, Frode Huse; Rodysill, Jade (2015): Fueling supply chain transformation. Predictive analytics energizes dynamic networks. In : Exploring the Big Data Revolution. APICS Suppy Chain Council, pp. 36-43.

Domingue, John; Lasierra, Nelia; Fensel, Anna; van Kasteren, Tim; Strohbach, Martin; Thalhammer, Andreas (2016): Big Data Analysis. In José María Cavanillas, Edward Curry, Wolfgang Wahlster (Eds.): New Horizons for a Data-Driven Economy: A Roadmap for Usage and Exploitation of Big Data in Europe. s.l.: Springer Open, pp. 63–86.

Domschke, Wolfgang; Drexl, Andreas; Klein, Robert; Scholl, Armin (2015): Einführung in Operations Research. 9., überarbeitete und verbesserte Auflage 2015. Berlin, Heidelberg: Springer Gabler.

Domschke, Wolfgang; Scholl, Armin (2005): Grundlagen der Betriebswirtschaftslehre: Eine Einführung aus entscheidungsorientierter Sicht. 3., verb. Aufl. Berlin, Heidelberg, New York: Springer.

Dougherty, John R. (2012): Lessons from the Pros. How to win with sales and operations planning. In APICS Suppy Chain Council (Ed.): How to be an S&OP champion, pp. 15–18.

Drew, John; McCallum, Blair; Roggenhofer, Stefan (2004): Journey to lean. Making operational change stick. Basingstoke: Palgrave Macmillan.

Drucker, Peter F. (1966): The practice of management. Reprint. London: Heinemann.

Drucker, Peter F.; Maciariello, Joseph A. (2008): Management. Rev. ed. Pymble, NSW, New York: HarperCollins e-books.

Drury, Colin (2012): Management and cost accounting. 8. ed. Hampshire: Cengage Learning.

Dubeauclard, Raoul; Kubik, Kerstin; Schrader, Ulf (2014): Agility: A response to the volatile world. In Knut Alicke, Thomas Ebel, Ulf Schrader, Ketan Shah (Eds.): Finding Opportunity in Uncertainty. A New Paradigm for Pharmaceutical Supply Chains, pp. 32–45.

Dües, Christina Maria; Tan, Kim Hua; Lim, Ming (2013): Green as the new Lean. How to use Lean practices as a catalyst to greening your supply chain. In Journal of Cleaner Production 40, pp. 93–100. DOI: 10.1016/j.jclepro.2011.12.023.

Dunning, John H. (2002): The selected essays of John H. Dunning. Cheltenham: Edward Elgar.

Dweekat, Abdallah Jamal; Park, Jinwoo (2016): Internet of Things-Enabled Supply Chain Performance Measurement Model. In : ICIMSA 2016. International Conference on Industrial Engineering, Management Science and Application (ICIMSA). Jeju, South Korea. Piscataway, NJ: IEEE, pp. 1–3.

Eckerson, Wayne W. (2007): Predictive Analytics. Extending the Value of Your Data Warehousing Investment. TDWI The Data Warehouse Institute (TDWI Best Practices Report). Available online at https://www.microstrategy.com/Strategy/media/downloads/products/MicroStrategy-TDWI-Best-Practices-Report-Predictive-Analytics-Data-Warehousing.pdf, checked on 8/16/2017.

Edgar, Thomas F.; Himmelblau, David Mautner; Lasdon, Leon S. (2001): Optimization of chemical processes. 2nd ed. Dubuque, Iowa: McGraw-Hill (McGraw-Hill chemical engineering series).

Edmonds, J.; Wilkinson, J. (2016): What part does human factors play within chemical and process industries? In Janette Edmonds, The Keil Centre (Eds.): Human factors in the chemical and process industries. Making it work in practice. 1st ed. Amsterdam, Oxford, Cambridge: Elsevier, pp. 13–24.

EEFA – Energy Environment Forecast Analysis GmbH & Co. KG (2013): Wettbewerbsfähige Stromkosten – Voraussetzung für die Zementherstellung am Standort Deutschland. EEFA. Münster.

Einstein, Albert (1916): Die Grundlage der allgemeinen Relativitätstheorie. In Annalen der Physik 49 (7), pp. 769-822.

Eisenhardt, Kathleen M. (1989): Building Theories from Case Study Research. In The Academy of Management Review 14 (4), pp. 532–550.

Epstein, Marc J.; Lee, John Y. (Eds.) (2000): Advances in Management Accounting, Volume 9. Greenwich, Conn., London: JAI (Advances in Management Accounting, 9).

Eßer, Gerd (2015): Soziotechnisches Potenzial cyber-physischer Systeme. In ZWF 110 (3), pp. 142–144.

European Union Chamber of Commerce in China (2017): China Manufacturing 2025. Putting Industrial Policy Ahead of Market Forces. Available online at http://www.europeanchamber.com.cn/en/china-manufacturing-2025, checked on 8/16/2017.

EVO - Efficiency Valuation Organization (2012): International Performance Measurement and Verification Protocol. Concepts and Options for Determining Energy and Water Savings, Volume 1. EVO 10000 - 1:2012.

Executive Office of the President: President's Council of Advisors on Science and Technology (2011): Report to the President on Ensuring American Leadership in Advanced Manufacturing. Available online at https://energy.gov/sites/prod/files/2013/11/f4/pcast_june2011.pdf, checked on 8/16/2017.

Executive Office of the President: President's Council of Advisors on Science and Technology (2014): Report to the President: Accelerating U.S. Advanced Manufacturing. Available online at https://obamawhitehouse.archives.gov/sites/default/files/microsites/ostp/PCAST/amp20_report_final.pdf, checked on 8/16/2017.

Fayyad, Usama; Piatetsky-Shapiro, Gregory; Smyth, Padhraic (1996): From Data Mining to Knowledge Discovery in Databases. In AI Magazine 17 (3), pp. 37-54.

Feldmann, Robert; Hammer, Markus; Somers, Ken; van Niel, Joris (2016): Buried treasure: Advanced analytics in process industries. McKinsey & Company. Available online at http://www.mckinsey.com/business-functions/operations/our-insights/buried-treasure-advanced-analytics-in-process-industries, checked on 8/16/2017.

Feldmann, Robert Markus (2013): Energetische Verbrauchsoptimierung bei industriellen Prozessen durch Einsatz künstlicher Intelligenz. In Ludger Pautmeier (Ed.): Praxis Energiemanagement. Köln: TÜV Media.

Fercoq, Alain; Lamouri, Samir; Carbone, Valentina (2016): Lean/Green integration focused on waste reduction techniques. In Journal of Cleaner Production 137, pp. 567–578. DOI: 10.1016/j.jclepro.2016.07.107.

Ferdows, Kasra; Thurnheer, Fritz (2011): Building factory fitness. In Int Jrnl of Op & Prod Mnagemnt 31 (9), pp. 916–934. DOI: 10.1108/01443571111165 820.

Ferrari, Elisabeth; Sparrer, Insa; Varga von Kibed, Matthias (2015): Simply More Complex: A SySt® Approach to VUCA. In Oliver Mack, Anshuman Khare, Andreas Krämer, Thomas Burgartz (Eds.): Managing in a VUCA World. Aufl. 2015. Cham: Springer International Publishing, pp. 21–38.

Finlay, Steven (2014): Predictive Analytics, Data Mining and Big Data. London: Palgrave Macmillan UK.

Floyd, Raymond C. (2010): Liquid lean. Developing lean culture in the process industries. New York: Productivity Press.

Forrester, Jay W. (1961): Industrial dynamics. Sixth printing, September 1969. S.l.: M.I.T. Press.

Franks, Bill (2014): The Analytics Revolution. How to Improve Your Business By Making Analytics Operational In The Big Data Era. 1., Auflage. New York, NY: John Wiley & Sons.

Fransoo, Jan C.; Rutten, Werner G.M.M. (1994): A Typology of Production Control Situations in Process Industries. In Int Jrnl of Op & Prod Mnagemnt 14 (12), pp. 47–57. DOI: 10.1108/01443579410072382.

Freeman, John (2007): Theory of Constraints and Throughput Accounting. CIMA - The Chartered Institute of Management Accountants. London (Topic Gateway Series, 26). Available online at http://www.cimaglobal.com/ Documents/ImportedDocuments/26_Theory_of_Constraints_and_Through put_Accounting.pdf, checked on 8/16/2017.

Friedli, Thomas; Schuh, Günther (2012): Wettbewerbsfähigkeit der Produktion an Hochlohnstandorten. Berlin, Heidelberg: Springer.

Friess, Peter (2013): Internet of Things Strategic Research and Innovation Agenda. In Ovidiu Vermesan, Peter Friess (Eds.): Internet of things. Converging technologies for smart environments and integrated ecosystems. Aalborg: River Publishers (River Publishers series in information science and technology), pp. 7–152.

Galloway, David; Waldron, David (1988a): Throughput Accounting Part 2: Ranking products profitably. In Management Accounting (December), pp. 34–35.

Galloway, David; Waldron, David (1988b): Throughput Accounting: The need for a new language for manufacturing. In Management Accounting (November), pp. 34–35.

Gandomi, Amir; Haider, Murtaza (2015): Beyond the hype. Big data concepts, methods, and analytics. In International Journal of Information Management 35 (2), pp. 137–144. DOI: 10.1016/j.ijinfomgt.2014.10.007.

Gantz, John; Reinsel, David (2012): THE DIGITAL UNIVERSE IN 2020: Big Data, Bigger Digital Shadows, and Biggest Growth in the Far East. Sponsored by EMC Corporation. IDC. Available online at https://www.emc-technology.com/collateral/analyst-reports/idc-the-digital-universe-in-2020.pdf, checked on 8/16/2017.

Gartner (2007): 'Dirty Data' is a Business Problem, Not an IT Problem, Says Gartner. Available online at http://www.gartner.com/newsroom/id/501733, checked on 8/16/2017.

Gartner (2016): Top 10 Strategic Technology Trends for 2017. Gartner. Available online at https://www.gartner.com/doc/reprints?id=1-3KW579O&ct=161028&st=sb, checked on 8/16/2017.

Gartner (2017): Gartner Says 8.4 Billion Connected "Things" Will Be in Use in 2017, Up 31 Percent From 2016. Available online at http://www.gartner.com/newsroom/id/3598917, checked on 8/16/2017.

Gausemeier, Jürgen; Klocke, Fritz (2016): Industrie 4.0. International Benchmark, Options for the Future and Recommendations for Manufacturing Research. Available online at http://www.acatech.de/fileadmin/user_upload/Baumstruktur_nach_Website/Acatech/root/de/Publikationen/Sonderpublikationen/INBENZHAP_E_web.pdf, checked on 8/16/2017.

Gigerenzer, Gerd (2007): Gut feelings. The intelligence of the unconscious. New York: Viking.

Gilchrist, Alasdair (2016): Industry 4.0. Berkeley, CA: Apress.

Gladen, Werner (2003): Kennzahlen- und Berichtssysteme: Grundlagen zum Performance Measurement. 2., überarb. Aufl. Wiesbaden: Gabler (Lehrbuch).

Goldratt, Eliyahu M. (1988): Computerized shop floor scheduling. In International Journal of Production Research 26 (3), pp. 443–455. DOI: 10.1080/00207548808947875.

Goldratt, Eliyahu M. (1990): What is this thing called theory of constraints and how should it be implemented. Great Barrington, MA: North River.

Goldratt, Eliyahu M.; Cox, Jeff (2004): The goal. A process of ongoing improvement. 3rd rev. ed., 20th anniversary ed. Great Barrington MA: North River Press.

Gordon, Adam (2009): Future savvy. Identifying trends to make better decisions, manage uncertainty, and profit from change. New York: AMACOM.

Gorecky, Dominic; Schmitt, Mathias; Loskyll, Matthias (2014): Mensch-Maschine-Interaktion im Industrie 4.0 Zeitalter. In Thomas Bauernhansl, Michael ten Hompel, Birgit Vogel-Heuser (Eds.): Industrie 4.0 in Produktion, Automatisierung und Logistik. Anwendung, Technologien, Migration. Wiesbaden: Springer Vieweg, pp. 525-542.

Gray, K.; Wilkinson, J. (2016): Managing organizational change. In Janette Edmonds, The Keil Centre (Eds.): Human factors in the chemical and process industries. Making it work in practice. 1st ed. Amsterdam, Oxford, Cambridge: Elsevier, pp. 335–355.

Groll, Karl-Heinz (2003): Kennzahlen für das wertorientierte Management. ROI, EVA und CFROI im Vergleich; ein neues Konzept zur Steigerung des Unternehmenswertes. München: Hanser.

Groover, Mikell P. (2001): Automation, production systems, and computer-integrated manufacturing. Upper Saddle River, NJ: Prentice Hall.

Gundersen, Thorvald F. (2017): Best Strategic Decisions in Management of Complex Operations. In Louis Brennan, Alessandra Vecchi (Eds.): International Manufacturing Strategy in a Time of Great Flux. 1st ed. 2017: Springer International Publishing (Measuring Operations Performance), pp. 85-104.

Gutenberg, Erich (1963): Der Absatz. Sechste Auflage. Berlin, Heidelberg: Springer (Grundlagen der Betriebswirtschaftslehre).

Guzzo, Richard A. (2016): How Big Data Matter. In Scott Tonidandel, Eden King, Jose M. Cortina (Eds.): Big data at work. The data science revolution and organizational psychology. New York and London: Routledge; Taylor & Francis (SIOP organizational frontiers series), pp. 336–349.

Haberfellner, Reinhard; Weck, Olivier de; Fricke, Ernst; Vössner, Siegfried (Eds.) (2012): Systems Engineering: Grundlagen und Anwendung. 12., völlig neu bearb. u. erw. Aufl. Zürich: Orell Füssli.

Hall, Robert W. (2010): Compression. Meeting the challenges of sustainability through vigorous learning enterprises. Boca Raton: CRC Press.

Hallam, Cory; Contreras, Carolina (2016): Integrating lean and green management. In Management Decision 54 (9), pp. 2157–2187. DOI: 10.1108/MD-04-2016-0259.

Hammer, Markus; Karre, Hugo; Ramsauer, Christian (2017a): Resource Productive Operations - How Lean, Green and Constraint Management Approaches Blend Together. In Proceedings International Scientific Conference MOTSP 2017, 5-7 April 2017, Dubrovnik, Croatia.

Hammer, Markus; Rutten, Paul; Somers, Ken (2014): Bringing lean thinking to energy. In McKinsey Quarterly (2), pp. 103–105.

Hammer, Markus; Somers, Ken (2015): More from less: Making resources more productive. In McKinsey Quarterly (3), pp. 14–20.

Hammer, Markus; Somers, Ken (2016): Unlocking Industrial Resource Productivity. 5 core beliefs to increase profits through energy, material, and water efficiency: McKinsey Publishing.

Hammer, Markus; Somers, Ken; Karre, Hugo; Ramsauer, Christian (2017b): Profit Per Hour as a Target Process Control Parameter for Manufacturing Systems Enabled by Big Data Analytics and Industry 4.0 Infrastructure. In Procedia CIRP 63, pp. 715–720.

Hawking, S. W. (1988): Eine kurze Geschichte der Zeit. Die Suche nach der Urkraft des Universums. Hamburg: Rowohlt.

Heinen, Edmund (Ed.) (1991): Industriebetriebslehre als entscheidungsorientierte Unternehmensführung. 9. vollst. neu bearb. u. erw. Aufl. Wiesbaden: Gabler (Industriebetriebslehre: Entscheidungen im Industriebetrieb).

Heinen, Tobias; Wulf, Serjosha (2011): Mehr Energieeffizienz in Fabriken. Ein Plädoyer. In ZWF 106 (07-08), pp. 502–505.

Heldmann, Stefan (2017): Informiert - Monitoring als Schnittstelle zum unsicheren Geschäftsumfeld. In Christian Ramsauer, Detlef Kayser, Christoph Schmitz (Eds.): Erfolgsfaktor Agilität. Chancen für Unternehmen in einem volatilen Marktumfeld. 1. Auflage. Weinheim: Wiley-VCH, pp. 161-200.

Heldmann, Stefan; Hammer, Markus; Ramsauer, Christian (2017): Eine strategische und operative Perspektive zur Anwendung von Big Data in der Industrie. In ZWF 112 (1-2), pp. 79–85.

Heldmann, Stefan; Rabitsch, Christian; Ramsauer, Christian (2015): Big-data basiertes Monitoring. Ein neuer Ansatz für agile Industrieunternehmen in der volatilen Welt. In Industrie 4.0 Management 31 (5), pp. 35–39.

Henke, Nicolaus; Bughin, Jacques; Chui, Michael; Manyika, James; Saleh, Tamim; Wiseman, Bill; Sethupathy, Guru (2016a): The Age of Analytics: Competing in a Data-Driven World. Edited by McKinsey Global Institute. McKinsey & Company. Available online at http://www.mckinsey.com/business-functions/mckinsey-analytics/our-insights/the-age-of-analytics-competing-in-a-data-driven-world, checked on 8/16/2017.

Henke, Nikolaus; Libarikian, Ari; Wiseman, Bill (2016b): Straight talk about big data. In McKinsey Quarterly (3), pp. 42–51.

Hernández Morales, Roberto (2003): Systematik der Wandlungsfähigkeit in der Fabrikplanung. Düsseldorf: VDI Verlag (Fortschr.-Ber. VDI. Reihe 16, Technik und Wirtschaft, Nr. 149).

Hey, Robert Bruce (2017): Performance Management for the Oil, Gas, and Process Industries. Cambridge, MA: Gulf Professional Publishing.

Hilbert, Martin; Lopez, Priscila (2011): The world's technological capacity to store, communicate, and compute information. In Science (New York, N.Y.) 332 (6025), pp. 60–65. DOI: 10.1126/science.1200970.

Hitomi, K. (1996): Manufacturing Systems Engineering: A Unified Approach to Manufacturing Technology, Production Management and Industrial Economics. London: Taylor & Francis.

Höller, Jan; Tsiatsis, Vlasios; Mulligan, Catherine; Karnouskos, Stamatis; Avesand, Stefan; Boyle, David (2014): From Machine-to-Machine to the Internet of Things. Introduction to a New Age of Intelligence. Amsterdam: Elsevier Academic Press.

Horngren, Charles T.; Datar, Srikant M.; Rajan, Madhav V. (2015): Cost accounting. A managerial emphasis. 15th ed., Global ed. Harlow, Essex: Pearson Education Limited.

Horvath, Peter; Michel, Uwe; Aschenbrücker, Andreas (2015): Big Data - Potenzial für den Controller. Ideenwerkstatt im Internationalen Controller Verein (ICV). In Controlling - Zeitschrift für erfolgsorientierte Unternehmenssteuerung 27 (2), pp. 103-106.

Hu, W.; Almansoori, A.; Kannan, P. K.; Azarm, S.; Wang, Z. (2012): Corporate dashboards for integrated business and engineering decisions in oil refineries. An agent-based approach. In Decision Support Systems 52 (3), pp. 729–741. DOI: 10.1016/j.dss.2011.11.019.

Hutchinson, Robert (2007): The Impact of Time-Based Accounting on Manufacturing Performance. Dissertation. University of Toledo.

Iafrate, Fernando (2014): A Journey from Big Data to Smart Data. In Pierre-Jean Benghozi, Daniel Krob, Antoine Lonjon, Hervé Panetto (Eds.): Digital Enterprise Design & Management. Proceedings of the Second International Conference on Digital Enterprise Design and Management DED&M 2014, pp. 25-34.

IBM Institute for Business Value (2012): Analytics: Big Data in der Praxis. Wie innovative Unternehmen ihre Datenbestände effektiv nutzen. In Zusammenarbeit mit der Said Business School an der Universität Oxford. Available online at http://www-935.ibm.com/services/de/gbs/thoughtleadership/GBE03519-DEDE-00.pdf, checked on 8/16/2017.

ICV - Internationaler Controller Verein (2016): Business Analytics. Der Weg zur datengetriebenen Unternehmenssteuerung. Available online at https://www.icv-controlling.com/fileadmin/Assets/Content/AK/Ideenwerkstatt/Dream_Car_Business_Analytics_DE.pdf, checked on 8/16/2016.

IIC - Industrial Internet Consortium (2016): The Industrial Internet of Things, Volume B01: Business Strategy and Innovation Framework (IIC:PUB:B01: V1.0:PB:20161115). Available online at http://www.iiconsortium.org/pdf/Business_Strategy_and_Innovation_Framework_Nov_2016.pdf, checked on 8/16/2017.

ITU-T (2012): ITU-T Rec. Y.2060 (06/2012) Overview of the Internet of things. Next Generation Networks – Frameworks and functional architecture models. International Telecommunication Union. Available online at https://www.itu.int/rec/T-REC-Y.2060-201206-I, checked on 8/16/2017.

Jackson, George C.; Low, James T. (1993): Constraint Management. A Description and Assessment. In Int Jrnl Logistics Management 4 (2), pp. 41–48. DOI: 10.1108/09574099310804975.

Jäger, Jens; Schöllhammer, Oliver; Lickefett, Michael; Bauernhansl, Thomas (2016): Advanced Complexity Management Strategic Recommendations of Handling the "Industrie 4.0" Complexity for Small and Medium Enterprises. In Procedia CIRP 57, pp. 116–121. DOI: 10.1016/j.procir.2016.11.021.

Jain, Anil K.; Mao, Jianchang (1996): Artificial Neural Networks: A Tutorial. In Computer (March), pp. 31–44.

Johansen, Robert (2007): Get there early. Sensing the future to compete in the present. 1st ed. San Francisco: Berrett-Koehler.

Kagermann, Henning; Wahlster, Wolfgang; Helbig, Johannes (2013): Recommendations for implementing the strategic initiative INDUSTRIE 4.0. Available online at http://www.acatech.de/fileadmin/user_upload/Baumstruktur_nach_Website/Acatech/root/de/Material_fuer_Sonderseiten/Industrie_4.0/Final_report__Industrie_4.0_accessible.pdf, checked on 8/16/2017.

Kahneman, Daniel; Rosenfield, Andrew M.; Gandhi, Linnea; Blaser, Tom (2016): Noise: How to Overcome the High, Hidden Cost of Inconsistent Decision Making. In Havard Business Review (October 2016), pp. 38–46.

Kahneman, Daniel; Slovic, Paul; Tversky, Amos (Eds.) (1982): Judgement under uncertainty. Heuristics and biases. Cambridge: Cambridge University Press.

Kals, Johannes (2015): ISO 50001 energy management systems. What managers need to know about energy and business management. New York, NY: Business Expert Press.

Kaplan, Abraham (1998): The conduct of inquiry. Methodology for behavioral science. 4th printing 2009. New Brunswick, N.J.: Transaction.

Kaplan, Robert S.; Norton, David P. (1992): The Balanced Scorecard - Measures That Drive Success. In Havard Business Review (January - February 1992), pp. 71–79.

Karlsson, Christer (2016): Research in operations management. In Christer Karlsson (Ed.): Research methods for operations management. Second edition. New York: Routledge, pp. 7–45.

Kersten, Wolfgang; Koller, Hans; Lödding, Hermann (Eds.) (2014): Industrie 4.0. Wie intelligente Vernetzung und kognitive Systeme unsere Arbeit verändern. Berlin: Gito.

Khan, Shahyan (2016): Leadership in the digital age. A study on the effects of digitalisation on top management leadership. Stockholm Business School, Stockholm.

Kieninger, Michael; Michel, Uwe; Mehanna, Walid (2015): Auswirkungen der Digitalisierung auf die Unternehmenssteuerung. In Peter Horvath, Uwe Michel (Eds.): Controlling im digitalen Zeitalter. Stuttgart: Schäffer-Poeschel Verlag, pp. 3–13.

Kim, Seonmin; Mabin, Victoria Jane; Davies, John (2008): The theory of constraints thinking processes. Retrospect and prospect. In Int Jrnl of Op & Prod Mnagemnt 28 (2), pp. 155–184. DOI: 10.1108/01443570810846883.

Kleindienst, Bernd (2016): Performance Measurement und Management. Partizipative Entwicklung eines Systems zur Steuerung, Analyse und Kontrolle von Unternehmen. Dissertation. Montanuniversität, Leoben. Lehrstuhl Wirtschafts- und Betriebswissenschaften.

Kleindienst, Mario (2017): Digitization in manufacturing industry. A systemic approach to align digitization with corporate strategy in small and medium sized enterprises. Dissertation. Technische Universität, Graz. Institute of Innovation and Industrial Management.

Kleinemeier, Michael (2014): Von der Autmatisierungspyramide zu Unternehmenssteuerungsnetzwerken. In Thomas Bauernhansl, Michael ten Hompel, Birgit Vogel-Heuser (Eds.): Industrie 4.0 in Produktion, Automatisierung und Logistik. Anwendung, Technologien, Migration. Wiesbaden: Springer Vieweg, pp. 571-579.

Koller, Tim; Goedhart, Marc H.; Wessels, David (2015): Valuation. Measuring and Managing the Value of Companies. Sixth edition, University edition. Hoboken, New Jersey: Wiley (The Wiley finance series).

Kreitlein, Sven; Baumhoer, Fabian; Ultsch, Fabian; Franke, Jörg (2016): The Physical Model Concept for the Determination of the Least Energy Demand as Energy Efficiency Benchmark for Production Processes. In AMM 856, pp. 49–56. DOI: 10.4028/www.scientific.net/AMM.856.49.

Kremsmayr, Martin (2017): Unsicher - Auswirkungen einer veränderten Welt. In Christian Ramsauer, Detlef Kayser, Christoph Schmitz (Eds.): Erfolgsfaktor Agilität. Chancen für Unternehmen in einem volatilen Marktumfeld. 1. Auflage. Weinheim: Wiley-VCH, pp. 33-76.

Kubiak, T. M.; Benbow, Donald W. (2009): The certified six sigma black belt handbook. 2nd ed. Milwaukee Wis.: ASQ Quality Press.

Kumar, Maneesh; Antony, Jiju; Madu, Christian N.; Montgomery, Douglas C.; Park, Sung H. (2008): Common myths of Six Sigma demystified. In Int J Qual & Reliability Mgmt 25 (8), pp. 878–895. DOI: 10.1108/02656710810898658.

Lacy, Peter; Rutqvist, Jakob (2015): Waste to wealth. The circular economy advantage. New York: Palgrave Macmillan.

Lakhani, Karim R.; Panetta, Jill A. (2007): The Principles of Distributed Innovation. The Berkman Center for Internet and Society Research Paper No. 2007-7. In Innovations: Technology, Governance, Globalization Summer 2 (3). Available online at https://ssrn.com/abstract=1021034, checked on 8/16/2017.

Laney, Doug (2001): 3D Data Management: Controlling Data Volume, Velocity, and Variety. META Group Inc. Available online at http://blogs.gartner.com/doug-laney/files/2012/01/ad949-3D-Data-Management-Controlling-Data-Volume-Velocity-and-Variety.pdf, checked on 8/16/2017.

Lanquillon, Carsten; Mallow, Hauke (2015a): Advanced Analytics mit Big Data. In Joachim Dorschel (Ed.): Praxishandbuch Big Data. Wirtschaft -- Recht -- Technik. Wiesbaden: Springer Gabler, pp. 55–89.

Lanquillon, Carsten; Mallow, Hauke (2015b): Grenzen konventioneller Business-Intelligence-Lösungen. In Joachim Dorschel (Ed.): Praxishandbuch Big Data. Wirtschaft -- Recht -- Technik. Wiesbaden: Springer Gabler, pp. 255-263.

Laux, Helmut; Gillenkirch, Robert M.; Schenk-Mathes, Heike Yasmin (2012): Entscheidungstheorie. 8. Aufl. 2012. Korr. Nachdruck 2012. Berlin, Heidelberg: Springer (Springer-Lehrbuch).

LaValle, Steve; Lesser, Eric; Shockley, Rebecca; Hopkins, Michael S.; Kruschwitz, Nina (2011): Big Data, Analytics and the Path From Insights to Value. In MIT Sloan Management Review 52 (2), pp. 21–32.

Law, Averill M.; Kelton, W. David (1991): Simulation modeling and analysis. 2nd ed. New York, London: McGraw-Hill (McGraw-Hill series in industrial engineering and management science).

Lebas, Michel (1994): Managerial accounting in France Overview of past tradition and current practice. In European Accounting Review 3 (3), pp. 471–488. DOI: 10.1080/09638189400000032.

Lebas, Michel J. (1995): Performance measurement and performance management. In International Journal of Production Economics 41 (1), pp. 23–35.

Lee, Jay; Bagheri, Behrad; Kao, Hung-An (2015a): A Cyber-Physical Systems architecture for Industry 4.0-based manufacturing systems. In Manufacturing Letters 3, pp. 18–23. DOI: 10.1016/j.mfglet.2014.12.001.

Lee, Jay; Bagheri, Behrad; Kao, Hung-An; Lapira, Edzel (2015b): Industry 4.0 and Manufacturing Transformation. In Manufacturing Leadership Journal (February), pp. 36–43. Available online at http://www.mljournal-digital.com /meleadershipjournal/201502?folio=4&pg=37#pg37, checked on 8/16/2017.

Lepak, David P.; Smith, Ken G.; Taylor, M. Susan (2007): Value Creation and Value Capture: A Multilevel Perspective. In Academy of Management Review 32 (1), pp. 180–194.

Li, X.; McKee, D. J.; Horberry, T.; Powell, M. S. (2011): The control room operator. The forgotten element in mineral process control. In Minerals Engineering 24 (8), pp. 894–902. DOI: 10.1016/j.mineng.2011.04.001.

Lichtblau, Karl; Stich, Volker; Bertenrath, Roman; Blum, Matthias; Bleider, Martin; Millack, Agnes et al. (2015): Industrie 4.0 Readiness. IMPULS Stiftung. Available online at http://industrie40.vdma.org/documents/4214 230/5356229/Industrie%204.0%20Readiness%20Study%20English.pdf, checked on 8/16/2017.

Liker, Jeffrey K. (2004): The Toyota way. 14 management principles from the world's greatest manufacturer. New York, London: McGraw-Hill.

Lindstrom, Martin (2016): Big Data ist ein Ausdruck von Unsicherheit. In Havard Business Manager (April).

Losbichler, Heimo; Gänßlen, Siegfried (2015): Performance Measurement in Zeiten von Big Data. In CON 27 (6), pp. 307–312. DOI: 10.15358/0935-0381-2015-6-307.

Loshin, David (2013): Big data analytics. From strategic planning to enterprise integration with tools, techniques, NoSQL, and graph. Amsterdam: Elsevier Morgan Kaufmann.

Luczak, Dominik (2017): Agil - Erfolgsfaktor agiles Unternehmenssystem. In Christian Ramsauer, Detlef Kayser, Christoph Schmitz (Eds.): Erfolgsfaktor Agilität. Chancen für Unternehmen in einem volatilen Marktumfeld. 1. Auflage. Weinheim: Wiley-VCH, pp. 17-32.

Lunau, Stephan (Ed.) (2009): Six Sigma+Lean Toolset. Berlin, Heidelberg: Springer.

Maier, H. R.; Guillaume, J.H.A.; van Delden, H.; Riddell, G. A.; Haasnoot, M.; Kwakkel, J. H. (2016): An uncertain future, deep uncertainty, scenarios, robustness and adaptation. How do they fit together? In Environmental Modelling & Software 81, pp. 154–164. DOI: 10.1016/j.envsoft.2016.03.014.

Manyika, James; Chui, Michael; Bisson, Peter; Woetzel, Jonathan; Dobbs, Richard; Bughin, Jacques; Ahron, Dan (2015): Unlocking the potential of the Internet of Things. Edited by McKinsey Global Institute. McKinsey & Company. Available online at http://www.mckinsey.com/business-functions/digital-mckinsey/our-insights/the-internet-of-things-the-value-of-digitizing-the-physical-world, checked on 8/16/2017.

Manyika, James; Chui, Michael; Brown, Brad; Bughin, Jacques; Dobbs, Richard; Roxburgh, Charles; Hung Beyers, Angela: Big data: The next frontier for innovation, competition, and productivity. Edited by McKinsey Global Institute. McKinsey & Company. Available online at http://www.mckinsey.com/business-functions/digital-mckinsey/our-insights/big-data-the-next-frontier-for-innovation, checked on 8/16/2017.

Markkanen, Aapo (2015): IoT Analytics Today and in 2020. Competitive Edge from Edge Intelligence. ABI Research. Oyster Bay, NY.

Marlin, Thomas E.; Perkins, John D.; Barton, Geoff W.; Brisk, Michael L. (1991): Benefits from process control: results of a joint industry-university study. In J. Proc. Cont. 1 (March), pp. 68–83.

Marr, Bernard (2015): Big data. Using SMART big data, analytics and metrics to make better decisions and improve performance. Chichester: Wiley.

Marshall, Alfred (1895): Principles of Economics. Third Edition. London: Macmillan and Co.

Martin, Sean (2016): The ascendency of data lakes. The premise, the promise, the potential of new method for managing big data. In Analytics Magazine (January/February 2016), pp. 32–39.

Marx, Karl (1990): Capital - A critique of political economy - Volume One. Introduced by Ernest Mandel, Translated by Ben Fowkes. Reprinted ed. London: Penguin Books in association with New Left Review.

Mayer-Schönberger, Viktor; Cukier, Kenneth (2013): Big data. A revolution that will transform how we live, work and think. London: John Murray.

McAfee, Andrew; Brynjolfsson, Erik (2010): Big Data: The Management Revolution. In Havard Business Review 90 (10), pp. 61–67.

McDonough, William; Braungart, Michael (2002): Cradle to cradle. Remaking the way we make things. New York: North Point Press.

Meadows, Donella H.; Meadows, Dennis L.; Randers, Jorgen; Behrens III, William W. (Eds.) (1972): The limits to growth. A report for the Club of Rome's project on the predicament of mankind. New York: Universe Books.

Meir-Huber, Mario; Köhler, Martin (2014): Best Practice für Big Data Projekte. Leitfaden aus #Big Data in #Austria. Available online at https://www.ffg.at/sites/default/files/allgemeine_downloads/thematische%20programme/IKT/big_data_in_austria-leitfaden.pdf, checked on 8/16/2017.

Meredith, Jack (1998): Building operations management theory through case and field research. In Journal of Operations Management 16 (4), pp. 441–454. DOI: 10.1016/S0272-6963(98)00023-0.

Minelli, Michael; Chambers, Michele; Dhiraj, Ambiga (2013): Big data, big analytics. Emerging business intelligence and analytic trends for today's businesses / by Michael Minelli, Michele Chambers, Ambiga Dhiraj. Hoboken, N.J.: Wiley.

MIT Center for Digital Business and Capgemini Consulting (2011): Digital Transformation: A Roadmap for Billion-Dollar Organizations. Available online at https://www.capgemini.com/resource-file-access/resource/pdf/Digital_Transformation__A_Road-Map_for_Billion-Dollar_Organizations.pdf, checked on 8/16/2017.

Möller, Klaus; Müller-Stewens, Benedikt; Wirnsperger, Franz (2014): Chancen und Risiken des Performance Managements aus Sicht des Verwaltungsrats. In Der Schweizer Treuhänder 88 (5), pp. 435–440.

Monostori, L.; Kádár, B.; Bauernhansl, T.; Kondoh, S.; Kumara, S.; Reinhart, G. et al. (2016): Cyber-physical systems in manufacturing. In CIRP Annals - Manufacturing Technology 65 (2), pp. 621–641. DOI: 10.1016/j.cirp.2016.06.005.

Monroe, Bill (2015): Pass or Fail. Six software-project questions you must get right. In : Enhancing project management, pp. 59-62.

Moulijn, Jacob A.; Makkee, Michiel; van Diepen, Annelies (2013): Chemical process technology. Second edition. Chichester: Wiley.

Mowen, Maryanne M.; Hansen, Don R.; Heitger, Dan Lee (2013): Cornerstones of managerial accounting. 5th ed. Mason, OH: South-Western, Cengage Learning.

Neely, Andy; Gregory, Mike; Platts, Ken (1995): Performance measurement system design. In Int Jrnl of Op & Prod Mnagemnt 15 (4), pp. 80–116. DOI: 10.1108/01443579510083622.

Neugebauer, Reimund; Hippmann, Sophie; Leis, Miriam; Landherr, Martin (2016): Industrie 4.0 - From the Perspective of Applied Research. In Procedia CIRP 57, pp. 2–7. DOI: 10.1016/j.procir.2016.11.002.

Nof, Shimon Y. (2009a): Automation: What it Means to Us Around the World. In Shimon Y. Nof (Ed.): Springer Handbook of Automation. Berlin, Heidelberg: Springer, pp. 13-52.

Nof, Shimon Y. (Ed.) (2009b): Springer Handbook of Automation. Berlin, Heidelberg: Springer.

Novatsis, E.; Wilkinson, J. (2016): Human factors in incident investigation. In Janette Edmonds, The Keil Centre (Eds.): Human factors in the chemical and process industries. Making it work in practice. 1st ed. Amsterdam, Oxford, Cambridge: Elsevier, pp. 131–150.

Obermaier, Robert (2016): "Controlling 4.0" - Zu den Möglichkeiten eines regelungsbasierten Controllings (nicht nur) von Supply Chains in einer "Industrie 4.0". In CON 28 (6), pp. 301–307. DOI: 10.15358/0935-0381-2016-6-301.

Ohno, Taiichi (1988): Toyota production system. Beyond large-scale production. Cambridge, MA: Productivity Press.

Omri, Fouad (2015): Big Data-Analysen: Anwendungsszenarien und Trends. In Joachim Dorschel (Ed.): Praxishandbuch Big Data. Wirtschaft -- Recht -- Technik. Wiesbaden: Springer Gabler, pp. 104–112.

Panizzolo, Roberto (2017): Practices and Performance in Constraints Management Production Planning and Control Systems. In Louis Brennan, Alessandra Vecchi (Eds.): International Manufacturing Strategy in a Time of Great Flux. 1st ed. 2017: Springer International Publishing (Measuring Operations Performance), pp. 153-182.

Patela, Suresa (2016): The tactical guide to six sigma implementation. Portland: CRC Press (Productivity Press Book).

Perry, Matthew J. (2016): The Platform Transformation. Sebastopol, CA: O'Reilly Media, Inc.

Piketty, Thomas; Goldhammer, Arthur (2014): Capital in the twenty-first century. Cambridge Massachusetts: The Belknap Press of Harvard University Press.

Pittman, Paul H.; Atwater, J. Brian (2016): APICS dictionary. 15th ed. Chicago, IL: APICS.

Plenert, Gerhard Johannes (2011): Lean management principles for information technology. Boca Raton: CRC Press (Series on Resource management).

Pointner, Alexander (2017): Vorbereitet - Anwendung der Agilitätsstellhebel. In Christian Ramsauer, Detlef Kayser, Christoph Schmitz (Eds.): Erfolgsfaktor Agilität. Chancen für Unternehmen in einem volatilen Marktumfeld. 1. Auflage. Weinheim: Wiley-VCH, pp. 201–237.

Porter, Michael E.; Heppelmann, James E. (2014): How Smart, Connected Products Are Transforming Competition. In Havard Business Review (November 2014). Available online at https://hbr.org/2014/11/how-smart-connected-products-are-transforming-competition, checked on 8/16/2017.

Porter, Michael E.; Heppelmann, James E. (2015): How Smart, Connected Products are Transforming Companies. In Havard Business Review (October 2015). Available online at https://hbr.org/2015/10/how-smart-connected-products-are-transforming-companies, checked on 8/16/2017.

Pyzdek, Thomas (2011): The six sigma project planner. A step-by-step guide to leading a six sigma project through DMAIC. New York: McGraw Hill Professional.

Qin, S.Joe; Badgwell, Thomas A. (2003): A survey of industrial model predictive control technology. In Control Engineering Practice 11 (7), pp. 733–764. DOI: 10.1016/S0967-0661(02)00186-7.

Rabitsch, Christian (2016): Methodology for Implementing Agility in Manufacturing Companies. Doctoral Thesis. University of Technology, Graz.

Rahman, Shams-Ur (1998): Theory of constraints. A review of the philosophy and its applications. In Int Jrnl of Op & Prod Mnagemnt 18 (4), pp. 336–355. DOI: 10.1108/01443579810199720.

Rakar, Andrej; Zorzut, Sebastjan; Jovan, Vladimir (2004): Assessment of Production Performance by Means of KPI. In Proceedings of the Control 2004 Conference, University of Bath, UK. Available online at http://uk acc.group.shef.ac.uk/proceedings/control2004/Papers/073.pdf, checked on 8/16/2017.

Ramsauer, Christian (2009): Production Strategy. Mastering the Dynamics of Globalization. Graz: Verlag d. Technischen Universität Graz (Monographic Series TU Graz).

Ramsauer, Christian (2013a): Einleitung. In Christian Ramsauer (Ed.): Industrial Engineering und Innovation. Techno-Ökonomie an der TU Graz ; Festschrift anlässlich des 70. Geburtstages von Em.Univ.-Prof. Josef W. Wohinz. Graz: Verl. der Techn. Univ (Festschriften TU Graz), pp. 1-7.

Ramsauer, Christian (2013b): Industrie 4.0 – Die Produktion der Zukunft. In WINGbusiness (3), pp. 6–12.

Ramsauer, Christian; Kayser, Detlef; Schmitz, Christoph (Eds.) (2017): Erfolgsfaktor Agilität. Chancen für Unternehmen in einem volatilen Marktumfeld. Wiley-VCH. 1. Auflage. Weinheim: Wiley-VCH.

Ransbotham, S.; Kiron, D.; Prentice, P. K. (2016): Beyond the Hype: The Hard Work Behind Analytics Success. Reprint Number 57381. MIT Sloan Management Review, March 2016.

Rao, R. Venkata (2011): Advanced modeling and optimization of manufacturing processes. International research and development. London: Springer (Springer series in advanced manufacturing, 1860-5168).

Rao, R. Venkata (2013): Decision Making in Manufacturing Environment Using Graph Theory and Fuzzy Multiple Attribute Decision Making Methods. London: Springer.

Riesenberger, Carlos A.; Sousa, Sergio D. (2010): The 8D Methodology: An Effective Way to Reduce Recurrence of Customer Complaints? In Proceedings of the World Congress on Engineering 2010 III, pp. 2225–2230.

Roffel, Brian; Betlem, B. H. (2006): Process dynamics and control. Modeling for control and prediction. Chichester: John Wiley.

Rother, Mike; Shook, John (1999): Learning to See. Value stream mapping to add value and eliminate muda. Version 1.2. Brookline, MA: The Lean Enterprise Institute.

Rothschild, Michael Lee (1998): Profit by the minute. Forbes. Available online at https://www.forbes.com/asap/1998/1130/233_print.html, checked on 8/16/2017.

Rothschild, Michael Lee; Kumar, Ameet; Farmer, Jake Alan; Chan, Gilbert Gee-yin; Shwert, Mark (2015): Computer-Aided System for Improving Return on Assets. Applied for by Profit Velocity Solutions, LLC on 12/8/2015. App. no. 14/962,659. Patent no. US 2016/0092892 A1.

Rumsfeld, Donald H. (2002): DoD News Briefing - Secretary Rumsfeld and Gen. Myers. February 12, 2002 11:30 AM EDT (News Transcript). Available online at http://archive.defense.gov/Transcripts/Transcript.aspx?TranscriptID=2636, checked on 8/16/2017.

Sager, Benedikt; Hawer, Sven; Reinhart, Gunther (2016): A Performance Measurement System for Global Manufacturing Networks. In Procedia CIRP 57, pp. 61–66. DOI: 10.1016/j.procir.2016.11.012.

Scaife, R. (2016): Reducing human failure. In Janette Edmonds, The Keil Centre (Eds.): Human factors in the chemical and process industries. Making it work in practice. 1st ed. Amsterdam, Oxford, Cambridge: Elsevier, pp. 93–130.

Schäfer, Andreas; Knapp, Melanie; May, Michael; Voß, Angelika (2012): Big Data - Vorsprung durch Wissen. Innovationspotenzialanalyse. Available online at https://www.iais.fraunhofer.de/content/dam/iais/gf/bda/Downloads/Innovationspotenzialanalyse_Big-Data_FraunhoferIAIS_2012.pdf, checked on 8/16/2017.

Schaller, Robert R. (1997): Moore's Law: past, present, and future. In Spectrum 34 (6), pp. 52–59.

Schank, R.; Lyras, D.; Soloway, E. (2010): The Future of Decision Making. How Revolutionary Software Can Improve the Ability to Decide. 1st ed. New York: Palgrave Macmillan US; Palgrave Macmillan.

Schimank, Christof; Briem, Christian; Thiele, Philipp (2015): Eine Praxisstudie zur Effektivität des Volatilitätsmanagement. In Controller Magazin (Juli/August), pp. 41-44.

Schläfke, Marten; Silvi, Riccardo; Möller, Klaus (2012): A framework for business analytics in performance management. In Int J Productivity & Perf Mgmt 62 (1), pp. 110–122. DOI: 10.1108/17410401311285327.

Schmidhuber, Jürgen (2015): Deep learning in neural networks. An overview. In Neural networks : the official journal of the International Neural Network Society 61, pp. 85–117. DOI: 10.1016/j.neunet.2014.09.003.

Schmidt, Mario; Spieth, Hannes; Bauer, Joa; Haubach, Christian (2017): 100 Betriebe für Ressourceneffizienz - Band 1. Praxisbeispiele aus der produzierenden Wirtschaft. 1st ed. Berlin, Heidelberg: Springer.

Schonberger, Richard (2008): Best practices in lean six sigma process improvement. A deeper look. Hoboken, NJ: Wiley.

Schroeder, Roger G.; Linderman, Kevin; Liedtke, Charles; Choo, Adrian S. (2008): Six Sigma. Definition and underlying theory. In Journal of Operations Management 26 (4), pp. 536–554. DOI: 10.1016/j.jom.2007.06.007.

Schuh, Günther; Anderl, Reiner; Gausemeier, Jürgen; Hompel, Michael ten; Wahlster, Wolfgang (Eds.) (2017): Industrie 4.0 Maturity Index. Managing the Digital Transformation of Companies. acatech STUDY. Munich: Utz Verlag.

Schuh, Günther; Potente, Till; Fuchs, Sascha; Thomas, Christian; Schmitz, Stefan; Hausberg, Carlo et al. (2013): Self-Optimizing Decision-Making in Production Control. In Katja Windt (Ed.): Robust manufacturing control. Proceedings of the CIRP Sponsored Conference RoMaC 2012, Bremen, Germany, 18th-20th June 2012. 1st ed. Heidelberg, New York, Dordrecht, London: Springer (Lecture notes in Production Engineering, 114), pp. 443-454.

Schuh, Günther; Schmidt, Carsten (Eds.) (2014): Produktionsmanagement. Handbuch Produktion und Management 5. 2. Aufl. 2014. Berlin, Heidelberg: Springer (VDI-Buch).

Schurig, Matthias (2017): Definiert - Was man unter Agilität versteht. In Christian Ramsauer, Detlef Kayser, Christoph Schmitz (Eds.): Erfolgsfaktor Agilität. Chancen für Unternehmen in einem volatilen Marktumfeld. 1. Auflage. Weinheim: Wiley-VCH, pp. 77-99.

Schurig, Matthias; Rabitsch, Christian; Ramsauer, Christian (2014): Agile Produktion. In ZWF 109 (10), pp. 956-959.

Schwaninger, Markus (2013): Gibt es Modelle, denen wir vertrauen können? In Jens Vollmar, Roman Becker, Isabella Hoffend (Eds.): Macht des Vertrauens. Perspektiven und aktuelle Herausforderungen im unternehmerischen Kontext. Wiesbaden: Springer Gabler, pp. 53–63.

Schweitzer, Marcell; Krause, Hans-Ulrich (1997): Produktions- und Kostentheorie: Grundlagen - Anwendungen. 2., vollst. überarb. u. wesentl. erw. Aufl. Wiesbaden: Gabler.

Seborg, Dale E.; Edgar, Thomas F.; Mellichamp, Duncan A. (2004): Process dynamics and control. 2nd ed. Hoboken, NJ: Wiley.

Seufert, Andreas; Heinen, Markus; Muth, Andreas (2014): Information Rules: Die neue Anatomie der Entscheidung. In Controlling & Management Review (Sonderheft 1), pp. 16–24.

Shearer, Colin (2000): The CRISP-DM Model: The New Blueprint for Data Mining. In Journal of Data Warehousing 5 (4), pp. 13-22.

Sheffi, Yossi; Rice Jr., James B. (2005): A Supply Chain View of the Resilient Enterprise. In MITSloan Management Review 47 (1), pp. 41–48.

Shobrys, Donald E.; White, Douglas C. (2002): Planning, scheduling and control systems: why cannot they work together. In Computers and Chemical Engineering 26, pp. 149–160.

Sixta, Herbert (1998): Comparative Evaluation of Different Concepts of Sulfite Pulping Technology. In Lenzinger Berichte (78). Available online at https://www.lenzing.com/fileadmin/template/pdf/konzern/lenzinger_berichte/ausgabe_78_1998/LB_1998_03_Sixta.pdf, checked on 8/16/2017.

Skinner, Wickham (1969): Manufacturing - Missing link to corporate strategy. In Havard Business Review 47 (May-June), pp. 136–145. Available online at https://hbr.org/1969/05/manufacturing-missing-link-in-corporate-strategy, checked on 8/16/2017.

Skinner, Wickham (1978): Manufacturing in the corporate strategy. New York, Chichester: Wiley (Manufacturing management).

Skinner, Wickham (1986): The Productivity Paradox. In Havard Business Review (July), pp. 55–59. Available online at https://hbr.org/1986/07/the-productivity-paradox, checked on 8/16/2017.

Slack, Nigel; Chambers, Stuart; Johnston, Robert (2010): Operations management. 6th ed. Harlow England, New York: Financial Times Prentice Hall.

Slack, Nigel; Lewis, Michael (2011): Operations strategy. 3rd ed. Harlow: Financial Times Prentice Hall.

Stamatis, D. H. (2010): The OEE primer. Understanding overall equipment effectiveness, reliability, and maintainability. Boca Raton FL: CRC Press.

Stanton, Jeffrey (2016): Sensing Big Data: Multimodal Information Information Interfaces for Exploration of Large Data Sets. In Scott Tonidandel, Eden King, Jose M. Cortina (Eds.): Big data at work. The data science revolution and organizational psychology. New York and London: Routledge; Taylor & Francis (SIOP organizational frontiers series), pp. 158–177.

Stevens, Graham C. (1989): Integrating the Supply Chain. In IJPD & MM 19 (8), pp. 3–8.

Steyn, P. G. (1989): The Scope of Production and Operations Management. In Ray Wild (Ed.): International handbook of production and operations management. London: Cassell Educational Ltd, pp. 3-14.

Stuart, I.; McCutcheon, D.; Handfield, R.; McLachlin, R.; Samson, D. (2002): Effective case research in operations management. A process perspective. In Journal of Operations Management 20 (5), pp. 419–433. DOI: 10.1016/S0272-6963(02)00022-0.

Stuchtey, Martin; Enkvist, Per-Anders; Zumwinkel, Klaus (2016): A good disruption. Redefining growth in the twenty-first century. 1st ed. London: Bloomsbury.

Sull, Donald N. (2009): The upside of turbulence. Seizing opportunity in an uncertain world. 1. ed. New York: Harper Business.

Sull, Donald N. (2010): Competing through organizational agility. In McKinsey Quarterly (1), pp. 1–9. Available online at http://www.mckinsey.com/business-functions/organization/our-insights/competing-through-organizational-agility, checked on 8/16/2017.

Svrcek, William Y.; Mahoney, Donald P.; Young, Brent R. (2014): A real-time approach to process control. 3rd edition. Chichester: Wiley-Blackwell.

Taha, Hamdy A. (2007): Operations research. An introduction. 8th ed. Upper Saddle River, N.J., London: Pearson/Prentice Hall.

Tapscott, Don (2014): The digital economy - Anniversary Edition. Rethinking promise and peril in the age of networked intelligence. 2 edition. New York: McGraw-Hill.

Taylor, James (2012): Decision management systems. A practical guide to using business rules and predictive analytics. Upper Saddle River, N.J.: IBM Press/Pearson.

Terwiesch, Peter; Ganz, Christopher (2009): Trends in Automation. In Shimon Y. Nof (Ed.): Springer Handbook of Automation. Berlin, Heidelberg: Springer, pp. 127-143.

Thiede, Sebastian; Juraschek, Max; Herrmann, Christoph (2016): Implementing Cyber-physical Production Systems in Learning Factories. In Procedia CIRP 54, pp. 7–12. DOI: 10.1016/j.procir.2016.04.098.

Thomé, Antônio Márcio Tavares; Scavarda, Luiz Felipe; Fernandez, Nicole Suclla; Scavarda, Annibal José (2012): Sales and operations planning. A research synthesis. In International Journal of Production Economics 138 (1), pp. 1–13. DOI: 10.1016/j.ijpe.2011.11.027.

Thomé, Antônio Márcio Tavares; Sousa, Rui Soucasaux; Scavarda do Carmo, Luiz Felipe Roris Rodriguez (2014): The impact of sales and operations planning practices on manufacturing operational performance. In International Journal of Production Research 52 (7), pp. 2108–2121. DOI: 10.1080/00207543.2013.853889.

Thomson, William (1889): Popular lectures and addresses. London: Macmillan and Co. (1).

Tompkins, James A. (2016): Choice Overload. In Supply Chain Management Review (May/June 2016), pp. 38–43.

Töpfer, Armin (2004): Six Sigma: Projektmanagement für Null-Fehler-Qualität in der Automobilindustrie. In ZfAW 2, pp. 13–24.

Töpfer, Armin (2012): Erfolgreich Forschen. Ein Leitfaden für Bachelor-, Master-Studierende und Doktoranden. 3., überarb. und erw. Aufl. 2012. Berlin, Heidelberg: Springer (Springer-Lehrbuch).

Tschöpe, Sebastian; Aronska, Kateryna; Nyhuis, Peter (2015): Was ist eigentlich Industrie 4.0? In ZWF 110 (3), pp. 145-149.

Ulrich, Hans (1981): Die Betriebswirtschaftslehre als anwendungsorientierte Sozialwissenschaft. In Curt Sandig, Manfred N. Geist, Richard Köhler (Eds.): Die Führung des Betriebes. Curt Sandig zu seinem 80. Geburtstag gewidmet. Stuttgart: Poeschel, pp. 1–25.

Ulrich, Hans (2001): Systemorientiertes Management: Das Werk von Hans Ulrich. Bern, Stuttgart, Wien: Haupt.

United Nations Industrial Development Organization (2015): Role of technology and innovation in inclusive and sustainable industrial development. Vienna: United Nations Industrial Development Organization (Industrial development report, 2016).

van Donk, Dirk Pieter; Fransoo, Jan C. (2006): Operations management research in process industries. In Journal of Operations Management 24 (3), pp. 211–214. DOI: 10.1016/j.jom.2005.01.001.

Váncza, J.; Monostori, L.; Lutters, D.; Kumara, S. R.; Tseng, M.; Valckenaers, P.; van Brussel, H. (2011): Cooperative and responsive manufacturing enterprises. In CIRP Annals - Manufacturing Technology 60 (2), pp. 797–820. DOI: 10.1016/j.cirp.2011.05.009.

VDI/VDE-Gesellschaft Mess- und Automatisierungstechnik (2016a): Industrie 4.0 - Technical Assets. Basic terminology concepts, life cycles and administration models. Düsseldorf.

VDI/VDE-Gesellschaft Mess- und Automatisierungstechnik (2016b): Status Report - Chancen mit Big Data Use Cases. Düsseldorf.

Veeramachaneni, Kalyan (2016): Why You're Not Getting Value from Your Data Science. Havard Business Review. Available online at https://hbr.org/2016/12/why-youre-not-getting-value-from-your-data-science, checked on 8/16/2017.

Vercellis, Carlo (2009): Business intelligence. Data mining and optimization for decision making. Chichester: Wiley.

Verein Deutscher Zementwerke e.V. (2002): Zement-Taschenbuch 2002. Düsseldorf: Verlag Bau+Technik.

Vermesan, Ovidiu; Friess, Peter (Eds.) (2014): Internet of things. From research and innovation to market deployment. Aalborg: River Pub (River Publishers Series in Communications).

Vij, Sandeep; Bedi, Harpreet Singh (2016): Are subjective business performance measures justified? In Int J Productivity & Perf Mgmt 65 (5), pp. 603–621. DOI: 10.1108/IJPPM-12-2014-0196.

Vodafone (2016): Vodafone IoT Barometer 2016. Available online at http://www.internet-of-things-research.eu/pdf/Vodafone%20IoT%20Barometer%202016.pdf, checked on 8/16/2017.

Voss, Chris; Blackmon, Kate (1998): Differences in manufacturing strategy decisions between Japanese and Western manufacturing plants: the role of strategic time orientation. In Journal of Operations Management 16 (2-3), pp. 147–158.

Voss, Chris; Johnson, Mark; Godsell, Jan (2016): Case research. In Christer Karlsson (Ed.): Research methods for operations management. Second edition. New York: Routledge, pp. 165–197.

Walker, Russell (2015): From big data to big profits. Success with data and analytics. 1 edition: Oxford University Press.

Wallace, Tom (2012): Seven Sorry Suppositions About S&OP. In APICS Suppy Chain Council (Ed.): How to be an S&OP champion, p. 9.

Walter, Chip (2005): Kryder's Law. In Sci Am 293 (2), pp. 32–33. DOI: 10.1038/scientificamerican0805-32.

Wan, Jiafu; Humar, Iztok; Zhang, Daqiang (Eds.) (2016): Industrial IoT Technologies and Applications. Cham: Springer International Publishing (173).

Wang, Shiyong; Wan, Jiafu; Zhang, Daqiang; Di Li; Zhang, Chunhua (2016): Towards smart factory for industry 4.0. A self-organized multi-agent system with big data based feedback and coordination. In Computer Networks 101, pp. 158–168. DOI: 10.1016/j.comnet.2015.12.017.

Westkämper, Engelbert (2013a): Rahmenmodell der digitalen Produktion. In Engelbert Westkämper, Dieter Spath, Carmen Constantinescu, Joachim Lentes (Eds.): Digitale Produktion. Aufl. 2013. Berlin, Heidelberg: Springer, pp. 15-16.

Westkämper, Engelbert (2013b): Struktureller Wandel durch Megatrends. In Engelbert Westkämper, Dieter Spath, Carmen Constantinescu, Joachim Lentes (Eds.): Digitale Produktion. Aufl. 2013. Berlin, Heidelberg: Springer, pp. 7-16.

Westkämper, Engelbert; Decker, Markus (2006): Einführung in die Organisation der Produktion. Berlin, Heidelberg: Springer (Springer-Lehrbuch).

Westkämper, Engelbert; Zahn, Erich (Eds.) (2009): Wandlungsfähige Produktionsunternehmen. Das Stuttgarter Unternehmensmodell. Berlin, Heidelberg: Springer.

Whiteman, Wayne E. (1998): Training and Educating Army Officers for the 21st Century: Implications for the United States Military Academy. Carlisle Barracks PA.

Wiendahl, H.-P.; Hernández, R. (2002): Fabrikplanung im Blickpunkt. In wt Werkstatttechnik 92 (4), pp. 133–138.

Wiendahl, Hans-Peter; Reichardt, Jürgen; Nyhuis, Peter (2014): Handbuch Fabrikplanung. Konzept, Gestaltung und Umsetzung wandlungsfähiger Produktionsstätten. 2., überarb. und erw. Aufl. München, Wien: Hanser.

Wiener, Norbert (1994): Cybernetics. Or control and communication in the animal and the machine. 2. ed., 7. print. Cambridge Mass.: MIT Press.

Wildemann, Horst (2010): Produktionssysteme. Leitfaden zur methodengestützten Reorganisation der Produktion. 8., Aufl. München: TCW.

Wise, Richard; Baumgartner, Peter (1999): Go Downstream: The New Profit Imperative in Manufacturing. In Havard Business Review 77 (September-October), pp. 133–141. Available online at https://hbr.org/1999/09/go-downstream-the-new-profit-imperative-in-manufacturing, checked on 8/16/2017.

Wohinz, Josef W. (Ed.) (2011): Industriebetriebslehre 2011. Technische Universität Graz. Graz: Verl. der TU (Monographic series TU Graz : Techno-ökonomie und industrielles Management).

Womack, James P.; Jones, Daniel T. (2003): Lean thinking. Banish waste and create wealth in your corporation. 1st Free Press ed., rev. and updated. New York: Free Press.

Womack, James P.; Jones, Daniel T.; Roos, Daniel (1990): The Machine that changed the world. Based on the Massachusetts Institute of Technology 5-million dollar 5-year study on the future of the automobile. New York: Rawson Associates.

World Economic Forum (2013): Building Resilience in Supply Chains Report. Available online at http://www3.weforum.org/docs/WEF_RRN_MO_BuildingResilienceSupplyChains_Report_2013.pdf, checked on 8/16/2017.

World Economic Forum (2015): Deep Shift. Technology Tipping Points and Societal Impact. Available online at http://www3.weforum.org/docs/WEF_GAC15_Technological_Tipping_Points_report_2015.pdf, checked on 8/16/2017.

World Economic Forum (2016): Unlocking $100 Trillion for Business and Society from Digital Transformation. Digital Transformation Initiative. In collaboration with Accenture. Available online at http://reports.weforum.org/digital-transformation/wp-content/blogs.dir/94/mp/files/pages/files/dti-executive-summary-website-version.pdf, checked on 8/16/2017.

World Economic Forum (2017): The Global Risks Report 2017. 12th Edition. Available online at http://www3.weforum.org/docs/GRR17_Report_web.pdf, checked on 8/16/2017.

Yadav, Neetu; Sagar, Mahim (2013): Performance measurement and management frameworks: Research trends of the last two decades. In Business Process Management Journal 19 (6), pp. 947–971. DOI: 10.1108/BPMJ-01-2013-0003.

Yarger, Harry R. (2006): Strategic theory for the 21st century. The little book on big strategy. Carlisle Barracks PA: Strategic Studies Institute U.S. Army War College (Letort papers, no. 12).

Yin, Robert K. (2003): Case study research. Design and methods. 3rd ed. Thousand Oaks, Calif., London: SAGE (Applied social research methods series, v. 5).

Zhou, Ji (2013): Digitalization and intelligentization of manufacturing industry. In Adv. Manuf. 1 (1), pp. 1–7. DOI: 10.1007/s40436-013-0006-5.

Zimmerman, Jerold L. (2011): Accounting for decision making and control. 7th ed. New York: McGraw-Hill/Irwin.

Züst, Rainer (1997): Einstieg ins Systems-Engineering. Systematisch denken, handeln und umsetzen. Zürich: Verl. Industrielle Organisation.

# Appendix: Pulp Manufacturing Case Study

## Appendix A: Readiness Assessment

| # | Dimension | Level 1 (poor) | Level 2 | Level 3 | Level 4 (target) | Comments |
|---|---|---|---|---|---|---|
| 1 | **Sensors for data capture:** Are readings from operations available? What kind of sensors are used? | Malfunctioning and/or incomplete sensor installation | Basic sensors | Smart components | End-to-end | - |
| 2 | **Coverage of data capture:** To what extent are production parameters captured? | Below 50% coverage | 70-80% | 80-90% | Above 90% coverage | - |
| 3 | **Granularity of measuring:** At what granularity level is the process flow measured? | Only basic, high level mapping | Department wise mapping | Equipment level mapping | Component level mapping | - |
| 4 | **Data collection:** At what frequency is data stored? | Unknown or inconsistent | Days or batch wise | Hours or minutes | Seconds or more frequent | - |


M. Hammer, *Management Approach for Resource-Productive Operations*, Industrial Management, https://doi.org/10.1007/978-3-658-22939-9

| | | | | | | |
|---|---|---|---|---|---|---|
| 5 | **Accuracy of data:** How accurate is the stored data? | Undefined or not known | +/-10-5% | +/-5-1% | +/- 1% | A few measurement devices, e.g., for consistency with lower accuracy |
| 6 | **Streaming and accessibility of data:** Is data being streamed? How accessible is the stream? | Locally stored files | Plant level access | Site level access | Network or cloud access | Network with secure remote access capability |
| 7 | **Structural data practices:** How is data structured, stored and accessed? | No central plan | Central structured (SQL) | High-performance databases, e.g., Hadoop | NoSQL for mixed data | SQL database with ability to include unstructured data |
| 8 | **Data cleaning:** How is data cleaned and blended? | Questionable / no structured cleaning | Ad-hoc data cleansing | Inconsistent and duplicate data removed. Smart value replacement for missing data | Time dependencies automatically removed | Data free of duplicates. Fixed dead time and retention time correction. Opportunity to make variable as a function of production output |
| 9 | **Focus of analysis:** What is the objective function and focus for any analysis and modelling? | Close gap to current best in class | Long term production efficiency | Basic profit modelling | Full variable profit maximization model | Mostly data mining for cost |

| | | | | | | |
|---|---|---|---|---|---|---|
| 10 | **Depth of analysis:** What level of dependents are used in the modelling and analysis? How is the element of time taken into account? | Unknown | 1st level parameters | 2nd/3rd level parameters | 3rd/4th level parameters | All data is analyzed |
| 11 | **Type of modelling used:** How advanced are the modelling techniques? | Unclear if/ what modelling is used | Linear modelling, e.g., in MS Excel | Statistical/ correlation modelling and FMEA in MatLab or specific software | Neural Network developed genetic model, combining multiple approaches | Machine learning methods used |
| 12 | **Degree of automated analysis:** To what degree are the analysis and modelling automated? | No analysis performed | Analysis made manually | Ad hoc automated analysis | Full automation | Specific analysis conducted ad hoc. KPI calculations, such as OEE automatically updated |
| 13 | **Presenting results:** How are the results presented and insights derived? | Data files (unstructured) | Consolidated data ready for analysis | Clear analysis with charts | Real-time interactive dashboards | |
| 14 | **Leveraging insights for operational decisions:** How is the model output used for operational decision-making? | Operational decisions made based on experience | Considered but not systematically used or fully trusted | Data-driven decision-making but manual adjustment of settings | Full automation of process steering | Simulation used to build trust with operators prior to eventual automation of controls |

| | | | | | | |
|---|---|---|---|---|---|---|
| 15 | **Leveraging insights for long-term decision-making:** How are insights incorporated into longer term operational strategy, e.g., plant optimization through capital investments? | Unclear | Used as input | Considered in capital expenditure cases but not mandatory element | Fact-based decision making for capital investments based on model results | Maximum sustained rate (MSR), efficiencies, and bottleneck as focus for operational and capital expenditures |
| 16 | **Capabilities and understanding:** Are in-house capabilities to run advanced analytics and modelling available? | Questionable | Basic ad hoc competence | Key resources with intermediate level capabilities | Dedicated personnel (e.g., Data Scientists) with strong expertise | Process engineers with skills required in engineering, process control, automation and data analytics. Opportunity to automate data analysis. |
| 17 | **Staff development:** What initiatives are used to increase knowledge and awareness of the possibilities to optimize the production processes? | None | Some training has occurred but driven by individuals | Training is available, delivery ad-hoc when needed | Everyone has received basic training on analytics. Skills needs are defined by role. A structured training program is in place. Standard software solution is available to all. | Initial training prior to launch of project, subsequently on demand |

| | | | | | | |
|---|---|---|---|---|---|---|
| 18 | **Objectives and vision:** Are advanced analytics incorporated into the company's strategic vision and culture? | Unclear | Analytics is spoken about by management team, but no clear link made to strategic objectives | Analytics is part of strategic objective but not well cascaded. Success case have been communicated, less than 3 per year. | Analytics is built into strategic objectives and cascaded into the organization. Leaders communicate a compelling story regarding analytics as part of improvement efforts and celebrate success cases. | |

Table 41: Readiness assessment from case study in pulp manufacturing

## Appendix B: Interview Questions and Answers

| # | Question | Answer |
|---|---|---|
| 1 | Under what conditions does a profit per hour management approach help to take the best available decisions? When does it fail? | The approach is suitable for continuous operations for the integrated optimization of cost and production (output). Ideally, both production and maintenance is covered in the improvement efforts as companies suffer from equipment reliability/plant availability issues. |
| 2 | In practice, what keeps companies from implementing a profit per hour approach? What are the pre-conditions and why? | In my opinion the limiting factor is not the availability of data, as all internal data is available and external data such as market prices are publicly accessible. I think it is a lack of awareness of the approach, the traditional focus on production output and cost, rather than profit per hour; and perhaps concerns about profit transparency. |
| 3 | How would companies implement a profit per hour operations management approach? | The first step would be to collect the process data and external data. Thereafter, a crucial step is to blend them together for analyses. Once the data is consolidated, data mining and calculations can be performed. Artificial neural networks, fuzzy and other logical algorithms/controllers can be applied. |
| 4 | Does the presented approach work? Why? | Yes, it does, because it considers the entire process end-to-end (from preparation to shipping). The approach analyses every parameter relevant, gaps, helps develop process improvement, and links back to ROIC. |
| 5 | What are the strengths of the approach? | The key strength is the clear link to the end goal of generating profits, which is the prime stakeholder expectation of for-profit companies. For example, the prime asset of forestry companies is wood and besides producing pulp there are other ways to generate profit from it. |
| 6 | Are there any limitations or weaknesses? What can be improved further? | Wood cellulose is a commodity product and its price is heavily exposed to external markets. We see large volatility in the time horizon of 3-5 years. In my opinion, it might be required to fix the price to a certain extent in the optimization modelling. |
| 7 | What else would you like to share? | A profit per hour model for the entire plant is required. So far I have seen machine learning algorithms like this only in the area of energy management. |

Table 42: General interview questions and answers from case study in pulp manufacturing

| # | Question | Answer |
|---|---|---|
| 1 | Does a profit per hour KPI help to make trade-off decisions between conflicting targets (e.g., throughput, energy, yield, ...)? | The approach helps as it is holistic and avoids shifting costs within the process, i.e. the savings in one area do not lead to higher costs in another. |
| 2 | If time is the constraint (e.g., continuous operations, high OEE), would a profit per hour KPI be helpful? Why, why not, and how? | In general, yes! However in situations with a high amount of downtime and shutdowns, it seems less helpful as maintenance and reliability improvements are of higher priority. |
| 3 | Is "real time" (or hourly) decision making required (e.g. due to high volatility, process changes)? Why, why not, and how? | Today targets and key decisions are made daily. Real-time decision support would be interesting in case of unexpected downtime helping to evaluate scenarios. Analyzing internal data in real-time, yes – external data due to variability, no. |
| 4 | Is cumulative profit maximization the desired long term goal? | Yes, it is, but the constraints of optimization have always to be considered, e.g. to avoid damaging equipment. That is the reason why we use the concept of MSR (maximum sustainable rate) to also guarantee long equipment lifetime. |
| 5 | Is it meaningful to use profit per hour as a KPI in industries (e.g. process industries) where invested capital (fixed cost) and/or resource intensity (variable cost) is high? Why, why not, and how? | Indeed, to have just one, integrated KPI is meaningful in these industries with high investment cost. |
| 6 | Are companies not following a profit per hour management approach, because it is not meaningful to them? Why, why not? | I see two reasons: 1) while companies already have all data, they struggle to blend it together. Typically, 3-4 different IT systems including SAP and DCS among others are in use. So, there is a need to integrate data. 2) They are not aware of the approach and opportunity. |
| 7 | Do companies lack infrastructure (e.g. sensors/meters) and/or data (e.g., volume, frequency, quality) to compute a profit per hour metric? Why, and what? | In general, in process industries, the necessary measurements are in place. As said, the challenge is to combine the data from different sources. Some measurement devices are still not as accurate as needed, e.g., the device for consistency measures has a variation in accuracy of +/- 10% |

| | | |
|---|---|---|
| 8 | Do manufacturers have access to and use (advanced) algorithms to calculate profit per hour as a target function? Why, why not? | Most of our clients do not have or use machine/deep learning algorithms yet. |
| 9 | Do companies lack an implementation process (e.g., methodology) or fail in the change management process? Why, why not? | Large sites have processes for topics such as improvement, innovation, idea generation and root cause problem solving, e.g., using Ishikawa diagrams. What is lacking is demonstrating the importance of change top-down by management. |
| 10 | Is there a lack in required skills (e.g., IT, analytics, functional expertise)? Why, why not? | There are fewer and fewer process engineers and they focus on domain know-how, and not data science skills. Often external providers are brought in to provide help with data analytics. |
| 11 | Can the business case for using analytics to solve for profit per hour be proven (e.g., measure & verify financial savings over time)? Why, why not, and how? | Yes, it can be proven and makes sense for overall optimization. As said, it helps validate savings and avoid shifting between different cost buckets. |
| 12 | Would companies benefit from and apply a standardized, repeatable, step-by-step process methodology? Why, why not? | A range of aspects can be covered with existing methodologies, e.g., DMAIC which is easy to follow. However, a comprehensive guideline, like a recipe for implementation, would help to reduce trial and error. New tools, such as the gap analysis and the readiness assessment are useful! |
| 13 | Are producers considering a live decision cockpit as a key tool for managers/ operators? Why, why not? | A main dashboard for a plant using profit per hour should allow access to a second level with profit per hour by area, and even include a more detailed third level to look at notifications, reasons, and the database. |
| 14 | Are fully automated advanced process controls (e.g., closed loop) an option? Why, why not? | Yes, that is the vision and end-goal to reach autonomous operations. |
| 15 | What specific rules and ongoing procedures would need to be adopted (e.g., Sales & Operations Planning linking internal and external requirements)? Why? | S&OP is important to link the sales and cost teams. Predictive information could help in sales and procurement negotiations, e.g., to get discounts for raw materials. |
| 16 | What else would be required to implement a "profit per hour" management approach following the DMAIC logic? | People need to be convinced and trained as it is a complex process. They need to understand the benefits, change their mindset/thinking from production output to profit maximization. All would share a common, aligned KPI instead of specific process indicators. |

Table 43: Specific interview questions and answers from case study in pulp manufacturing

MIX
Papier aus verantwortungsvollen Quellen
Paper from responsible sources
FSC® C105338

If you have any concerns about our products,
you can contact us on
**ProductSafety@springernature.com**

In case Publisher is established outside the EU,
the EU authorized representative is:
**Springer Nature Customer Service Center GmbH**
**Europaplatz 3, 69115 Heidelberg, Germany**

Printed by Libri Plureos GmbH
in Hamburg, Germany